The US Lobby and Australian Defence Policy

"Vince Scappatura provides some much-needed fresh thinking on Australia's strategic relationship with the United States. This book would be an important contribution to a rather small and frequently uncritical literature at any time. In the Trump era it is essential reading – especially for those who are likely to disagree with its carefully researched conclusions."

Professor Mark Beeson
University of Western Australia

The US Lobby and

Australian Defence Policy

Vince Scappatura

MONASH University Publishing

The US Lobby and Australian Defence Policy
© Copyright 2019 Vince Scappatura

Monash University Publishing
Matheson Library and Information Services Building
40 Exhibition Walk
Monash University
Clayton, Victoria 3800, Australia
www.publishing.monash.edu

Monash University Publishing brings to the world publications which advance the best traditions of humane and enlightened thought.

Monash University Publishing titles pass through a rigorous process of independent peer review.

ISBN: 9781925523522 (paperback)
ISBN: 9781925523560 (pdf)
ISBN: 9781925523577 (epub)

www.publishing.monash.edu/books/usladp-9781925523522.html

Series: Investigating Power

Series Editor: Clinton Fernandes

Design: Les Thomas

Cover design: Les Thomas

A catalogue record for this book is available from the National Library of Australia.

Printed in Australia by Griffin Press an Accredited ISO AS/NZS 14001:2004 Environmental Management System printer.

The paper this book is printed on is certified against the Forest Stewardship Council ® Standards. Griffin Press holds FSC chain of custody certification SGS-COC-005088. FSC promotes environmentally responsible, socially beneficial and economically viable management of the world's forests.

CONTENTS

ABBREVIATIONS

A2/AD	Anti-Access/Area-Denial
AALD	Australian American Leadership Dialogue
ACRI	Australia-China Relations Institute
ADF	Australian Defence Force
AILF	Australia Israel Leadership Forum
ALP	Australian Labor Party
ANZAM	Anglo, New Zealand, Australia, Malaya Area
ANZUS	Australia, New Zealand, United States Security Treaty
APEC	Asia–Pacific Economic Cooperation
ASEAN	Association of Southeast Asian Nations
ASIC	Australian Security and Investments Commission
ASIO	Australian Security Intelligence Organisation
ASIS	Australian Secret Intelligence Service
ASPI	Australian Strategic Policy Institute
AUSFTA	Australia United States Free Trade Agreement
AUSMIN	Australia United States Ministerial Consultations
AWD	Air-Warfare Destroyer
AWU	Australian Workers Unions
CPI	Committee on Public Information
CCP	Chinese Communist Party
CSIS	Centre for Strategic and International Studies
DOA	Defence of Australia
DPRK	Democratic People's Republic of Korea
IMF	International Monetary Fund
IRS	Internal Revenue Service
ISIS	Islamic State of Iraq and Syria
IVLP	International Visitor Leadership Program
IVP	International Visitor Program
JAM-GC	Joint Concept for Access and Manoeuvre in the Global Commons

LHD	Landing Helicopter Dock
NAFTA	North American Free Trade Agreement
NATO	North Atlantic Treaty Organisation
NIC	Newly Industrialised Country
PRC	People's Republic of China
SCAP	Supreme Commander for the Allied Powers
SEATO	Southeast Asia Treaty Organisation
T1	Track One Diplomacy
T2	Track Two/Second Track Diplomacy
T3	Track Three Diplomacy
ToDs	Tracks of Diplomacy
UNCLOS	United Nations Convention on the Law of the Sea
UNIDIR	United Nations Institute for Disarmament Research
USIA	United States Information Agency
USSC	United States Studies Centre
YLD	Young Leadership Dialogue

ACKNOWLEDGEMENTS

I owe this book to the following people.

The initial idea originated with my PhD supervisor and intellectual mentor, Dr Scott Burchill. I had never come across the Australian American Leadership Dialogue before Scott suggested that I investigate its role in socialising Australian leaders. That seed grew into a 300 page manuscript and I am grateful for Scott's valuable insights and guidance along the way.

Were it not for the initiative and support provided by Professor Clinton Fernandes my PhD would have remained an unpublished manuscript. I am grateful for Clinton's confidence in my intellectual abilities and his willingness to give me the break I needed. Without his support this book would never have seen the light of day.

To Dr Nathan Hollier and Monash University Publishing, thank you for giving me the opportunity to have my research reach a wider audience. Your patience and understanding as I prepared this book were invaluable.

Thank you to my parents, Rocco and Laura Scappatura, who came from humble backgrounds and sacrificed so much to provide me with the privileges and opportunities that I now enjoy. I hope I have made you proud.

Above all, I thank my wife, Leila Lotfi, who had to endure my long absences for much longer than either of us anticipated. You believed in me when I didn't believe in myself. I can say without any hint of exaggeration that without your love and support, my PhD, and this book, would never have made it to completion.

To my children, Leo and Luca, it is you who remind me every day why this world is worth fighting for. I hope I can make it a little better for you both.

PREFACE

The debate about China's rising power and influence

Research for this book was undertaken as part of a PhD thesis completed in 2016. Aside from changes in structure, format and style, the essential content remains the same. There have been significant developments in the dynamics of the Australia-US relationship since the time this manuscript was completed. Specifically, the ascendency of Donald J. Trump to the White House has injected further impetus into an ongoing debate about the value and importance of Australia's relationship with the United States. That debate was initiated several years ago as a result of the apparent shift in strategic power from the US to China currently underway in the "Indo-Pacific". The major foreign policy debate in Australia today is whether or not an irresolvable clash exists between Australia's most important strategic partner – the United States – and its most important trading partner: China.

As this book argues, and as I have written elsewhere, the threat posed by China to Australia and the current US-dominated regional order is exaggerated.[1] The fear of a Chinese invasion of Australia is fantastical. The possibility of Beijing undertaking a unilateral and unprovoked act of aggression against Australia is remote. The only realistic contingency where Australia might come under attack by China is in the event of a general US-China conflict where there is a stated expectation of active Australian participation. In this scenario, "Beijing simply [could not] ignore the possibility of potentially decisive amounts of US air power being staged from northern Australia".[2] It is only *because of the alliance* and the deep level of Australian politico-military integration with the US that China poses a potentially significant and direct threat to Australian security.

---

1   Vince Scappatura, The US "Pivot" to Asia, the China Spectre and the Australian-American Alliance, *The Asia–Pacific Journal*, vol. 12, issue 36, no. 3, 9 September 2014, <http://apjjf.org/2014/12/36/Vince-Scappatura/4178/article.html>, accessed 1 April 2018.

2   Timothy J. Blizzard, The PLA, A2/AD and the ADF: Lessons for Future Maritime Strategy, *Security Challenges*, vol. 12, no. 3, 2016, p. 66.

In terms of the regional strategic order, China's growing military strength does pose challenges for America, specifically by making it increasingly difficult for the US navy to operate freely in the seas close to China. In the worldview of the US Department of Defence, Beijing's capacity to counter US "power projection capabilities" in the air and sea approaches to the Chinese homeland is a threat to US national interests.[3] Apart from this "threat", US military superiority in the Asia–Pacific remains unchallenged. As China's military power continues to grow, the South and East China Seas will become a more contested battlespace, but there is no evidence of China achieving military hegemony or anything like it over the Western Pacific.[4]

Similarly, many loose predictions about China's emergence as the next global superpower due to its extraordinary economic growth, and America's relative economic decline, are misleading because they fail to take seriously the impact of American-led globalisation.[5] The increasing dominance of transnational corporations (TNCs) and global supply chains means that national accounts no longer accurately reflect national economic power. Foreign-owned TNCs dominate key sectors of China's domestic and export markets and capture most of the value added. For example, even though China exports almost all of the world's iPhones, it is Apple that reaps the majority of the profits.

In the era of neoliberal globalisation, national power is more accurately measured by the ownership and profit-share of TNCs. A survey of the top 2000 global corporations reveals that America's transnationals enjoy unrivalled supremacy, leading or dominating in over 70 per cent of the major sectors of the international economy. It is only by taking the globalisation of corporate ownership into account that one can explain why American GDP accounts for "only" 22 per cent of global GDP, even as an incredible 46 per cent of the world's top corporations are owned by American firms, and a whopping 42 per cent of the world's millionaires are American (only 4 per cent are Chinese). In sum, "American power hasn't declined – it globalised".[6]

---

3 US Department of Defence, Sustaining US Global Leadership: Priorities for 21st Century Defence, January 2012, p. 4, <http://www.defense.gov/news/Defense_Strategic_Guidance.pdf>, accessed 1 April 2018.

4 Stephen Biddle and Ivan Oelrich, Future Warfare in the Western Pacific: Chinese Antiaccess/Area Denial, US AirSea Battle, and Command of the Commons in East Asia, *International Security*, vol. 41, no. 1, Summer 2016, pp. 7-48.

5 See, for example, Hugh White, Without America: Australia in the New Asia, *Quarterly Essay*, vol. 68, 2017, p. 31.

6 Sean Starrs, American Economic Power Hasn't Declined – It Globalised! Summoning the Data and Taking Globalisation Seriously, *International Studies*

While it may appear contradictory, China's capitalist rise signifies the realisation of America's global vision for hegemony. In the 1940s, American state planners recognised that the growth of other major economies served to benefit and solidify US power, as long as they remained open to American capital. The primary threat to the expansion of capitalism was communism and third world nationalism. By the end of the Cold War, both of these challenges had largely collapsed in the face of the American military and economic juggernaut. Today, the world's former peasant societies, including in China, have rapidly transformed into masses of workers and consumers. The entire planet is now virtually integrated into global capitalism under American influence and leadership. American business has overwhelmingly benefited from the capitalist rise of others, more or less as was envisioned in the 1940s. The growth of China and other emerging markets doesn't reflect the end of the American empire, but the end of the beginning of the "American Century".[7]

Of course, US global dominance is not guaranteed. America is free to squander its immense advantages by any number of ill-conceived domestic and foreign policy decisions, such as reverting to economic isolationism or engaging in imperial overstretch. If left unabated, deepening domestic political and social issues – the result of a neoliberal assault over the past four decades and recurring economic crises wrought by the financialisation of capitalism – might unleash extreme right-wing forces that lead the United States down an irreversibly self-destructive path. However, absent such mortally self-inflicted blows, no country is likely to acquire the means to challenge US hegemony in the foreseeable future. Indicators that take into account net rather than gross measures of national power illustrate that the United States is in a league of its own when it comes to economic and military capabilities, and future trends are generally in its favour.[8]

Apart from strategic and economic considerations, China's rise has raised concerns about its growing "soft power" influence in Australia. Since completing the core research for this manuscript, a debate has exploded on the front pages of Australia's major newspapers on the influence of the Chinese Communist Party (CCP) in Australia. The issue was brought to

---

Quarterly, vol. 57, 2013, pp. 817-830.

7   Sean Starrs, "The Rise of Emerging Markets Signifies the End of the Beginning of the American Century: Henry Luce and the Emergence of Global Capitalism" in Salvador Santino, F. Reglime Jr and James Parisot, *American Hegemony and the Rise of Emerging Powers: Cooperation or Conflict*, New York: Routledge, 2018, pp. 76-101.

8   Michael Beckley, *Unrivaled: Why America Will Remain The World's Sole Superpower*, Ithaca: Cornell University Press, 2018.

prominence when a joint investigation by *Fairfax Media* and *Four Corners* revealed what was described as a "covert campaign of influence in Australia" and an "aggressive form of soft power" waged by the CCP.[9] There were some concerning revelations in those reports that were certainly newsworthy. However, what's most remarkable about the debate is how uneven it is. As Professor of International Politics, Mark Beeson, has noted, it's difficult not to be struck by the fact that China's degree of institutionalised influence in Australia pales in comparison to that enjoyed by the United States.[10] Australia, after all, hosts American, not Chinese bases.

When this fact was pointed out to the Director of Foreign Policy and Defence at the United States Studies Centre at Sydney University, Ashley Townshend, the response was that America's presence at the Joint Defence Facility Pine Gap and in Darwin shouldn't be considered "foreign interference".[11] It is a viewpoint reminiscent of the remarks expressed by former Australian Prime Minister Tony Abbott, that "few Australians would regard America as a foreign country."[12] According to Ely Ratner, a former American national security advisor and senior fellow at the Council of Foreign Relations, even the debate on the margins of Australian commentary about American foreign interference in Australia is "deeply disturbing from [a] US perspective, and good evidence China's influence ops [sic] in Australia are succeeding".[13]

Clive Hamilton's *Silent Invasion: China's Influence in Australia*, published in early 2018, to much fanfare and controversy, provides further illustration that Washington's influence in Australia is so pervasive and internalised that it is not even perceived or otherwise recognised as problematic. Hamilton alleges that the CCP "is engaged in a systematic campaign to infiltrate, influence and control the most important institutions in Australia" in an attempt to "break our alliance with the United States and turn this country

---

9   Nick McKenzie, et al., China's Operation Australia, *Sydney Morning Herald*, June 2017, <http://www.smh.com.au/interactive/2017/chinas-operation-australia/>, accessed 1 April 2018.

10   Mark Beeson, Soft Power and the Institutionalisation of Influence, *The Conversation*, 12 September 2016, <https://theconversation.com/soft-power-and-the-institutionalisation-of-influence-65208>, accessed 1 April 2018.

11   Ashley Townshend, Twitter Post, 11 June 2017, <https://twitter.com/ashleytownshend/status/873820094459019264>, accessed 1 April 2018.

12   Tony Abbott, Speech to The Heritage Foundation, Washington DC, 18 July 2012, <http://australianpolitics.com/2012/07/18/abbott-foreign-policy-speech-heritage-foundation.html>, accessed 1 April 2018.

13   Ely Ratner, Twitter Post, 10 June 2017, <https://twitter.com/elyratner/status/873515255812456448>, accessed 1 April 2018.

into a tribute state".[14] One of the central strategies of the CCP is to utilise the "art of relationship management", building personal relationships with prominent figures in politics, business, the media and academia who can be persuaded to disseminate Beijing's position. According to Hamilton, the CCP has successfully cultivated a cohort of pro-Beijing voices among elites and opinion makers who are now the loudest voices in Australia.[15]

That the CCP would like to drive a wedge into the Australian-American alliance is unsurprising, but the notion that it is anywhere close to succeeding is nothing short of fantastical. It is the position of the pro-US lobby that constitutes the loudest voice among Australian elites and opinion makers. As this book illustrates, there has existed for decades a broad and deep pro-US security consensus among Australia's foreign policy and national security elite. The elite consensus is rooted in an alliance orthodoxy that conceives of the Australian-American alliance as indispensable to Australian security and bound by a "special relationship" forged in shared values and underpinned by benign US regional power.

For those who sustain it, the alliance orthodoxy is not subject to external measures of validity. Threat-centric explanations for the alliance are not convincing, and the exercise of US regional power has been far from benign. Rather, the alliance orthodoxy is driven by elite interests deeply rooted in historical legacies and myriad institutionalised relationships with Washington, built over decades. One of the central ways the United States acts to bind Australia to US foreign policy interests is by cultivating the same kinds of "networks of influence" that Hamilton argues typify the strategy of the CCP to break Australia's alliance with the United States. The "soft power" wielded by Washington, however, is of a quantity and quality unmatched by the CCP.

If it were otherwise, Australia's integration with the United States at the political, military and intelligence levels would not have *accelerated* over the period of China's rapidly growing influence during the last two decades. Consider the remarks by Kim Beazley, who stepped down as Australia's Ambassador to the US in 2016 after six years in office. Beazley recounted his "shock" as he first arrived in Washington to discover that Australia was "vastly more deeply engaged with the Americans than we were during the

---

14   Clive Hamilton, *Silent Invasion: China's Influence in Australia*, Kindle Edition, Melbourne: Hardie Grant Books, 2018, Kindle Locations 142-143.

15   Hamilton, chapter 12, especially the "China Club" and Kindle Locations 5137-5140.

Cold War".[16] Over the course of the 21st century, Beazley was witness to the emergence of a "deep state" between Australia and the United States that has cemented the alliance irrespective of who may occupy the White House in Washington or The Lodge in Canberra. Beazley describes the "deep state" in the following terms:

> [The] seamless interconnection between Australian and US armed forces, intelligence services, exploitation of the joint facilities and capability acquisition ... that stands aside from processes most immediately affected by elected governments.[17]

After nearly two decades of fighting the "war on terror", primarily in the battlegrounds of Afghanistan and Iraq, the ADF has achieved an unprecedented degree of integration with the armed forces of the United States; organisationally, operationally and materially. Even so, as Australia and the US shift focus to Asia and jointly prepare to confront the rise of China, the degree of military integration is set to undertake a "step-change" in every area from Special Forces to amphibious strike, air combat, force projection and ballistic-missile defence.[18]

Perhaps the most salient expression of this deepening integration is the dramatic expansion in the size, capability and function of America's military presence in Australia, including in what is the most important intelligence facility outside of the United States – Pine Gap. Australia is now "literally and institutionally hardwired into the US global surveillance system and military operations, with consequent legal and moral responsibilities".[19] Nuclear war planning, drone assassinations, mass surveillance and the militarisation of space are all now a central feature of Australia's alliance with the United States.

---

16   Kim Beazley, Vernon Parker Oration, Australian Naval Institute, 22 June 2016, <http://navalinstitute.com.au/full-text-of-2016-vernon-parker-oration-kim-beazley/>, accessed 1 April 2018.

17   Kim Beazley, "Sovereignty and the Alliance" in Peter J. Dean, Stephan Fruling and Brendan Taylor (eds), *Australia's American Alliance: Towards a New Era?*, Kindle Edition, Melbourne: Melbourne University Publishing Digital, 2016, Kindle Locations 4383-4389.

18   Peter Jennings, Turnbull Sees New Opportunity to Grow The US Alliance, *The Australian*, 1 March 2018, <https://www.theaustralian.com.au/national-affairs/defence/turnbull-sees-new-opportunity-to-grow-the-us-alliance/news-story/fe9a4871acc58bc4bb9c166f45781285>, accessed 1 April 2018.

19   Richard Tanter, Our Poisoned Heart: The Transformation of Pine Gap, *Arena Magazine*, 2016, <https://arena.org.au/our-poisoned-heart-by-richard-tanter/>, accessed 1 April 2018.

As a result of former Prime Minister Julia Gillard's decision in November 2011 to form a central plank in President Obama's "Pivot" to Asia – read containment of China – Australia now hosts 1500 US Marines in Darwin, scheduled to increase to a full Marine Air-Ground Task Force (MAGTF) of 2,500 by 2020, including command, ground combat and air combat elements available for rapid deployment and expeditionary combat. They constitute what Admiral Samuel J. Locklear, former Commander of US Pacific Command, describes as "the point of the arrow" of US forward-deployed forces, representing "credible deterrence and the 'fight tonight' force necessary for immediate crisis and contingency response".[20]

America's military presence in Darwin is part of a global network of over 800 foreign military bases in more than 70 countries.[21] Following the Roman practice of nominally respecting the sovereign independence of its weaker allies by requiring only a patch of ground for a Roman fortress, Washington too has sought little or no territory, instead establishing hundreds of military bases scattered across the planet. Leaders in Canberra may argue that there are no American bases in Australia, only "joint facilities", but like a Roman vassal state, by granting patches of ground to host US military forces and intelligence facilities, Australia undoubtedly constitutes a part of America's global empire.[22]

There is a stark difference in the way that Chinese and American influence in Australia is perceived by national security elites. While Beijing's soft power influence may be "silent" or clandestine, and extends into espionage and surveillance, it is immediately recognised and condemned as malign. The influence exercised by the United States, on the other hand, is open and consensual; rarely condemned because it is considered mutually beneficial and benign. Australians need not be concerned about America's influence, let alone the broader Australia-US alliance, because according to our national elites it reflexively serves the national interest.

For those who are less sanguine about the current bi-partisan consensus on Australia's relationship with the United States, and where that relationship is heading, acknowledging and understanding the nature of American influence in Australia is paramount. The objective of US "soft power",

---

20   Scappatura, The US "Pivot" to Asia.

21   In comparison to the approximately 30 foreign bases of all non-US countries combined. David Vine, *Base Nation: How US Military Bases Abroad Harm America and the World*, New York: Metropolitan Books, 2015.

22   For a comparative historical analysis of the American Empire see, Alfred W. McCoy, *In the Shadows of the American Century: The Rise and Decline of US Global Power*, Chicago: Haymarket Books, 2017.

and the pro-US lobby, is not to hijack and transform Australia's national security policy but to preserve and protect the status quo, instilling and reinforcing the alliance orthodoxy among the public and especially in the minds of the next generation of elites and alliance managers. The point is to insulate the alliance from any serious critical reflection on its costs and benefits, head off any potential opposition and bind Australia to an ever-closer relationship with America.

The debate about foreign influence in Australia is entirely hypocritical on this dimension of "soft power". Attempts by the pro-China lobby to harden the ideological position of those who agree with the CCP's view on an issue are portrayed as a "weaponised narrative attack".[23] In contrast, critics who point to similar efforts by the pro-US lobby are levelled with the charge of "anti-Americanism".[24] While US influence passes without criticism, both major political parties have responded to the threat of foreign interference by authoritarian regimes – namely China and Russia – by enacting sweeping and draconian changes to national security legislation that threaten to suppress dissent and political communication but ignore the much larger threat to democratic processes posed by corporate political activity.[25]

There are good reasons why the pro-US lobby in Australia concentrate their efforts on maintaining a strong elite consensus on the alliance. Global research suggests that political opponents and social movements who have attempted to challenge the pro-US positions of their national governments are much less likely to be successful when a broad and deep national security consensus exists about the centrality of their nation's alliance with the United States. Even in the face of a broad-based mass social movement, if the security consensus is strong, elites will likely dig their heels in and attempt to resist, co-opt or simply wait out any mass opposition.

However, if social movements manage to take advantage of an open political window, forge alliances with sympathetic elites and break the consensus, the likelihood for success is greatly increased. Cracks in

23   Chris Zappone, Is the Talk of Australia's 'Anti-China Bias' a Weaponised Narrative? *Sydney Morning Herald*, 19 May 2018, <https://www.smh.com.au/world/asia/is-talk-of-australia-s-anti-china-bias-a-weaponised-narrative-20180503-p4zd4a.html>, accessed 20 September 2018.

24   Clive Hamilton, Chinese Communist Party Influence: Why the Critics Are Wrong, *Policy Forum*, 9 April 2018, <https://www.policyforum.net/chinese-communist-party-influence-critics-wrong/>, accessed 20 September 2018.

25   James Goodman, Contesting Accusations of "Foreign Interference": The New Agenda for Australian Civil Society, *Cosmopolitan Civil Societies: An Interdisciplinary Journal*, vol. 10, no. 1, 2018, pp. 64-84.

the national security consensus can occur by slow moving forces like a generational change in attitudes, or more quickly in response to changes in the external security environment, or other external "shocks", that might cause some elites to recalibrate their existing beliefs and perceptions about the value of the alliance.[26]

America's "pivot" to Asia to confront China's growing power – increasing the alliance burden on Australia and the risk of being dragged into a major regional war – combined with the more immediate "shock" of Trump in the White House, may provide a small political window for a broad-based social movement in Australia to exploit and weaken the security consensus in order to redefine Australia's relationship with the United States.

Increased public debate on the value of the alliance to Australia, and public opinion polls that indicate majority opposition to Australian part-icipation in any future US wars in Asia, have certainly been noted with alarm by members of the pro-US lobby. Rory Medcalf, Head of the National Security College at ANU, has observed that:

> [G]overnments in Canberra and Washington can no longer assume that the Australian public will go along with whatever policy decisions officials and political leaders reach when it comes to the shape of the alliance or the way it operates in an increasingly contested Asia.[27]

The election of President Donald J. Trump has significantly elevated these concerns. It's now "an open question how long the relationship can prosper under the weight of Mr Trump's behaviour", warns Michael Fullilove and Alex Oliver from the Lowy Institute of International Affairs.[28] Consequently, "the challenge ahead is how do we preserve and protect the alliance through a difficult phase."[29] Australia's former top defence official, Dennis Richardson, responded to Trump's election by issuing what

---

26 Andrew Yeo, *Activists, Alliances, And Anti-US Base Protests*, Cambridge: Cambridge University Press, 2011.

27 Rory Medcalf, Australia and the United States: Navigating Strategic Uncertainty, Asian Alliances Working Paper Series, Paper 4, *Brookings Institute,* July 2016, p. 6, <https://www.brookings.edu/wp-content/uploads/2016/07/Paper-4v3.pdf>, accessed 1 April 2018.

28 Michael Fullilove and Alex Oliver, Trump Tarnishes America's Standing Down Under, *The Wall Street Journal*, 20 June 2017, <https://www.wsj.com/articles/trump-tarnishes-americas-standing-down-under-1497975866>, accessed 1 April 2018.

29 Rory Medcalf, The Future of Australia's Alliance with the United States, Speech at the National Press Club, Canberra, 21 February 2017, <https://crawford.anu.edu.au/news-events/news/9214/future-australias-alliance-united-states>, accessed 1 April 2018.

amounted to a clarion call to the pro-US lobby. "Those who believe in the alliance", he proclaimed, "must be prepared to engage in the public debate and to make the case. Perhaps more so than of any time over the past 70 years, this is one of those times."[30]

Even more ominous was the warning issued by two former senior advisers from the US and Australia, Michael Green and Andrew Shearer respectively, who had the following to say in May 2017:

> [We] have each held senior positions in our respective governments and have generally downplayed concerns about public support for the US-Australia alliance over the past 10 years. Candidly, we are now growing concerned. No other US ally in the Pacific has had, in recent history, two former prime ministers actively attacking their country's alliance with the US. [While there is] broad support for the alliance in Australia, it [is] not deep – particularly among millennials. We will need our leaders to go beyond reconfirming our indispensable alliance and to begin charting a compelling path forward together.[31]

The challenge for Australians who want a chart a *different* path for Australia's national security policy, and its alliance with the United States, is to articulate an alternative national security discourse that can replace the current US alliance orthodoxy. Actually, Australians don't have to look far. In his book *Unnecessary Wars*, Henry Reynolds highlights that Australia possesses a small but articulate alternative national security culture within its historical experience. Reynolds brings attention to the band of mid-to-late 19th century Australian republicans and nationalists who rejected the dominant discourse of the time, which stressed security through dependence and support for British imperialism. Instead, in Reynolds' words, they presciently argued that:

> [P]roximity to the empire carried its own risks and would inevitably drag Australia needlessly into wars, whereas the isolation of the continent could allow for neutrality or at least non-intervention. The

---

30   Fergus Hunter, Top Defence Official Warns of "Big Mistake" of Questioning US Alliance Over Donald Trump, *The Canberra Times*, 24 November 2016, <http://www.canberratimes.com.au/federal-politics/political-news/top-defence-official-warns-of-big-mistake-of-questioning-us-alliance-over-donald-trump-20161124-gswog5.html>, accessed 1 April 2018.

31   Michael Green and Andrew Shearer, Turnbull-Trump: The Alliance Needed A New Start, And Got One, *The Interpreter*, Lowy Institute for International Policy, 6 May 2017, <https://www.lowyinstitute.org/the-interpreter/turnbull-trump-alliance-needed-new-start-and-got-one>, accessed 1 April 2018.

empire itself was a potent source of danger. Security would come from remaining at home and using the armed forces purely for defence of the homeland. The continent, not the empire, had to be the main concern of all international relations. Australian interests could be distinguished from those of Britain and should be given priority.[32]

There has in fact been an enduring history in Australia of dissident "strategic subcultures" that have challenged the dominant strain of reliance on "great and powerful friends", advocating instead that Australia provide for its own security.[33] Be it "Fortress Australia", "armed and independent" or "unarmed and neutral", there have always been alternatives to "bandwagoning" on the global or regional hegemonic power. The New Zealand experience since leaving ANZUS is also instructive.[34] Each alternative holds advantages and drawbacks, but the debate must begin with an acknowledgement of both Australia's relatively benign security environment and the heavy costs of continuing the American embrace, not only to Australians, but especially to the victims of American power abroad; and also to Americans themselves.

An unfortunate irony of the "special relationship" narrative is that while claiming to be the "true friends" of America, Australian leaders have consistently pleaded with the US to maintain its enormous global military presence, ignoring the difficulties endured by the American people under the extraordinary burden of maintaining a vast military-industrial complex. Far from encouraging restraint, Australia has acted as a "hound dog" by "beseeching, urging, encouraging US military adventurism", including into the most disastrous and costly foreign military conflicts in American history since World War Two – Vietnam and Iraq.[35]

The mounting political, economic and social problems inside the United States are currently being compounded by the radical insurgency of President Trump's Republican Party, which is systematically dismantling

---

32   Henry Reynolds, *Unnecessary Wars*, Kindle Edition, Sydney: NewSouth Publishing, 2016, Kindle Locations 253-256.

33   Peter J. Dean, "The Alliance, Australia's Strategic Culture and Way of War" in Peter J. Dean, Stephan Fruling and Brendan Taylor (eds), *Australia's American Alliance: Towards a New Era?*, Kindle Edition, Melbourne: Melbourne University Publishing Digital, 2016.

34   Mark Beeson, Australia's Defence: Should we go down the Kiwi Road? *The Strategist*, Australian Strategic Policy Institute, 10 December 2015, <https://www.aspistrategist.org.au/australias-defence-should-we-go-down-the-kiwi-road/>, accessed 1 April 2018.

35   Lloyd Cox and Brendon O'Connor, Australia, the US, and the Vietnam and Iraq Wars: "Hound Dog not Lapdog", *Australian Journal of Political Science*, vol. 47, No. 2, 2012, p. 185.

America's social institutions to further enrich the top 1 per cent and increase the already gargantuan military budget, all the while racing to the precipice of global environmental catastrophe and nuclear Armageddon.[36] In June 2018, the Trump administration saw the US Senate pass a US$716 billion defence budget for fiscal year 2019, representing a US$82 billion increase from the previous year. The *increase* in US military spending alone over the past two years (US$165 billion) is bigger than the entire annual military budget of China (US$150 billion).[37]

Trump's decision to "take the gloves off the Pentagon" saw the US military dropping 44,096 bombs in his first year in office alone; an average of 121 bombs per day, or one bomb every 12 minutes. By comparison, during the George W. Bush and Barack Obama administrations, the US military dropped an average of 8,750 and 12,500 bombs per year, respectively.[38] Unsurprisingly, Trump's more muscular approach to the "war on terror", specifically in directing the US military to loosen its rules of engagement, has led to the killing of large numbers of civilians.[39]

Meanwhile, Australia's Defence Industry Minister, Christopher Pyne, reaffirmed the "special relationship" after Trump's shock victory by lauding his election commitment to "a massive expansion of US military capability", beaming that it "could bring with it remarkable opportunities for the Australian defence industry".[40] Similarly, Australia's longest serving foreign minister, Alexander Downer, praised Trump's massive tax cuts for corporate

36   Noam Chomsky and David Barsamian, Noam Chomsky Diagnoses the Trump Era, *The Nation*, 3 October 2017, <https://www.thenation.com/article/noam-chomsky-diagnoses-the-trump-era/>, accessed 1 April 2018.

37   Matt Taibbi, Can You Think of Any Other Ways to Spend $716 Billion?, *Rolling Stone*, 21 June 2018, <https://www.rollingstone.com/politics/politics-news/can-you-think-of-any-other-ways-to-spend-716-billion-666079/>, accessed 20 September 2018.

38   Lee Camp, Trump's Military Drops a Bomb Every 12 Minutes, and No One Is Talking About It, Truthdig, 19 June 2018, <https://www.truthdig.com/articles/trumps-military-drops-a-bomb-every-12-minutes-and-no-one-is-talking-about-it/>, accessed 20 September 2018.

39   Margaret Sullivan, Middle East Civilian Deaths Have Soared Under Trump. And The Media Mostly Shrug, *Washington Post*, 16 March 2018, <https://www.washingtonpost.com/lifestyle/style/middle-east-civilian-deaths-have-soared-under-trump-and-the-media-mostly-shrug/2018/03/16/fc344968-2932-11e8-874b-d517e912f125_story.html>, accessed 20 September 2018.

40   Christopher Pyne, Speech to the Submarine Institute of Australia, 16 November 2016, <http://www.contactairlandandsea.com/2016/11/16/transcript-christopher-pyne-submarine-institute-speech/>, accessed 1 April 2018.

America, as well as his "aggressive commitment to American military power" and "huge increase in defence spending", as "good for Australia".[41]

Notwithstanding such grotesque and distorted expressions of national self-interest, the pro-US lobby in Australia is generally alarmed by the Trump administration; not because of the grave risks and costs of further American militarisation, but due to the fear that Trump's "America first" approach will reduce American military presence and undermine American leadership in Asia. The anxiety and condemnation that accompanied Trump's announcement to suspend provocative military exercises in South Korea – exercises that are intended to demonstrate the capacity to "decapitate" the North Korean leadership and overthrow the Kim regime – is an apt illustration of how wedded Australian national security elites are to US hegemony.[42] Following the logic of the alliance orthodoxy, the prospect of a peace treaty on the Korean peninsula and the evaporation of the North Korean threat would be dangerous for Australia, and against our long-term interests, because it might lead to a weakening of America's military presence in Asia.[43]

Australians who criticise the US alliance and challenge the belief in America as a benign hegemonic power are often portrayed as "anti-American". However, if the term has any relevance, it is more applicable to Australian leaders and opinion makers who seek to exploit America's power at the expense of the American people. A true friend of America would seek to challenge, not cheer, the forces of militarism and neoliberalism at home and abroad. The pro-US lobby's attempt to advance these forces by strengthening the alliance makes Australia an ally of the worst kind. Former Prime Minister Gough Whitlam's invocation, at the height of the then Liberal government's enthusiasm for America's disastrous war in Vietnam, remains just as pertinent today: "Heaven save the United States from such allies".[44]

---

41   Alexander Downer, Donald Trump's Much Better for Australia Than Barack Obama Was, *Australian Financial Review*, 5 August 2018, https://www.afr.com/opinion/columnists/donald-trumps-much-better-for-australia-than-barack-obama-was-20180805-h13kii>, accessed 20 September 2018.

42   Debra Killalea, Trump-Kim Meeting: What It All Means For Australia, *9News*, 13 June 2018, <https://www.9news.com.au/national/2018/06/13/11/23/trump-kim-meeting-what-it-means-for-australia>, accessed 20 September 2018.

43   Brendan Taylor, The Kim-Trump Summit: Implications For Australia, *Australian Outlook*, 20 June 2018, <https://www.internationalaffairs.org.au/australianoutlook/trump-kim-summit-implications-australia/>, accessed 20 September 2018.

44   James Curran, *Unholy Fury: Whitlam and Nixon at War*, Kindle Edition, Melbourne: Melbourne University Press, 2015, Kindle Locations 1837-1840.

INTRODUCTION

What this book is about

This book challenges the conventional conception of the Australian-American alliance as indispensable to Australian security and bound by a "special relationship" forged in shared values and underpinned by benign US regional power. It also challenges many critiques of the alliance that argue Canberra's enthusiastic support for Washington's foreign policy objectives can be explained primarily by an insecurity complex and other cultural predispositions that lend themselves to dependency on "great and powerful friends". Instead, this book argues that the alliance can be best understood in the unsentimental "realist" terms of power politics, as an expression of the complementary objectives of preserving Western control over global, and particularly regional, strategic and economic affairs, and extending Australia's influence abroad.

While the general public in Australia views the alliance primarily in terms of providing a security guarantee in the event of an attack, foreign policy and national security elites highlight the privileged access it provides to strategic councils in Washington and advanced US military technologies and cutting-edge defence science, and vastly enhanced intelligence collection capabilities that bolster Australia's strategic and diplomatic influence. Security concerns are not primarily conceived of by national security elites in terms of a direct threat to Australia – an eventuality that has remained remote since World War Two – but threats to US regional hegemony and Australia's status as a leading "middle power".

Although material interests and the desire to advance state power and influence form the basis of elite support for the alliance, the breadth and depth of that support is sustained by a pro-US security consensus and alliance orthodoxy, rooted in domestic institutions, ideologies and historical legacies, that serves to constrain Australian national security policymakers and prevent them from departing too far from the status quo. Together with prominent voices in the media, academia, defence, think-tanks and non-government organisations that promote the alliance orthodoxy, this loose network of elites and institutional relationships can be broadly described as the "US Lobby" which functions to further entrench Australia's "special relationship" with America.

Arguably the most important private institution dedicated to reinforcing the alliance orthodoxy in the minds of Australian leaders is the Australian American Leadership Dialogue (AALD), which forms the central subject of this book's analysis on the US Lobby as a whole. For over a quarter of a century, the AALD has helped to build and solidify personal relationships between present and up-and-coming leaders in both Australia and the United States, strengthening the bi-lateral relationship at the elite level and in conformity with the alliance orthodoxy. Although just one small element of the US Lobby, the nature and function of the AALD, laid bare in this book, provides crucial insights into the wider role and significance of the Lobby and American "soft power" influence in Australia. It also sheds light on the ways and means by which the alliance orthodoxy constrains Australian foreign policy choices.

The AALD and its role and function in managing Australia's alliance with the United States has never been subject to a major study or exposed to sustained critical attention in the media and in scholarship. This is despite the fact that the AALD is widely lauded as "arguably the most valuable private-sector foreign policy initiative ever undertaken in Australia",[1] "a central institution in the US-Australia relationship"[2] and "the most important of all non-government organisations dedicated to the strengthening of the Australia-US alliance in all its manifestations; civil, political and commercial".[3] Paradoxically, the AALD is also largely unknown beyond a small group of interested participants and observers. Supporters of the AALD concede that it is a "vital but largely invisible part of the alliance infrastructure"[4] and a "semi-secret of the alliance".[5]

This book is an attempt to raise awareness and understanding of the role and function of the AALD, particularly in managing elite opinion in Australia. Based in part on interviews with current and former participants,

---

1   Stephen Loosley, Support Grows For Free Trade, *Sunday Telegraph*, 19 August 2001.

2   Greg Sheridan, Financial Shadow On Alliances, *The Australian*, 25 September 2008.

3   Glenn Milne, Rudd's Relevance Deprivation Syndrome, *The Drum, ABC*, 29 September 2010, <http://www.abc.net.au/unleashed/35454.html>, accessed 1 April 2018.

4   Peter Hartcher, In With The New, And No Hard Feelings, *Sydney Morning Herald*, 26 January 2008, <http://www.smh.com.au/news/opinion/in-with-the-new-and-no-hard-feelings/2008/01/25/1201157663391.html>, accessed 1 April 2018.

5   Greg Sheridan, *The Partnership: The Inside Story of the US-Australian Alliance Under Bush and Howard*, Sydney: UNSW Press, 2007, p. 311.

and informed by existing literature on lobby groups, informal diplomacy and public diplomacy, this book identifies three central ways the AALD influences elite opinion. First, the AALD carefully frames discussion and debate about the value of the alliance to Australia. Second, it facilitates the socialisation of Australian elites into the alliance orthodoxy. And finally, it serves as a "gatekeeper" of the status quo and a litmus test on the alliance loyalty of potential future leaders.

What is the alliance orthodoxy?

Central to the analysis of this book is the concept of alliance orthodoxy. The intellectual foundations of the concept lie in the security consensus framework developed by Andrew Yeo in his book *Activists, Alliances, and Anti-US Base Protests*.[6] In attempting to understand why some social movements opposed to the hosting of US foreign bases succeed, and others fail, Yeo argues that the degree of pro-US security consensus among host-nation elites plays a key role. Yeo defines the pro-US security consensus in the following terms:

> [The] pro-US security consensus [is] based on the shared perception and understanding of US-host-state relations among national elites. For example, do political elites agree that US alliance relations function as an integral component of their national security strategy? Do host-government elites value a long-term strategic partnership with the United States? As a corollary, states characterized by a high degree of security consensus tend to accept the hosting of US military bases as an important component of their relationship with the United States.[7]

The degree of security consensus is captured by its breadth, measured by the number of elite individuals and groups who share the consensus, and its depth, measured by the level of embodiment in domestic institutions, ideologies and historical legacies. The depth of the security consensus in particular helps solidify collective beliefs and prevent elites from deviating too far from the status quo.[8]

---

6   Andrew Yeo, *Activists, Alliances, And Anti-US Base Protests*, Cambridge: Cambridge University Press, 2011.

7   Yeo, p. 14.

8   Yeo, p. 28.

While all national elites may share a similar outlook with respect to the centrality of the security relationship with the United States, Yeo defines the relevant holders of the pro-US security consensus as government or political elites within the foreign policy or national security establishments.[9] In this book, a distinction is made between the national security *establishment* and the national security *elite* which is a broader term that includes prominent voices in the media, academia, think-tanks and non-government organisations – the bulk of the US Lobby.

Although Yeo does not include Australia in his assessment, focussing instead on American security relations with the Philippines, Japan, Ecuador, Italy and South Korea, Australia undoubtedly fulfils the criteria for possessing a pro-US security consensus. In answering the three questions posed by Yeo, the alliance with the United States is considered indispensable to Australia's national security, highly valued in terms of its long term strategic value, and the hosting of US bases in Australia, specifically Pine Gap, is widely accepted to be the "heart" or "strategic essence" of the alliance.[10]

Utilising Yeo's measures, the pro-US security consensus enjoys extraordinary breadth and depth among Australian's foreign policy and national security elite. In terms of breadth, the alliance is widely understood to constitute the cornerstone of Australia's entire foreign and strategic policy since the 1950s. A strong belief in the alliance is held by key foreign policy elites in both major parties, senior figures in the bureaucracy and influential non-government organisations.[11] Strong public opinion, electoral politics and elite preferences combine to underpin what one scholar has described as the "Canberra consensus": the belief "that a very strong military relationship with the USA is necessary for Australia's well-being".[12]

The pro-US security consensus is also deeply embodied in domestic institutions, ideologies and historical legacies. Further evidence of this is provided in chapter two which explores the mythology of the alliance as a "special relationship", grounded in shared values and bound by blood ties forged in war. Even for a number of strong supporters of Australia's relationship with the United States, the alliance has become an "ideology" and an "article of faith" in Australian politics:

---

9   Yeo, p. 15.

10 Desmond Ball, The Strategic Essence, *Australian Journal of International Affairs*, vol. 55, no. 2, 2001.

11 Nick Bisley, An Ally For All The Years To Come: Why Australia Is Not A Conflicted US Ally, *Australian Journal of International Affairs*, vol. 67, no. 4, 2013, pp. 410-412.

12 Bisley, p. 410.

It has ceased to be just a practical arrangement for the mutual benefit of two sovereign states, or a signal of the close cultural and historical ties between Australia and the US. It has become an idée fixe, with neither side of politics capable of articulating a vision for Australian foreign policy that does not presume an ever-closer relationship.[13]

Beyond the security realm, the Australia-US relationship has penetrated Australia's diplomatic, military, social, political, economic and cultural spheres. Accordingly, writes Australian historian Peter Edwards, it is "far more than just another bilateral relationship ... it has become a political institution in its own right, comparable with a political party or the monarchy".[14] Consequently, anyone who transgresses the norm of bipartisanship towards the alliance, and Australia's national security policies more generally, is criticised and delegitimised, with compliance monitored and reinforced by prominent voices in the media, academia and the defence industry.[15]

While Yeo accurately locates the foundations of the security consensus in the relationship between threat-perceptions, identity and ideology, he does not go far enough in addressing the importance of interests in shaping the beliefs of elites.[16]

I contend that material interests and the desire to advance state power and influence best explain Australia's alliance with the United States. If that is the case, what is the relationship between belief in the alliance orthodoxy and the material interests that motivate elite support for the alliance?

The relationship between elite interests and beliefs is convincingly dealt with by Natasha Hamilton-Hart in her in-depth study of American power in Southeast Asia.[17] Hamilton-Hart investigates the foundational beliefs

13 Sam Roggeveen, Tony Abbott and the US Alliance, *The Interpreter*, Lowy Institute for International Policy, 21 August 2013, <https://www.lowyinstitute.org/the-interpreter/tony-abbott-and-us-alliance>, accessed 1 April 2018.

14 Peter Edwards, *Permanent Friends? Historical Reflections on the Australian-American Alliance*, Lowy Institute Paper 8, Lowy Institute for International Policy, Sydney, 13 December 2005, p. 2, <http://www.lowyinstitute.org/publications/permanent-friends-historical-reflections-australian-american-alliance>, accessed 1 April 2018.

15 Andrew Carr, Is Bipartisanship on National Security Beneficial? Australia's Politics of Defence and Security, *Australian Journal of Politics and History*, vol. 63, no. 2, 2017, pp. 258-259.

16 In all fairness, the theoretical framework Yeo presents is more concerned with evaluating the strength or weakness of the security consensus rather than its origins. Yeo, p. 15.

17 Natasha Hamilton-Hart, *Hard Interests, Soft Illusions*: Southeast Asia and American Power, New York: Cornell University Press, 2012.

of elites in six Southeast Asian nations regarding the international role and power of the United States.[18] In each case, just as in Australia, the foundational belief of the majority of foreign policy-makers and practitioners is that the exercise of American power is fundamentally benign and necessary for regional stability and prosperity.

Hamilton-Hart argues that these foundational beliefs are not straight-forward reflections of an external reality but a manifestation of the int-erests and position of ruling elites and their key constituencies who have disproportionately benefited from the exercise of American power. In other words, they are self-serving beliefs. As Hamilton-Hart explains:

> Our motives and interests impinge on the way we gather, absorb, and evaluate information. While we do not simply see the world as conforming to the way we would like it to be, there is ample evidence that what we see and what we believe can be influenced by what we want.[19]

In terms of Southeast Asian elites, the exercise of US power during the Cold War, often through the provision of military and economic aid, secured the political power of ruling parties and their key constituents as they brutally repressed popular political opposition movements.[20] Over the longer term, the particular capitalist order and patterns of growth sup-ported by the United States enriched state elites, large corporate enterprises and the urban middle class while marginalising labour, the poor and rural populations.[21] In these domestic political conflicts, the exercise of US power has undoubtedly been benign for a privileged minority but simultaneously destructive for the majority of others.

In Australia's case, the global order crafted and sustained by American military, political and economic power since World War Two has served the tangible interests of some, even many, Australians. This fundamental fact is often ignored by those critics who argue policymakers in Canberra are driven by an irrational insecurity complex that leads to dependence on, and even subservience to, Washington. Indeed, it would be rather strange if Australian policymakers persistently failed to correctly perceive

---

18   Indonesia, Malaysia, the Philippines, Thailand, Singapore and Vietnam.

19   Hamilton-Hart, p. 29.

20   Although playing an indispensable role, the heavy lifting in the case of Singapore and Malaysia was carried out by Great Britain rather than the United States. Vietnam, of course, is an exception.

21   Hamilton-Hart, chapter 3.

these interests over many decades; and yet that is precisely what those who subscribe to such dependency theories argue.

The tangible interests derived from the alliance, however, cannot sensibly be defined in terms of the "national interest" that is repeatedly invoked by policymakers but does not exist in any objective sense. The term national interest is used by political leaders as a euphemism for serving the interests of state power, closely aligned with the interests of concentrated private economic power.[22] The interests that drive belief in the alliance orthodoxy and America's benign hegemony are thus primarily the interests of the state-corporate nexus managed by the foreign policy and national security establishment.

From this perspective, the most tangible benefits of the alliance for Australia are twofold. First, the alliance provides privileged access to strategic councils in Washington, advanced US military technologies and cutting-edge defence science, and vastly enhanced intelligence collection capabilities that bolster Australia's strategic and diplomatic influence. The "clout" that Australia derives from its connection to the United States is underpinned and complemented by a favourable regional strategic order sustained by American power. More generally, but perhaps even more important, American power sustains an open global trading and investment environment beneficial to dominant Australian corporate interests. That this constitutes the driving force behind Australia's alliance with the United States – not the alliance orthodoxy and "special relationship" narrative – is one of the central arguments of this book.

Nevertheless, the alliance orthodoxy does play an important role in sustaining elite support for the alliance because it assists in the reduction of cognitive dissonance; the need to bring beliefs and actions into concordance.[23] This does not mean that adherence to the alliance orthodoxy is necessarily insincere or merely an instrumental rationalisation for pursuing self-serving interests. Interests influence beliefs, but how they do so is contingent on numerous factors, including available information and the social organisation and practices of the professional milieu that surrounds policy-makers.[24]

Individual foreign policy practitioners are certainly capable of adjusting their beliefs in the face of compelling evidence, even if it is unwelcome and

---

22   Scott Burchill, *Australia's International Relations: Particular, Common and Universal Interests*, East Melbourne: Australian Institute of International Affairs, 1994.

23   Hamilton-Hart, pp. 30-31.

24   Hamilton-Hart, p. 2.

contrary to their interests. However, the circumstances conducive to this kind of "corrective feedback" do not typically characterise the social world inhabited by national security elites, which is highly insular, self-referential and tends to reinforce rather than question foundational beliefs.[25] This is one of the central reasons why US "soft power" and the pro-US lobby in Australia focus on the management and institutionalisation of elite relationships.

How this book is structured

This book is divided into three parts. Part I is a detailed critical examination of the various elements that form the alliance orthodoxy and the conventional understanding of the Australia-US alliance held by elites. Chapter one addresses the first half of the alliance orthodoxy, the apparent indispensability of the alliance to Australian security. Chapters two and three deal with the second half of the alliance orthodoxy which conceives of Australia's relationship with the United States as a "special relationship" built on an historical foundation of mutual security interests and shared values.

After providing a critique of the alliance orthodoxy in Part I, an alternative interpretation of the alliance is presented in Part II. The fundamental purpose of the alliance has been to preserve a regional strategic and economic order favourable to Australian interests and beneficial to a particular form of Australian capitalism and, relatedly, to fulfil an ambition on the part of the foreign policy and national security establishment in Canberra to exercise independent regional influence as a leading "middle power".

In chapter four I argue that, threat perceptions aside, the Australian leadership's primary interest in the two decades after 1945 was to impose an Anglo-American order in Asia from which Australian vested interests would benefit. While restoring British power and prestige in the Far East was the primary objective initially, as British power receded, maintaining US hegemony in Asia became the sole motivating interest.

Chapters four and five together illustrate the evolution of Australia's "strategic dependence" on the US from the 1950s and 1960s – undertaken with the objective of restoring Western influence in Asia – through to Australia's emergence as a strategically independent "middle power" fully integrated into the US-led capitalist world order from the 1970s onwards.

---

25   Hamilton-Hart, p. 193.

In the context of Australia's enduring benign security environment and expansionist strategic doctrine, the alliance is best understood in terms of a desire to bolster Australia's strategic and diplomatic influence abroad as an Asia–Pacific regional power.

After arguing the primacy of material interests driving support for Australia's relationship with the United States, Part III turns to the importance of established beliefs in sustaining elite support for the alliance. Specifically, Part III investigates how and why the alliance orthodoxy detailed in Part I is transmitted and reproduced among Australian foreign policy and national security elites, using the AALD as a case study.

Chapter six provides the historical background, operation and objectives of the AALD. It reveals that, motivated by the fear that the alliance was at risk in the hands of a generation of leaders who were not steeped in the alliance orthodoxy and the "special relationship" narrative, the AALD set out to strengthen the personal foundations of the alliance at the elite level in order to preserve the status quo. Chapter seven identifies the significance of the AALD as an elite institution backed by large corporate interests, founded by Phillip Scanlan; a committed alliance loyalist and neoliberal activist.

Drawing on the literature of informal diplomacy, chapter eight demonstrates how the AALD seeks to preserve rather than challenge official policy perspectives and eschews critical discussion and debate. Chapter nine investigates the socialisation function of the AALD and its role in managing the alliance via a number of important material and psychological inducements. This chapter also explains how the AALD prevents adverse changes to orthodox government policymaking by measuring the alliance loyalty of future leaders.

PART I:

The Alliance Orthodoxy

Chapter One

THREATS WITHOUT ENEMIES

Australia's enduring security

The Australia-US alliance is unusual when compared to other bilateral security relationships.[1] Typically, alliances exist to confront an external threat or contain or balance one or more rival powers.[2] In contrast, the Australia-US alliance did not dissolve when the major threats offered as justification for its creation – Japanese militarism and Soviet/Chinese communist aggression – were no longer officially a concern. Australia's enthusiastic embrace of the alliance continued into the post-Cold War era despite the security pay-offs becoming increasingly unclear and the costs remaining high.[3]

Nevertheless, conventional wisdom maintains that the alliance is indispensable as a deterrent against attack and, more importantly, for maintaining Australia's self-reliant defence capability against all levels of potential threat. Indirectly, the alliance is seen to underpin Australia's favourable regional security environment via its contribution to the American-led system of bilateral alliances in Asia. According to Australia's 2016 Defence

---

1   "The Australia-US alliance", "the US alliance" and simply "the alliance" are used interchangeably throughout this book.

2   On the traditional role of alliances in international relations and the shifting nature of the Australia-US alliance and other Western security partnerships, see William Tow, "Alliances and Alignments in the Twenty-First Century" in Brendan Taylor (ed), *Australia as an Asia Pacific Regional Power: Friendship in Flux?*, London: Routledge, 2007, pp. 14-16. For a classic neo-realist understanding of the role of alliances in international relations, see Stephen M. Walt, Why Alliances Endure or Collapse, *Survival: Global Politics and Strategy*, vol. 39, no. 1, 1997, pp. 156-179.

3   On the peculiar nature of the US alliance system in Asia and the limits of traditional alliance theory for understanding its persistence, see Mark Beeson, Can Asia's Alliances Still Keep the Peace?, *Global Asia*, vol. 9, no. 3, 2014; Mark Beeson, Invasion by Invitation: The Role of Alliances in the Asia–Pacific, *Australian Journal of International Affairs*, vol. 69, no. 3, 2015, pp. 100-107.

White Paper, American primacy is indispensable for ensuring a peaceful, prosperous and stable Asia–Pacific and a "rules-based global order".[4] Former Prime Minister Malcolm Turnbull reiterated that Australia's alliance with the United States is "the bedrock of our national security".[5] This is a central element of the alliance orthodoxy and perhaps the most salient point in the minds of the Australian public about the value of the alliance with the US.

It is a viewpoint amplified in the media by prominent national security elites. Former Chief of the Defence Force, Sir Angus Houston, and Professor Rory Medcalf, write in the *Australian Financial Review* that the alliance remains a "powerful security insurance" for Australia.[6] Professor Brendan Taylor, also writing in the *Australian Financial Review*, has argued that Australia could not "secure the continent" in the absence of the alliance without a major military build-up in the order of an additional $70-100 billion dollars in defence spending per annum, quoting estimates made by the esteemed strategic and defence studies expert, Professor Paul Dibb.[7] Going by 2017 global military spending figures, a military budget of that size would elevate Australia to the third largest military spender in the world, behind the US and China and in front of Saudi Arabia and Russia.[8]

As discussed in chapter four, Australia has a long tradition of relying on a powerful ally for its security despite the absence of any direct threats. For obvious historical and cultural reasons, Australia held fast to strategic dependence on Britain from the time of European colonisation through to World War Two. Australians harboured a keen sense of vulnerably to the prospect of attack and yet, in the words of the Colonial Defence Committee in London in the late-nineteenth century, "there is no British territory so little liable to aggression as that of Australia".[9] There was no

---

4   Commonwealth of Australia, *2016 Defence White Paper*, Canberra: Department of Defence, 2016, p. 121.

5   Malcolm Turnbull, Radio Interview with David and Will, 5AA Breakfast, Prime Minister of Australia, 16 May 2017, <https://www.pm.gov.au/media/radio-interview-david-and-will-5aa-breakfast>, accessed 1 April 2018.

6   Angus Houstan and Rory Medcalf, The Unaffordable Price of Australia Abandoning ANZUS Over Donald Trump, *Australian Financial Review*, 21 February 2017, http://www.afr.com/opinion/columnists/the-unaffordable-price-of-australia-abandoning-anzus-over-donald-trump-20170220-gugqnp, accessed 1 April 2018.

7   Brendan Taylor, Why Australia's Defence Capability Without ANZUS is Greatly Overrated, *Australian Financial Review*, 6 February 2017, <http://www.afr.com/opinion/why-australias-defence-capability-without-anzus-is-greatly-overrated-20170205-gu5rpq>, accessed 1 April 2018.

8   International Institute for Strategic Studies, Chapter Two: Comparative Defence Statistics, *The Military Balance*, 2018, p. 19.

9   Tom O'Lincoln, *The Neighbour From Hell: Two Centuries of Australian Imperialism*, Melbourne: Interventions, 2014, pp. 18-20, quote p. 19.

credible German threat to Australia during World War One and, although confronted by Japanese imperialism during World War Two, there was no planned Japanese invasion of Australia.[10]

Conventional, threat-centric explanations for the existence of the alliance are problematic, to say the least. Japan, the Soviet Union and the People's Republic of China (PRC) did not represent a credible direct threat to Australia during the Cold War. Other potential regional threats, such as Indonesia, lacked both the intent and the capability to launch a serious attack on mainland Australia. Although presented as a direct threat in public, communism was privately understood by authorities as a threat to Western interests as a whole and not to Australia directly. Today, strategic concerns with respect to China's rise are primarily about the potential threat Beijing poses to US primacy in Asia rather than any specific threat to Australia.[11]

Threat perceptions: 1950s and 1960s

The formal defence treaty signed by Australia, New Zealand and the US in 1951 (ANZUS) was carefully worded, on the insistence of the Americans, to avoid any binding obligations to come to one another's aid.[12] This is not an atypical arrangement for the US, which often crafts its alliance treaties to contain loopholes or vague commitments in order to avoid becoming entangled in a war that it does not perceive to be in its interests.[13] Australian leaders at the time publicly presented ANZUS as a defence treaty identical to that of NATO. Minister for External Affairs, Richard Casey, for example, remarked to the Australian parliament in July 1951 that like NATO, the "intention" of the ANZUS Treaty "is that an attack on one should be regarded as an attack on all".[14] In fact, ANZUS merely stipulates

---

10   Greg Lockhart, "We're So Alone" Two Versions of the Void in Australian Military History, *Australian Historical Studies*, vol. 33, no. 120, 2002, pp. 390-391.

11   Jae Jeok Park and Hyun Chung Yoo, The Resilience of the US Australia Alliance: Does a (Potential) China Threat Provide a Rationale for the Alliance?, *The Korean Journal of Defence Analysis*, vol. 27, no. 4, December 2015, pp. 417-434.

12   Gregory Pemberton, *All the Way: Australia's Road to Vietnam*, Sydney: Allen & Unwin, 1987, pp. 25-26.

13   Michael Beckley, The Myth of Entangling Alliance: Reassessing the Security Risks of US Defence Pacts, *International Security*, vol. 39, no. 4, 2015, pp. 18-19.

14   Gary Brown, *Breaking the American Alliance: An Independent National Security Policy for Australia*, Canberra: Australian National University, 1989, p. 62.

that in the event of an attack each country will "act to meet the common danger in accordance with its constitutional processes".[15]

Australian leaders nonetheless took the alliance to be a security blanket so long as certain obligations were fulfilled, particularly support for US foreign military interventions and, later, the hosting of US bases on Australian soil. In practice, given the reality of Australia's strategic environment, the ANZUS Treaty was of little value to Australia in providing protection against a direct attack. As one historian and political scientist presciently observed in 1952, "It seems certain, almost beyond reasonable doubt, that circumstances under which Australia may invoke American assistance under the Pact will not arise".[16]

Apart from guaranteeing protection in the event of an attack, Australian policy-makers saw the alliance as crucial for forestalling the emergence of threats to Australia in its immediate strategic environment. In the context of the early period of the Cold War during the 1950s and 1960s, the primary concern was Soviet and/or Chinese communist infiltration into Southeast Asia from which an attack on Australia might have been mounted. Consequently, the alliance played a central role in Australia's strategic doctrine of "forward defence". A memorandum concerning Australian security submitted by the Defence Committee in January 1962, stated:

> [Protection against communist expansion] can be best achieved by a forward defence strategy which involves the containment of enemy forces as far from our immediate environs as possible. The adoption of this forward defence strategy extends our strategic interests to Southeast Asia as the centre and closest part of the Allied defence line extending from Pakistan to Japan, and as the area most immediately threatened. While Southeast Asia is held, defence in depth is provided for Australia.[17]

As the memorandum suggests, the doctrine dictated sending Australian forces, in cooperation with its allies, to confront communism as far forward of Australia as possible in order to maintain "defence in depth". By

---

15   1951 Security Treaty between Australia, New Zealand and the United States (ANZUS), article IV. Reproduced at Australian Politics, ANZUS Treaty, <http://australianpolitics.com/topics/foreign-policy/anzus-treaty-text>, accessed 1 April 2018.

16   D.C.S. Sissons, The Pacific Pact, *Australian Outlook*, vol. 6, no. 1, 1952, p. 21.

17   Peter Edwards with Gregory Pemberton, *Crises and Commitments: The Politics and Diplomacy of Australia's Involvement in Southeast Asian Conflicts 1948-1965*, Sydney: Allen & Unwin, 1992, p. 247.

continuing to support America's involvement in the region, it was reasoned, the US would be more likely to retain a significant military presence in Southeast Asia and come to Australia's aid in a time of need.[18]

Although allying itself to the greatest power in world history undoubtedly provided a level of protection to Australia that was otherwise unavailable, the actual defence benefits the alliance provided against realistic threat scenarios were minimal. The dual threats of potential Japanese militarism and Soviet/Chinese communism that led to the establishment of the ANZUS Treaty and formed the primary defence justification for the alliance in the 1950s and 1960s were far less significant than was, and continues to be, typically presented. As Stephan Fruhling states, when the term "threat" was used in official Australian strategic assessments, "it often meant the contribution to allied action in support of wider interests, rather than a direct possibility of harm to Australia itself".[19]

In the case of Japan, its defeat and occupation by American forces after World War Two virtually eliminated any potential threat from that country:

> [T]he overwhelming US presence in Japan, the exceptional powers exercised by McArthur as SCAP [Supreme Commander for the Allied Powers], the American trusteeship of Japanese territories and the presence of US forces in the Asia–Pacific region confirmed the inadequacy of the proposition that Japan could constitute a threat to Australia.[20]

Although Australia's Minister for External Affairs, and self-declared "father" of the ANZUS Treaty, Sir Percy Spender, required some convincing, he and most members of Cabinet eventually came to accept that a Japanese threat to Australian security was remote.[21] In line with US

18 Graeme Cheeseman, From Forward Defence to Self-Reliance: Changes and Continuities in Australian Defence Policy 1965-90, *Australian Journal of Political Science*, vol. 26, no. 3, 1991, p. 430.

19 Stephan Fruhling, *A History of Australian Strategic Policy Since 1945*, Canberra: Defence Publishing Service, Department of Defence, 2009, fn 4, p. 2.

20 James Wood, "Australian Aims During the Occupation of Japan 1945-1952: From Occupier to Protector" in Christine De Matos and Robin Gerster (eds), *Occupying the "Other": Australia and Military Occupations From Japan to Iraq*, Cambridge Scholars Publishing: Newcastle upon Tyne, UK, 2009, p. 38.

21 David McLean, Anzus Origins: A Reassessment, *Australian Historical Studies*, vol. 24, no. 94, 1990, p. 77; Philip Dorling, *The Origins of the ANZUS Treaty: A Reconsideration*, South Australia: Flinders Politics Monographs, Flinders University, 1989, pp. 76, 80, 104.

thinking, the Australian government increasingly came to view Japan as a bulwark against communist aggression and, as early as November 1946, "fell into line with the prevailing geopolitical position that Japan should be treated as a loyal ally within the changing strategic balance, rather than too harshly as a defeated enemy".[22]

When it came to the potential security threat posed by communist countries, from as early as 1947 high-level strategic planning assessments concluded that there was no direct threat to Australia from the Soviet Union and, from 1949, added that communist control over the Chinese mainland, and any further extension of communist influence in Asia, "would not materially affect Australia's comparatively secure strategic position in the short to medium term".[23] The outbreak of war on the Korean peninsula in 1950 did not fundamentally change these assessments.[24] After the attack on South Korea by the DPRK, Menzies reiterated that "International Communism" did not possess great naval power and that "the principal purpose of an Australian Army is not to repel a land invasion, but to cooperate with other democratic forces in those theatres of war where the fate of mankind may be fought out".[25]

The ANZUS Treaty was not understood by Spender as primarily a defence pact to protect Australia in the event of a direct attack but, rather, as a means to secure Australian access and influence over American global strategic planning. In October 1950, American diplomat George Perkins wrote in a memorandum to US Secretary of State Dean Acheson that, while Spender's initial concern was to gain assurance that the US would defend Australia, it was "no longer important in Spender's or other Australian eyes". Although Spender "is still interested in the Pacific Pact, what he really wants is closer participation in all stages of high-level Washington planning which might later involve the disposition of Australian forces or material", likely in the Middle East, to assist the UK in the event of global war.[26] Spender later addressed the House of Representatives expressing the same concerns and desires.[27]

As Australia became increasingly concerned with instability in Southeast Asia, the ANZAM area of strategic interest came to serve as the basis of

---

22   Wood, "Australian Aims During the Occupation of Japan", p. 38.
23   Dorling, *The Origins of the ANZUS Treaty*, pp. 26-27, 32-33, quote p. 33.
24   Dorling, pp. 44-68.
25   Dorling, p. 64.
26   Dorling, p. 82.
27   Dorling, pp. 85-87.

Australia's defence policy throughout the 1950s and 1960s. Ostensibly, the purpose of ANZAM was to provide for the common defence of Australia, New Zealand and Malaya against the threat from Soviet or Chinese communism. However, as Australian military historian Greg Lockhart points out, the ANZAM concept "was based on the *absence* of an external threat to those places". Both high-level Australian and British assessments confirmed there was "no possible land threat to the mainland of Australia" and "the external threat to Malaya from Chinese armies operating over long and difficult lines of communications is not likely to be very great".[28]

Even in the case of Indonesia, with whom relations were significantly strained over the question of Dutch New Guinea and the establishment of the Malaysian Federation, the official assessment from 1950 onwards was that there was "no immediate threat of external aggression". Indonesia was identified as posing a potential direct threat to Australia in a slightly revised assessment in October 1964, however its capacity to attack Australia was still acknowledged to be negligible.[29] Significantly, at a popular level, less than ten per cent of Australians considered Indonesia to be a possible threat in the 1960s and early 1970s despite it having one of the largest communist parties in the world until 1965.[30]

Despite frequent public pronouncements by Australian conservative governments throughout the 1950s and 1960s of the need for a great power alliance to protect Australia against communist aggression from the North, official but classified strategic assessments – although deficient and exaggerated – continued to present the likelihood of high-level threats to Australia as remote.[31] Evidence that Australia's secure position was understood by policy-makers at the time can be deduced from defence outlays and ADF manpower statistics which were not high and thus not indicative of a nation that was seriously concerned with a high-level threat.[32]

In sum, while Australia's involvement in Southeast Asia in the 1950s and 1960s is commonly portrayed as a response to genuinely perceived military threats from Asia, and the ANZUS Treaty the "bolt on the back door" to those threats, "low defence budgets confirmed what the electorate and the

---

28   Greg Lockhart, *The Minefield: An Australian Tragedy in Vietnam*, Crows Nest, Sydney: Allen & Unwin, 2007, p. 9. Emphasis in original.

29   Lockhart, p. 12.

30   Simon Philpott, Fear of the Dark: Indonesia and the Australian National Imagination, *Australian Journal of International Affairs*, vol. 55, no. 3, 2001, p. 379.

31   Brown, *Breaking the American Alliance*, pp. 24-25.

32   Brown, pp. 18-19; David McLean, Australia in the Cold War: A Historiographical Review, *The International History Review*, vol. 23, no. 2, 2001, pp. 318-319.

Australian Chiefs of Staff well knew: that Japan was pacifist, China did not have a navy, Indonesia was also too poor to invade, and there was never any sign of a Viet Cong Pacific armada".[33]

Apart from Japan and communist aggression, the other concern to Australian policy-makers, generally acknowledged privately, was the process of decolonisation and the rise of independent Asian nationalism. Minister for External Affairs, Richard Casey, made the point in his private notes that ANZUS "protects us against Com Russia, Asian aggression, Indonesia (Dutch) – *as well as* Japan".[34] In a candid private exchange with New Zealand officials, Secretary of the Department of External Affairs, Sir Alan Watt, stated in March 1951 that "Australia wanted an American security guarantee for three reasons: against a rearmed Japan, against communist imperialism in Asia, and against Asian expansionism generally". Watt revealed that the third reason was "the strongest", although this "could not ... be made public".[35]

In the official rhetoric of Western leaders, Asian nationalist movements were typically conflated with communist aggression emanating from Moscow and Beijing. However, Australian policymakers correctly acknowledged a difference between the two on a number of occasions. Conceding this distinction at a lecture at Michigan State University in the late 1950s, Minister for External Affairs Richard Casey warned that "non-Communist extreme anti-Western nationalist forces in Asia could pose as great a danger as Communism", making it quite clear he was referring to Indonesia.[36]

Casey's concerns reflected Australia's official strategic assessments which, in Fruhling's words, by the late 1950s began to "recognise decolonisation and the establishment of new, independent countries in Asia as a separate strategic concern from the Cold War ... and then replace the latter as the main focus of Australia's defence policy".[37] As explored in chapter four, independent Asian nationalism posed little threat to Australian security, but it did threaten the imperial order in Asia, to which Australia was deeply committed.

---

33   Lockhart, "We're So Alone", p. 392.

34   McLean, Anzus Origins: A Reassessment, pp. 78-79. Emphasis in original.

35   See Roger Holdich, Vivianne Johnson and Pamela Andre (eds), *Documents on Australian Foreign Policy: The ANZUS Treaty 1951*, Department of Foreign Affairs and Trade, 2001, fn 3, p. 130.

36   Pemberton, *All the Way*, p. 79.

37   Fruhling, *A History of Australian Strategic* Policy, p. 44.

Threat perceptions: 1970s to the end of the Cold War

Beginning in the early to mid-1970s, forward defence gradually receded as the basis of Australia's defence policy in favour of the Defence of Australia (DOA) and "self-reliance" doctrines. These doctrines shifted the focus of Australia's defence strategy from expeditionary combat to the protection of the homeland, placing primary importance on the ability of the armed forces to independently defend the northern air and maritime approaches to Australia from which an attack would most likely be mounted.[38] The change in strategic doctrine reflected an official acknowledgment in Australia that it could not and should not rely on the US to guarantee its security. The shift in attitude was reflected in official Australian defence papers which downgraded the alliance from a "guarantee" (1956) and the "assured foundation of Australia's security" (1972) to "substantial grounds for confidence" (1976) and later just "confidence" (1987) that the US would come to Australia's aid.[39]

The catalyst for the shift from strategic dependence to self-reliance was the announcement of President Richard Nixon's "Guam doctrine", requiring allies like Australia to take on more of the "burden sharing" for regional security. The Guam doctrine was a tactical change on the part of Washington. The US fully intended to remain dominant in the region, only now its allies – backed by American aid and technology – would have to assume a greater proportion of the costs in both lives and resources.[40] While the Cold War continued to dominate Australian threat perceptions, the détente between the superpowers, the discrediting of the "domino theory" and "monolithic communism" in the aftermath of the Vietnam War, and the resumption of diplomatic ties with the PRC, severely undermined the perceived threat of communist aggression in Southeast Asia.

As assurances of American military aid were downgraded, and in the light of Australia's changing strategic environment, greater attention was

38   Peter Edwards, *Permanent Friends? Historical Reflections on the Australian-American Alliance*, Lowy Institute Paper 8, Lowy Institute for International Policy, Sydney, 13 December 2005, pp. 32-4, <http://www.lowyinstitute.org/publications/permanent-friends-historical-reflections-australian-american-alliance>, accessed 1 April 2018; Stephan Fruhling, Australian Defence Policy and the Concept of Self-Reliance, *Australian Journal of International Affairs*, vol. 68, no. 5, 2014, pp. 533-34.

39   Gary Brown and Laura Rayner, *Upside, Downside: ANZUS After Fifty Years*, Foreign Affairs, Defence and Trade Group, Department of the Parliamentary Library, Current Issues Brief, no. 3, 2001-02, p. 17; Brown, *Breaking the American Alliance*, pp. 62-65.

40   Virginia Brodine and Mark Selden (eds), *Open Secret: The Kissinger-Nixon Doctrine in Asia. Why We Are Never Leaving*, New York: Harper & Row, 1972.

placed on the benefits the US alliance provided Australia in terms of access to advanced defence technology, intelligence cooperation, defence science and military training. Greater attention to these benefits, states Peter Edwards, "had been gaining support in political and official circles for some years, but from the late 1970s they would be deployed more frequently in public debate".[41] While in the past the primary justification for the alliance was viewed in terms of a guarantee of protection against attack and its contribution to the global strategic balance, by the mid-1980s this had changed. As Desmond Ball observes:

> By the mid-1980s ... the importance of the US alliance derived from entirely different grounds – that only the United States could provide Australia with the intelligence, defence technology and professional military expertise which would enable Australia to independently handle regional threats.[42]

Specifically, these benefits were deemed critical for ensuring Australia could defend itself against more likely, but low-level, threat scenarios, while remaining prepared to meet the potential challenge of a serious, albeit remote, high-level attack.[43] In the latter scenario, advanced strategic intelligence capabilities required to determine foreign military strength and hostile intent were deemed crucial for ensuring an adequate lead time for force expansion.[44] The qualitative lead in military and intelligence capabilities – or regional "edge" – derived from the alliance has continued to be understood for the last forty years as a solution to mitigate both the disparity in Australia's landmass and maritime patrol zones and the relatively small size and capacity of its defence forces.[45]

Although the benefits derived from the alliance undoubtedly bolstered Australia's self-reliant defence posture, their actual value can only be properly evaluated in the context of Australia's continuing non-threatening

---

41   Edwards, *Permanent Friends?*, p. 34.

42   Desmond Ball, The Strategic Essence, *Australian Journal of International Affairs*, vol. 55, no. 2, 2001, p. 236.

43   Paul Dibb, *Review of Australia's Defence Capabilities*, Report to the Minister for Defence, Canberra: Australian Government Publishing Service, March 1986, pp. 46, 53-55.

44   Richard Brabin-Smith, Force Expansion and Warning Time, *Security Challenges*, vol. 8, no. 2, 2012, pp. 33-47.

45   John Hardy, Statements of Intent: The Politicisation of Australia's Strategic Edge in the era of Defence Self-Reliance, *Australian Political Studies Association (APSA) Annual Conference*, Melbourne, 30 September – 3 October 2013, pp. 1-42.

strategic environment. While fear and threat inflation frequently dominated political rhetoric during the 1970s and 1980s, official strategic assessments confirmed the low probability of contingencies that might arise concerning the defence of Australia.[46]

The potential value of the alliance in providing for Australia's defence was carefully appraised by Paul Dibb in his 1986 report, *Review of Australia's Defence Capabilities*.[47] Dibb pointed out that the deterrence capacity of the alliance in the "remote" and "improbable" case of a high-level threat emerging, while still valuable, was not particularly relevant, given strategic realities. Apart from its "obligations" under the ANZUS Treaty, the dramatic change in regional circumstances that would likely precipitate such a threat emerging would impinge on core US interests – specifically America's "own supremacy in the region" – that would automatically elicit a countervailing American response.[48] In the "very improbable" case of sustained conventional global war between the superpowers, Dibb deemed the chance of a direct Soviet threat as "limited" given the remoteness of Australia. In any case, during global war, "both the United States and its European allies would give first priority to their own military needs. We could not assume that they would give any priority to our military requirements".[49]

Given that a general war between the superpowers would in all likelihood quickly escalate into an all-out nuclear exchange, special importance was placed on the need to maintain an effective nuclear deterrence strategy. As Dibb highlighted in his report, the Australia-US "joint defence facilities" contributed to nuclear deterrence by helping to technically verify US-Soviet arms control agreements. They also made Australia a high-level Soviet nuclear target.[50] Left unmentioned in the Dibb report was the contribution these facilities made to enhancing America's capability for launching a disabling first-strike, undermining Australia's position on nuclear deterrence and increasing the chances of nuclear war.[51] Technical

---

46   Commonwealth of Australia, *Threats to Australia's Security: Their Nature and Probability*, Joint Committee on Foreign Affairs and Defence, Canberra: Australian Government Publishing House, 1981. On the mismatch between political rhetoric and official strategic assessments, especially during the Fraser and Hawke governments, see Brian Toohey and Marian Wilkinson, *The Book of Leaks: Exposes in Defence of the Public's Right to Know*, North Ryde: Angus and Robertson, 1987.

47   Dibb, *Review of Australia's Defence Capabilities*.

48   Dibb, pp. 1, 7, 175.

49   Dibb, pp. 31-32.

50   Dibb, p. 31.

51   Desmond Ball, *A Suitable Piece of Real Estate: American Installations in Australia*, Sydney: Hale & Iremonger, 1980; Desmond Ball, *Pine Gap: Australia and the US*

developments and changes in the global nuclear order since the end of the Cold War have further undermined the apparent contribution of these facilities to global nuclear stability.[52]

The most significant contribution of the alliance to Australia's direct security identified by Dibb were the "practical benefits" that augmented the ADF's defence capabilities. These were specifically identified and quantified as access to US intelligence resources, which contributed to the "potential effectiveness" of the ADF in combat; logistical support that provided Australia with "some assurance" of military supplies during conflict; and "considerable" access to advanced US military technology that contributed to Australia's efforts at maintaining a clear technological advantage over potential regional adversaries.[53] Although Dibb rather cautiously valued the practical benefits of the alliance in his 1986 report, subsequent government policy statements and speeches were less equivocal, asserting that self-reliance was only achievable with the benefits the alliance provided.[54]

The benefits identified by Dibb were deemed important particularly against more credible, but less serious, threat contingencies, from

Geostationary Signals Intelligence Satellite Program, Sydney: Allen & Unwin, 1988. Ball came to reluctantly support US installations in Australia, specifically Pine Gap, for what he considered its sole legitimate purpose in supporting arms control agreements at that time. More recently, Ball publicly abandoned his previous position, stating he could no longer justify Pine Gap given its dramatically expanded role in US warfighting worldwide. Richard Tanter, Reader Response: John Blaxland on Des Ball and Pine Gap, *The Strategist*, Australian Strategic Policy Institution (ASPI), 13 September 2017, <https://www.aspistrategist.org.au/reader-response-john-blaxland-des-ball-pine-gap/>, accessed 30 March 2019. Also see Richard Tanter, *The "Joint Facilities" Revisited – Desmond Ball, Democratic Debate on Security, and the Human Interest*, Nautilus Institute for Security and Sustainability, Special Report, 11 December 2012, <https://nautilus.org/napsnet/napsnet-special-reports/the-joint-facilities-revisited-desmond-ball-democratic-debate-on-security-and-the-human-interest/>, accessed 30 March 2019.

52   Richard Tanter, "Just in Case": Extended Nuclear Deterrence in the Defence of Australia, *Pacific Focus: Inha Journal of International Studies*, vol. XXVI, no. 1, April 2011, pp. 113-136; Richard Tanter, The US Military Presence in Australia: Asymmetrical Alliance Cooperation and its Alternatives, *The Asia–Pacific Journal*, vol. 11, issue 45, no. 1, 11 November 2013, <http://apjjf.org/2013/11/45/Richard-Tanter/4025/article.html>, accessed 1 April 2018.

53   Dibb, *Review of Australia's Defence Capabilities*, p. 46.

54   Graeme Cheeseman and Michael McKinley, Moments Lost: Promise, Disappointment and Contradictions in the Australian-United States Defence Relationship, *Australian Journal of International Affairs*, vol. 46, no. 2, 1992, p. 208. More recently, Dibb has argued that Australia's self-reliant defence posture is "immeasurably strengthened" as a result of the practical benefits the alliance provides. Paul Dibb, *US-Australia Alliance Relations: An Australian View*, Strategic Forum, Institute for National Strategic Studies, National Defence University, no. 216, August 2005, p. 1.

small-scale harassments and raids through to substantial, albeit well below the level of invasion, conventional military action. While small-scale harassments and raids were deemed within the current military capabilities of regional powers, larger-scale conventional military action, such as lodging and maintaining substantial forces in Australia, would require a significant and detectable military build-up over many years.[55]

It is important to note that the Dibb report emphasised the fact that no conflict at any level of threat was considered likely in the foreseeable future. Furthermore, the more credible low-level threat scenarios for which the alliance was deemed of most benefit were still conditioned on a then unforeseeable and substantial deterioration in strategic circumstances. All of the threat assessments "simply represented judgements of what might be possible, given potential military capacities, should conflict arise".[56]

Threat perceptions: the end of the Cold War to the present

The end of the Cold War virtually eliminated the threat of communism and global nuclear war that provided the primary justification for the alliance from the 1950s. No longer bound together by a common threat, the importance of the alliance as an anchor for regional stability now took on greater prominence.[57] In Northeast Asia, there was the apparent prospect of regional tensions erupting into outright conflict in the absence of the "balancing" effect of America's dominating military presence.[58] Closer to home, in Southeast Asia, Australian defence planners, it was argued, were confronted by a "bewildering array of momentous change", "profound uncertainty" and "extraordinary volatility", particularly as a result of developments such as the Asian Financial Crisis, the collapse of President Suharto's regime in Indonesia and the independence of East Timor. This "rapid strategic change" had consequently "brought into relief the complacent attitude towards the US alliance and the [sic] defence spending".[59]

---

55   Dibb, *Review of Australia's Defence Capabilities*, pp. 5, 53-55.

56   Dibb, p. 54.

57   John Baker and Douglas H. Paal, "The US-Australia Alliance" in Robert D. Blackwell and Paul Dibb (eds), *America's Asian Alliances*, Cambridge: MIT Press, 2000, pp. 89-90.

58   The typical formulation in the post-Cold War era has been that US military presence caps Japanese militarism, balances Chinese power and deters North Korea.

59   Desmond Ball, Australian Defence Planning: Problems and Prospects, *Pacifica Review*, vol. 12, no. 3, 2000, pp. 281, 290.

Despite these apparent dramatic changes within Australia's regional environment, the transition into the post-Cold War era did not bring about a major shift in Australia's strategic outlook. Rather, as had been the case since the 1970s, Australia continued to live in a "non-specific threat environment".[60] Concerns about an "arc of instability" in the South Pacific dominated political discourse in the late 1990s and 2000s, leading to a "new interventionism" that ignored the economic and social issues that lay at the root of conflict and instability in the region.[61] Nevertheless, how such instability to Australia's north might one day translate into an actual high-level threat to Australia remained unexplained.[62]

No Southeast Asian nation then or since has possessed the requisite military capability or hostile intent to threaten Australia in the foreseeable future. Crucially, this assessment includes Australia's largest near neighbouring country, Indonesia. Although the size and geographical proximity of Indonesia means it will always occupy a central place in Australian defence planning, threat perceptions are frequently driven by alarmist predictions about Indonesia's emergence as a major regional military power and economic powerhouse.[63] Meanwhile, serious concerns about domestic oppression, cronyism, inequality and religious radicalism are overlooked in order to maintain good strategic relations and a favourable trade and investment climate.[64]

Expectations about Indonesia's potential economic power have arisen from misplaced faith in neoliberal reforms, advocated by the likes of the US and Australia, that have served to concentrate economic and social power in the hands of powerful oligarchs and undermined sustainable national economic development.[65] Indonesia's armed forces are mostly concerned with protecting ruling elites from domestic threats, and its external concerns are focused towards the north on Malaysia, Singapore and

---

60　Robert Ayson, "Australasian Security" in Robert Ayson and Desmond Ball (eds), *Strategy and Security in the Asia–Pacific*, Sydney: Allen & Unwin, 2006, p. 242.

61　Joanne Wallis, The South Pacific: "Arc of Instability" or "Arc of Opportunity?", *Global Change Peace & Security: Formerly Pacifica Review: Peace, Security & Global Change*, vol. 27, no. 1, 2015, pp. 39-53.

62　Alan Dupont, Transformation or Stagnation? Rethinking Australia's Defence, *Australian Journal of International Affairs*, vol. 57, no. 1, 2003, pp. 55-76.

63　Hugh White, What Indonesia's Rise Means for Australia, *The Monthly*, June 2013, <https://www.themonthly.com.au/issue/2013/june/1370181600/hugh-white/what-indonesia-s-rise-means-australia>, accessed 1 April 2018.

64　Andre Vltchek, *Indonesia: Archipelago of Fear*, New York: Pluto Press, 2012.

65　Richard Robinson and Vedi R. Hadiz, Indonesia: A Tale of Misplaced Expectations, *The Pacifica Review*, vol. 30, no. 6, 2017, pp. 895-909.

China, not south with Australia. A careful appraisal of Indonesia's military capabilities, including its modernisation efforts, demonstrates that it poses very little direct threat to Australia.[66]

In the 2000s, fear of regional instability merged with fears of the threat of terrorism, the latter skilfully utilised by the conservative Howard government to justify Australia's participation in America's "war on terror".[67] The extraordinary rise and military success of ISIS from 2014 refocused the political debate on the threat of international terrorism and on Australian involvement in the Middle East. Although an important security concern, the threat of terrorism to Australia since the terrorist attacks against the US on 11 September 2001 has remained marginal, its prominence more a reflection of domestic politics than of genuine security concerns.[68]

The enduring absence of identifiable threats in Australian defence planning was summed up by Desmond Ball at the turn of the twenty-first century. Threats to Australia's national security, he pointed out, had for many decades played no role in the maintenance of the US alliance. In Ball's words:

[Since] the 1970s, when "forward defence" was replaced by the policy of "defence of Australia", official assessments have reiterated that Australia faces no foreseeable threats, and threat scenarios have played no part in the development of Australia's defence capabilities. The vitality of the alliance has been "threat insensitive".[69]

The general thrust of Ball's assessment remains true today. Certainly, the rise of China and the transformation of major power relations in the Asia Pacific have emerged as Australia's central strategic considerations for the foreseeable future. In all likelihood, the "unipolar" era of American dominance is

66   Benjamin Schreer, *Moving Beyond Ambitions? Indonesia's Military Modernisation*, Australian Strategic Policy Institute (ASPI), Canberra, November 2013, < https://www.aspi.org.au/report/moving-beyond-ambitions-indonesias-military-modernisation-0 >, accessed 1 April 2018.

67   Anthony Burke, *Fear of Security: Australia's Invasion Anxiety*, Cambridge: Cambridge University Press, 2008, pp. 207-233.

68   Christopher Michaelsen, The Triviality of Terrorism, *Australian Journal of International Affairs*, vol. 66, no. 4. 2012, pp. 431-449; Scott Burchill, Radical Islam and the West: The Moral Panic Behind the Threat, *The Conversation*, <https://theconversation.com/radical-islam-and-the-west-the-moral-panic-behind-the-threat-43113>, accessed 1 April 2018.

69   Ball, The Strategic Essence, p. 245.

a state of affairs that will continue well into the twenty-first century.[70] Nevertheless, the potential destabilising effects of China's rise, and the need to hedge against it, has taken on primary importance in Australian defence planning, particularly since the release of the 2009 Defence White Paper. As a number of strategic commentators argued at the time, the rise of China and the transformation of major power relations in the Asia–Pacific have been accepted by Canberra "as a fact requiring an Australian response in the form of an unprecedented military build-up over 20 years".[71]

Whatever the long-term consequences of the changing power relations in Asia may be, Australia faces the least strategic challenge from the rise of China of any regional power. China lacks the requisite military capability and hostile intent to present a realistic threat scenario to Australia now or in the foreseeable future.[72] Australia's latest Defence White Paper, while stressing the uncertainty inherent in the wider strategic environment of the Indo-Pacific, nevertheless reiterates that "there is no more than a remote prospect of a military attack by another country on Australian territory in the foreseeable future".[73] The fear of an invasion by China, or any other state for that matter, remains "close to fantasy".[74]

The only realistic contingency where Australia might come under attack by China is in the event of a general US-China conflict where there is a stated expectation of active Australian participation. In this scenario, "Beijing simply [could not] ignore the possibility of potentially decisive amounts of US air power being staged from northern Australia".[75] In other words, China poses a potentially significant direct threat to Australian security only because of the alliance and the deep level of politico-military integration with the US. It has been suggested that the ADF develop a

---

70   Michael Beckley, China's Century? Why America's Edge will Endure, *International Security*, vol. 36, no. 3, 2011, pp. 41-78.

71   John Langmore, Calum Logan and Stewart Firth, *The 2009 Australian Defence White Paper: Analysis and Alternatives*, Austral Policy Forum 10-01A, Nautilus Institute for Security and Sustainability, 15 September 2010, pp. 10-11, <http://nautilus.org/wp-content/uploads/2011/12/langmore-logan-firth.pdf>, accessed 1 April 2018.

72   Paul Dibb and John Lee, Why China Will Not Become the Dominant Power in Asia, *Security Challenges*, vol. 10, no. 3, 2014, pp. 1-21; Robert S. Ross, *The US Pivot to Asia and Implications for Australia*, Centre of Gravity Series, ANU Strategic and Defence Studies Centre, March 2013, <http://sdsc.bellschool.anu.edu.au/experts-publications/publications/1853/us-pivot-asia-and-implications-australia >, accessed 1 April 2018.

73   Commonwealth of Australia, *2016 Defence White Paper*, p. 15.

74   Langmore, et.al, *The 2009 Australian Defence White Paper*, p. 9.

75   Timothy J. Blizzard, The PLA, A2/AD and the ADF: Lessons for Future Maritime Strategy, *Security Challenges*, vol. 12, no. 3, 2016, p. 66.

similar Anti-Access/Area-Denial (A2/AD) capability to that of the PRC in order to defend Australia's northern defence infrastructure from Chinese surface ships in the event of such a conflict, particularly given the likelihood that Australia could not rely on the US for support in the early stages of a general war.[76]

Australia's growing economic relationship with China may pose greater problems, but here too, concerns are frequently exaggerated. Chinese attempts at economic coercion against other countries have often backfired in the long run and failed to achieve Beijing's strategic objectives.[77] While China is Australia's largest two-way trading partner in goods and services, the economic relationship is rather one-dimensional. Exports to China consist mostly of commodities while imports are of cheaply manufactured consumer goods. This one-dimensionality, together with the dynamic nature of the international commodities market, means that China's capacity to punish Australia economically is, in practice, "almost non-existent".[78]

China's rise has resurfaced long-standing but erroneous fears about Australia's apparent economic vulnerability to the disruption of international trade.[79] However, it is extremely unlikely China would attempt to shut down the free flow of trade in the South China Sea given it is highly dependent on such trade to sustain its economy. In any case, the significance of trade through the South China Sea is marginal to Australia when compared with other routes such as through the Indonesia archipelago via the Lombok Straight, despite much misleading commentary that argues otherwise.[80]

76   Blizzard; Paul Dibb and Richard Brabin-Smith, *Australia's Management of Strategic Risk in the New Era*, Australian Strategic Policy Institute, November 2017, p.11

77   Rory Medcalf, Chinese Money and Australia's Security, NSC Policy Options Paper 2, Australian National University, March 2017, <https://nsc.crawford.anu.edu.au/department-news/9880/chinese-money-and-australias-security>, accessed 1 April 2018; Linda Jackobson and Bates Gill, *China Matters: Getting it Right for Australia*, Carlton, VIC: Black Inc, 2017, chapter 5.

78   Nick Bisley, An Ally For All The Years To Come: Why Australia Is Not A Conflicted US Ally, *Australian Journal of International Affairs*, vol. 67, no. 4, 2013, p. 414.

79   Commonwealth of Australia, *Guarding Against Uncertainty: Australian Attitudes to Defence, Report on Community Consultations*, Canberra: Department of Defence, 2015, p. 17, <http://www.defence.gov.au/Whitepaper/docs/GuardingUncertainty.pdf>, accessed 1 April 2018. For an explanation of why Australia's economy is not especially vulnerable to disruption through the interdiction of overseas trade see Dibb, *Review of Australia's Defence Capabilities*, pp. 2, 39. Also see Commonwealth of Australia, *The Defence of Australia 1987*, Canberra: Department of Defence, 1987, p. 28.

80   James Laurenceson, Economics and Freedom of Navigation in East Asia, *Australian Journal of International Affairs*, vol. 71, no. 5, 2017, pp. 461-473.

Expressed concerns about Australia's economic dependence on China often fail to acknowledge the enormous scale of the Australia-US investment relationship. Bilaterally, it stands at $1.47 trillion, including $860 billion dollars of US investment in Australia. That's ten times more than China's investment stake. In fact, Australia is home to more US investment dollars than any other country in the entire Asia–Pacific. A report compiled by the United States Studies Centre at the University of Sydney lauds the fact that a "typical Australian household engages with US products or companies in almost every aspect of their life."[81]

Australian history is replete with fears of unrealistic threats. As two noted strategic experts write, "It is commonplace to assert in every era that Australia faces complex, uncertain and potentially dangerous strategic circumstances".[82] In reality, the absence of current and future threats is probably the most striking historic feature of Australia's strategic environment. Although it is rarely stated publicly and explicitly, the fact of the matter is that "for more than seventy years, the defining feature of Australia's strategic environment has been the absence of a threat against which to plan its defence".[83] It would likely come as a surprise to most Australians that the "direct defence of allies was never a focal point of the US-Australia alliance, as there was little direct threat to Australia".[84] Contrary to the traditional myth of Australia's indefensibility, its relative geographic isolation makes it "arguably more naturally secure than any other part of the planet".[85]

---

81   Richard Holden and Jared Mondschein, *Indispensable Economic Partners: The US-Australia Investment Relationship*, United States Studies Centre, 13 August 2017, <https://www.ussc.edu.au/analysis/indispensable-economic-partners-the-us-australia-investment-relationship?>, accessed 1 April 2018.

82   Paul Dibb and Richard Brabin-Smith, Australian Defence: Challenges for the New Government, *Security Challenges*, vol. 9, no. 4, 2013, p. 49.

83   Raoul Heinrichs, China's Defence White Paper is Historic for Australia, And Not in a Good Way, *The Interpreter*, Lowy Institute for International Policy, <http://www.lowyinterpreter.org/post/2015/06/03/Chinas-defence-white-paper-is-historic-for-Australia-and-not-in-a-good-way.aspx>, accessed 1 April 2018. Dibb and Brabin-Smith also write that "Despite major changes in Australia's circumstances, we have been free from threat of major military attack since the end of World War II". Dibb and Brabin-Smith, Australian Defence, p. 51.

84   Stephan Fruling, "Wrestling with Commitment: Geography, Alliance Institutions and the ANZUS Treaty" in Peter J. Dean, Stephan Fruling and Brendan Taylor (eds), *Australia's American Alliance: Towards a New Era?*, Kindle Edition, Melbourne: Melbourne University Publishing Digital, 2016, Kindle Locations 505-506.

85   Mark Beeson, American Hegemony: The View from Australia, *SAIS Review*, vol. 23, no. 2, 2003, p. 114.

Chapter Two

AUSTRALIA'S "SPECIAL RELATIONSHIP"

Blood ties

There is no question that Australia and the US enjoy a remarkably firm and enduring relationship. For more than sixty years, Australia has remained a stalwart ally and a stable element in Washington's system of bilateral relationships in Asia, serving to boost US diplomatic, strategic and economic engagement in the region.[1] Conversely, the alliance is widely understood to constitute the cornerstone of Australia's entire foreign and strategic policy since the 1950s.[2] All current indicators suggest the bilateral relationship at the political and military levels will continue to grow in strength, particularly as Australia's geopolitical value to the US increases amidst the rise of the "Indo-Pacific".

The unusual strength, persistence and intimacy of the alliance are commonly taken to denote a "special relationship" between both countries.[3] Although common interests and shared values are ordinarily taken to form the basis of the relationship, emphasis is often placed on the latter. Officialdom in both countries asserts that it is the existence of "shared values" and a "natural friendship between our peoples" that forms "the

1   On America's "hub-and-spokes" system of alliances in Asia, see Victor D. Cha, Powerplay: Origins of the US Alliance System in Asia, *International Security*, vol. 34, no. 3, 2010, pp. 158-196. For a summary of the diplomatic, strategic and economic benefits of the alliance to the United States, see John Baker and Douglas H. Paal, "The US-Australia Alliance" in Robert D. Blackwell and Paul Dibb (eds), *America's Asian Alliances*, Cambridge: MIT Press, 2000, pp. 90-3.

2   Michael Wesley, *There Goes the Neighbourhood: Australia and the Rise of Asia*, Sydney: New South, 2011, pp. 143-144.

3   Jeffrey D. McCausland, Douglas T. Stuart, William T. Tow and Michael Wesley (eds), *The Other Special Relationship: The United States and Australia at the Start of the 21st Century*, Strategic Studies Institute, US Army War College, February 2007.

foundation" of the relationship.[4] In July 2018, the US Senate passed a resolution recognising "100 years of mateship" between Australia and the United States.[5] The deep level of cooperation and the intimacy of leader-to-leader interactions are taken as evidence of a special affinity between both nations.[6]

This "values" conception of the Australia–US relationship is steeped in mythology and a selective reading of history, locating the foundations of the alliance in false mutual security interests and shared values first forged in the joint blood sacrifices of World War Two. Together with the conventional security justifications for the alliance outlined in the previous chapter, the "special relationship" narrative constitutes the second half of the alliance orthodoxy.

Former Prime Minister John Howard did more than any other Australian leader before or since to promote the notion of a special relationship. According to officials in Canberra who were present during his time in office, Howard successfully elevated Australia's alliance with the US to an unprecedented level.[7] Speaking in 2015, Howard reiterated his belief that:

> Nothing that I experienced when I was prime minister, and nothing that I have experienced since, has altered my view that the things that bind nations together more tightly than anything else are shared values and shared philosophies. On that basis it is self-evident that the relationship between Australia and the United States, based on common values, common beliefs, shared experiences in war and

---

4   Australia-United States Ministerial (AUSMIN) Consultations, 2011 Joint Communique, 15 September 2011, <http://dfat.gov.au/geo/united-states-of-america/ausmin/Pages/ausmin-joint-communique-2011.aspx>, accessed 1 April 2018.

5   100 years of Mateship: U.S. Senate Passes Resolution Recognising 100 Years of the United States-Australia Relationship, US Embassy and Consulate in Australia, 11 July 2018, <https://au.usembassy.gov/100-years-of-mateship-u-s-senate-passes-resolution-recognizing-100-years-of-the-united-states-australia-relationship/>, accessed 20 September 2018.

6   Andrew Shearer, *Unchartered Waters: The US Alliance and Australia's New Era of Strategic Uncertainty*, Lowy Institute Perspectives, Lowy Institute for International Policy, Sydney, August 2011, <http://www.lowyinstitute.org/publications/uncharted-waters-us-alliance-and-australias-new-era-strategic-uncertainty>, accessed 1 April 2018.

7   As noted at the time, "In official circles in Canberra, the view is firmly held that the Australian-US security relationship is probably in the best shape in its history". Rod Lyon and William T. Tow, The Future of the Australia-US Security Relationship, *Asian Security*, vol. 1, no. 1, 2005, p. 34.

peace … is as tight as any bilateral relationship anywhere in the world can be.[8]

For Howard and other ardent believers in the special relationship, the implication is that the alliance transcends strategic interests that typify other bilateral alliances. In the words of former Prime Minister Tony Abbott, Australia and America "are more than allies, we're family".[9] While the "enduring power" of the alliance "does derive from shared interests and mutual benefits", writes noted foreign policy commentator, Greg Sheridan, "at the deepest levels it derives from the fact that for all our differences, the values we share as nations are so great".[10]

The apparent central importance of the alliance to Australian security is reinforced by this sentimental understanding of the relationship. It is closely related to the view of the US as a benign hegemon, and the belief that Australia and the United States share a joint commitment to promote liberal ideals such as peace, democracy, human rights and the rule of law in the Asia–Pacific region and beyond. In this chapter I argue that interests, not values, are what have typically driven the Australia-US relationship; and the interests of both nations have not always coincided.

Permanent friends or permanent interests?

Australia and the US evidently share similarities when it comes to political institutions, language, culture and values. Australians have long admired the US as a leader and sought to emulate many of its political, economic and cultural innovations. From as early as the 1830s, a popular theme in political life was the notion of Australia as a "future America".[11] A century later, leading Australian figures were still proudly assuring Americans,

---

8   David Wroe, Former PM John Howard Defends Top Bureaucrat Michael Thawley Over China Remarks, *Sydney Morning Herald*, 2 July 2015, <http://www.smh.com. au/federal-politics/political-news/former-pm-john-howard-defends-top-bureaucrat-michael-thawley-over-china-remarks-20150702-gi3puy.html>, accessed 1 April 2018. Despite all the talk about shared values, Howard was prepared to criticise American gun culture. Alliance loyalists sometimes distinguish Australian from American values on domestic issues, but rarely when it comes to foreign policy.

9   Tony Abbott, Speech to the Heritage Foundation, Washington DC, 18 July 2012, <http://australianpolitics.com/2012/07/18/abbott-foreign-policy-speech-heritage-foundation.html>, accessed 1 April 2018.

10   Greg Sheridan, *The Partnership: The Inside Story of the US-Australian Alliance Under Bush and Howard*, Sydney: UNSW Press, 2006, p. 322.

11   Philip Bell and Roger Bell, *Implicated: The United States in Australia*, Melbourne: Oxford University Press, 1993, p. 20.

"What we are, you were; and what you are, we hope to be".[12] The inclination to look to America for inspiration accelerated in the post-World War Two period when, like other Western nations, Australia was subjected to the global phenomenon of "Americanisation", and its social development was heavily influenced by American models.[13]

Notwithstanding the long and intimate ties Australia shares with the US, the language of a special relationship papers over what are in fact complex and contradictory histories. Australia, unlike the US, did not experience revolution or civil war, nor did it sever its strong and influential ties to the British monarchy, events that profoundly shaped American attitudes and institutions. Divergent historical experiences, in fact, led to significant differences in cultures, values and even languages that belie the notion of a "natural" or inevitable friendship.[14]

The origin of the special relationship is frequently traced back to the "watershed" moment in 1908 when the then Prime Minister, Alfred Deakin, in an act of defiance towards Britain, invited America's "Great White Fleet" to visit Australia as part of a US tour of the Pacific.[15] Australians were decidedly frenzied about the prospect of a visit by their powerful white cousins, the event itself drawing bigger and more enthusiastic crowds than anything in Australian history, including the inauguration of the Commonwealth in January 1901.[16] Although the event captured the attention of the nation, it did not mark the beginning of an "enduring bond" between both nations. It is pertinent to recall that while Australians were preoccupied with attending to the everyday needs of their

---

12   Former Australian Prime Minister Billy Hughes, 1938. Quoted in Dennis Phillips, *Ambivalent Allies: Myth and Reality in the Australian-American Relationship*, Ringwood, Victoria: Penguin Books, 1988, p. 69.

13   Bell and Bell, *Implicated*, pp. 157-200; Joseph Camilleri, *Australian-American Relations: The Web of Dependence*, South Melbourne: Macmillan, 1980, pp. 16-19. On the growing influence and control of corporate America over Australia's economy in the post-World War Two era, see Greg Crough and Ted Wheelwright, *Australia: A Client State*, Melbourne: Penguin Books, 1982.

14   For an in-depth critique of the widely held view that Australia and the US share similar historical influences, cultures, values and languages, see Phillips, *Ambivalent Allies*.

15   Australian Consulate-General New York, Enduring Bond: 60 Years of ANZUS, 2012 photo exhibition, 17 April 2012, <http://www.newyork.usa.embassy.gov.au/nycg/EnduringBondEnduringBond.html>, accessed 1 April 2018.

16   Marilyn Lake and Henry Reynolds, *Drawing the Global Colour Line: White Men's Countries and the International Challenge of Racial Equality*, Cambridge: Cambridge University Press, 2008, pp. 200-209; David Walker, *Anxious Nation: Australia and the Rise of Asia 1850-1939*, St Lucia, Queensland: University of Queensland Press, 1999, pp, 93-7.

guests, the Americans used the opportunity to secretly gather intelligence for contingency plans to invade Australia and capture its major cities in the event of hostilities breaking out between the US and British-allied Japan. The anecdote is an apt reflection of Lord Palmerston's dictum that states have no permanent friends, only permanent interests.[17]

World War Two has similarly been mythologised as a defining historical moment in the development of the Australia-US alliance. According to the orthodoxy, Australia's special relationship with the US was "forged by our shared sacrifice during the Second World War" and "in the defining battles of the past century".[18] Fuelling this narrative is the persistent myth that the US helped to prevent a Japanese invasion of Australia during World War Two. In reality, the conquest of Australia was explicitly ruled out by Japan's military leaders, a fact revealed by US communication intercepts as early as April 1942 and accepted at the highest levels of the Australian government by mid-1942.[19]

America's decision to reinforce Australia's strategic position and establish General MacArthur's Southwest Pacific Command Area in early 1942 was due not to an inviolable commitment to Australia's defence and freedom but the result of strategic necessity; Australia was no more than a suitable base from which to hit Japan.[20] The myth of a Japanese invasion of Australia deterred by American intervention has "been used by conservatives ever since as a legitimising narrative for Australian adherence to the US alliance", writes Anthony Burke.[21]

---

17   Gary Brown and Laura Rayner, *Upside, Downside: ANZUS After Fifty Years*, Foreign Affairs, Defence and Trade Group, Department of the Parliamentary Library, Current Issues Brief, no. 3, 2001-02, pp. 1-2.

18   AUSMIN Consultations, 2011 Joint Communique.

19   Peter Stanley, "Dramatic Myth and Dull Truth: Invasion by Japan in 1942" in Craig Stockings (ed), *Zombie Myths of Australian Military History*, Sydney: UNSW Press, 2010, pp. 146-147; Anthony Burke, *Fear of Security: Australia's Invasion Anxiety*, Cambridge: Cambridge University Press, 2008, pp. 73-75. For a copy of the official Japanese consideration, and subsequent rejection, of an invasion of Australia on 7 March 1942, see Commonwealth of Australia, *Threats to Australia's Security: Their Nature and Probability*, Joint Committee on Foreign Affairs and Defence, Canberra: Australian Government Publishing House, 1981, Annex C, p. 62.

20   Peter Edwards, *Permanent Friends? Historical Reflections on the Australian–American Alliance*, Lowy Institute Paper 8, Lowy Institute for International Policy, 13 December 2005, p. 11, <http://www.lowyinstitute.org/publications/permanent-friends-historical-reflections-australian-american-alliance>, accessed 1 April 2018; Coral Bell, *Dependent Ally: A Study in Australian Foreign Policy*, St. Leonards: Allen & Unwin, 1993, p. 24; Bell and Bell, *Implicated*, p. 92.

21   Burke, *Fear of Security*, p. 74.

World War Two is frequently depicted as a decisive turning point in Australia's foreign relations, marking the end of strategic dependence on the UK and the beginning of a new dependent relationship with the US. Prime Minister John Curtin's infamous speech in 1941, when he declared that "Australia looks to America, free of the pangs as to our traditional links or kinship with the United Kingdom", is offered as evidence of this fact.[22] The quote, however, is taken out of context, making "Curtin seem much more anti-British and pro-American than he had probably intended".[23] While Curtin was looking to promote immediate and substantial strategic support from the US during a critical phase of the war, his loyalty remained firmly attached to Britain. His government did not consider Australia as "anything but an integral part of the British empire".[24]

Frequently missing from the popular wartime narrative is the fact that Australia and the US entertained major disputes over strategic and economic objectives, notably Canberra's opposition to the Anglo-American "Hitler first" strategy and Washington's attempts to challenge Australia's protectionist trade policies.[25] Australia and New Zealand wrought fervent opposition from Washington when they jointly signed the 1944 Australia-New Zealand Agreement, or ANZAC Pact, in an attempt to preserve their spheres of influence in the South Pacific and check American expansionism.[26] Examining these and other divergent interests between the US and Australia in detail in his major study of the period, Roger Bell came to the following conclusion concerning the wartime alliance:

> [It] did not constitute a decisive turning-point as has often been implied. No special or enduring bilateral political, security or economic relationship developed as a result of effective collaboration

---

22   Fraser, for example, writes Curtin's speech was the moment when "Australia transferred its dependence to America". Malcolm Fraser with Cain Roberts, *Dangerous Allies*, Melbourne: Melbourne University Press, 2014, p. 74.

23   Edwards, *Permanent Friends?*, p. 10

24   Roger J. Bell, *Unequal Allies: Australian-American Relations and the Pacific War*, Melbourne: Melbourne University Press, 1977, p. 47.

25   Other disagreements included the Anglo-American opposition to Canberra's decision to relocate its last remaining division in the Middle East to Australia for continental defence, and disagreements with Washington over the extent of Australian and British participation in the counter-offensive against Japan. See Bell, *Unequal Allies*.

26   Norman Harper, *A Great and Powerful Friend: A Study of Australian American Relations Between 1900 and 1975*, St Lucia, Queensland: University of Queensland Press, 1987, pp. 124-33.

against Japan. Nor was Australia's wartime alliance with the US unusual or unique.[27]

Australia and the US remained mutually ambivalent about their relationship in the immediate post-war period. While keen to see the US commit to upholding regional security, Ben Chifley's Labor government remained concerned about American economic imperialism and potential US interference in what was considered Australia's local sphere of influence.[28] Australia was particularly concerned that America's trade liberalisation agenda would undermine the ability of the government to utilise interventionist measures to promote industrialisation.[29] American hegemony was a serious concern, Australia anxious about the capacity of Washington "to exert political and economic pressure on virtually every other country in the capitalist world".[30]

Washington was entirely uninterested in formalising the wartime alliance with Australia after the common enemy, Japan, was defeated. The Australian Labor government attempted and failed on numerous occasions to entice the US into a Pacific security arrangement. This was despite fierce and persistent lobbying on the part of External Affairs Minister H. V. Evatt, including efforts to utilise the American base on Manus Island as a bargaining chip. The US was simply not interested in any security pact or any Australian representation in US defence planning circles.[31]

Evatt's conservative successor, Sir Percy Spender, was more amenable to Washington but also faced the same intransigence. It was only the exigencies of the Cold War that finally persuaded the US to accede to Australian pressure, with this resulting in the 1951 ANZUS Treaty and delivering success to Spender's adept negotiating tactics.[32] Even so, the

---

27   Roger J. Bell, *Unequal Allies*, pp. 226-227.

28   Bell, *Dependent Ally*, 1993, pp. 38-39; Camilleri, *Australian-American Relations*, pp. 2-6; Joseph M. Siracusa, The ANZUS Treaty Revisited, *Security Challenges*, vol. 1, no. 1, 2005, pp. 89-97.

29   Ann Capling, *Australia and the Global Trade System: From Havana to Seattle*, Cambridge: Cambridge University Press, 2001, pp. 18, 25, 32-33.

30   Capling, p. 21.

31   Gregory Pemberton, *All the Way: Australia's Road to Vietnam*, Sydney: Allen & Unwin, 1987, pp. 4-5.

32   Siracusa, The ANZUS Treaty Revisited. More recent scholarship reveals that Washington was in fact more amenable to a Pacific alliance system from 1949-50 than previously assumed, albeit not due to sentiments of American "goodwill" toward Australia; it was derived from a reassessment of the benefits a Pacific security system would provide to Washington's Cold War strategy in Asia. David McLean, Anzus Origins: A Reassessment, *Australian Historical Studies*, vol. 24, no. 94, 1990, pp. 64-82.

US refused to provide a security arrangement on a par with NATO or the access to strategic decision making that Australia had sought.[33] The US Joint Chiefs of Staff strongly opposed an equal partnership with Australia with respect to global, or even Pacific, military planning, and made sure that any language in the draft versions of the ANZUS Treaty that alluded to this, was removed.[34]

Australia's decision to strategically align itself more closely to the US in the aftermath of World War Two was a reflection of changes in geopolitics, not sentiment. Historian Norman Harper noted in 1947 that the effective decline of British influence in the Far East indicated to Australia that the UK "will be unable to play a permanent and major role in the balance of Pacific power". The US, on the other hand, had emerged as the "greatest military and industrial world power", whose interest in overseas markets made it "perfectly clear that America in policy has become an expanding imperial state with every intention of playing a major role in Far Eastern affairs".[35]

Although Australian leaders recognised a shift was taking place in the regional balance of power, there was no significant transference of loyalty or change in strategic planning. When the ANZUS Treaty came into force on 29 April 1952, Australian Minister for External Affairs, Richard Casey, declared that the treaty "will not in any way weaken or diminish the close ties of kinship and cooperation which bind Australia to the other members of the British Commonwealth". Rather, it was his "hope" that the treaty would "add an important and intimate association" with the US.[36]

Regional defence planning in the first two decades of the post-war era proceeded to be primarily coordinated with the British and other Commonwealth nations.[37] Australia fought twice in Southeast Asia, not under ANZUS, but in support of its Commonwealth partners during the Malayan "Emergency" (1948-1960) and the Indonesian-Malaysian "Konfrontasi" (1963-1966). When the interests of its two great power allies

---

33   Wayne Reynolds, Loyal to the End: The Fourth British Empire, Australia and the Bomb, 1943–57, *Australian Historical Studies*, vol. 33, no. 119, 2002, pp. 42-44.

34   Pemberton, *All the Way*, pp. 27-31.

35   N.D. Harper, Australian Policy Towards Japan, *Australian Outlook*, vol. 1, no. 4, 1947, p. 16.

36   Statement by Richard Casey, 29 April 1952, in Roger Holdich, Vivianne Johnson and Pamela Andre (eds), *Documents on Australian Foreign Policy: The ANZUS Treaty 1951*, Department of Foreign Affairs and Trade, 2001, p. 227.

37   Peter Edwards, seminar on the ANZUS Alliance presented to the Defence Sub-Committee of the Joint Standing Committee on Foreign Affairs, Defence and Trade, Canberra, 11 August 1997, pp. 10-18.

conflicted during the 1956 Suez crisis, Australia firmly sided with the UK against the US (and virtually the rest of the world), clearly demonstrating the conservative Menzies government's continuing loyalty to British imperial interests.[38]

It was London's decision to withdraw "east of Suez" in 1967, foreshadowed many years earlier, that marked a significant shift in Australia's prior reliance on the UK as the basis of its regional defence planning.[39] Simultaneously, Australia entered a peak period of dependence on the US, Canberra having made a major commitment to America's war in Vietnam. The period from 1945 to the mid-1960s was a transition phase in which Australia saw value in supporting for as long as possible the declining British Empire as well as the reigning American one. The steps by which Australia came to rely primarily on Washington for its security are glossed by McLean:

> Between 1957 and 1963 Australia standardised its military equipment with the US, adopted American military organisational practices, entered into close cooperation with America in the exchange of information and in other defence-related areas, and agreed to the establishment of the North West Cape naval communications station on terms which surrendered all Australian rights to a say in the operation of the base. The dispatch of Australian troops to support US military involvement in Vietnam – a war in which Britain did not participate – highlighted the extent of the transformation of Australia's strategic relations since the formation of ANZUS.[40]

Australian and American forces have fought together in every significant conflict since World War One. Officially, this reflects the enduring strength of the alliance as well as the common values and shared interests between both countries.[41] Another interpretation is that Australia, as the substantially weaker power, has felt obligated to fight alongside the US in

---

38   Alan Renouf, *The Frightened Country*, South Melbourne: MacMillan, 1979, pp. 370-83.

39   Derek McDougall, Australia and the British Military Withdrawal from East of the Suez, *Australian Journal of International Affairs*, vol. 51, no. 2, 1997, pp. 183-194.

40   David McLean, From British Colony to American Satellite? Australia and the USA during the Cold War, *Australian Journal of Politics and History*, vol. 52, no. 1, 2006, p. 66.

41   Commonwealth of Australia, *2016 Defence White Paper*, Canberra: Department of Defence, 2016, p. 124; US Department of State, US Relations with Australia, Fact Sheet, Bureau of East Asian and Pacific Affairs, 25 February 2016, <http://www.state.gov/r/pa/ei/bgn/2698.htm>, accessed 1 April 2018.

order to maintain Washington's allegiance.[42] In any case, it is a clear rebuke of the special relationship that on those rare occasions when Australian and American strategic interests have failed to converge, Australia's long record of loyalty to the US has counted for very little.

A particularly instructive example occurred in the early 1960s when, after twenty years of being a loyal and dependable ally, Australia was unable to sway the US to oppose Indonesia's claims over West New Guinea. Australia faced the prospect of becoming entangled in a war with Jakarta without the support of a major ally. Placating Sukarno in order to prevent the "loss" of Indonesia to communism ultimately proved of far greater importance to the US than Australia's security concerns. It was a "sobering" lesson for Canberra, Gregory Pemberton writes, that "in the most dangerous international crisis Australia had faced since the [Second World] War, the US alliance was of little value as an instrument of Australian diplomacy because of the conflict in Australian-US interests".[43]

A more recent incident occurred when US President Bill Clinton rebuffed Australia's request for American troops to support the 1999 intervention into East Timor. The Clinton administration's reasoning was that Indonesia, a populous and mineral-rich nation, was of much greater strategic importance than the tiny, impoverished territory of East Timor.[44] After intense lobbying by both Australia and Portugal, along with significant pressure emanating from Congress, Washington belatedly decided to act and provide the political, logistical and intelligence support necessary to make the Australian-led intervention a success.[45] Prime Minister John Howard was nonetheless taken aback and intensely disappointed at America's refusal to provide "boots on the ground", believing it was a "violation of the alliance's spirit" after so many decades of "unbroken military support for the United States".[46]

---

42   As two prominent strategic experts put it, "Australian decision-makers have seen involvement in conflict as a premium that needs to be paid for the security guarantee and other benefits Australia accrues from its relationship with the US". Nick Bisley and Brendan Taylor, *Conflict in the East China Sea: Would ANZUS Apply?* Australia-China Relations Institute (ACRI), Ultimo, NSW, 2014, p.25.

43   Pemberton, *All The Way*, p. 101.

44   Noam Chomsky, Hypocrisy of the West: East Timor, Horror and Amnesia, *Le Monde Diplomatique*, October 1999, October 1999, <http://mondediplo. com/1999/10/02chomsky/>, accessed 1 April 2018.

45   Clinton Fernandes, *Reluctant Saviour: Australia, Indonesia and the independence of East Timor*, Carlton North, Victoria: Scribe Publications, 2004, pp. 97-99.

46   Paul Kelly, *The March of Patriots: The Struggle for Modern Australia*, Melbourne: Melbourne University Press, 2009, p. 508.

The gravest and most revealing variance in Australia's relationship with the US occurred in the early to mid-1970s, when the progressive Whitlam government attempted to shake off Australia's client status after two decades of unadulterated conservative support for the alliance. The Whitlam government's public criticism of US foreign policy in Indochina and dissent over the operation of US intelligence facilities in Australia raised grave concerns in Washington. Concern over Whitlam's intent to publicly reveal Pine Gap as a CIA operation was perhaps so great that the CIA sought to have Whitlam removed.[47] There is no conclusive evidence of this, but new research reveals that the CIA had certainly planned specific covert operations against Australia, and senior policymakers in Washington had contemplated such action, although it was deemed, at least at one point, to be counterproductive and too risky to carry out.[48]

Whitlam's agenda to pursue a more independent foreign policy within the alliance was perhaps most notably reflected in his government's attempts at "resources diplomacy".[49] The objective was to increase Australia's returns on mineral exports and help Australian corporations "go multinational", transforming Australia into a regional sub-metropolitan power. While the goal was to avoid satellite status, resources diplomacy was crucially dependent upon the continuation of American power in the region. Whitlam thus sought to create a more balanced Australia-US relationship while maintaining Australia's increasingly important role as a beneficiary and protector of America's regional security and economic order. Nowhere was this more apparent than with respect to Indonesia, where the Whitlam government moved immediately to strengthen Suharto's New Order regime to the benefit of Western strategic and economic interests; expanding economic and military aid, assisting in the rapid expansion of trade and investment, forging strong diplomatic relations and praising Suharto's achievements while whitewashing his crimes.[50]

---

47   Brian Toohey and Marian Wilkinson, *The Book of Leaks: Exposes in Defence of the Public's Right to Know*, North Ryde: Angus and Robertson, 1987, pp. 81-109; John Pilger, *A Secret County*, Great Britain: Vintage, 1989, pp. 187-238.

48   James Curran, *Unholy Fury: Whitlam and Nixon at War*, Kindle Edition, Melbourne: Melbourne University Publishing, 2015, Kindle Locations 4881-4891.

49   Robert Catley and Bruce McFarlance, *From Tweedledum to Tweedledee: The New Labor Government in Australia. A Critique of its Social Model*, Sydney: Australia and New Zealand Book Company, 1974; Jim Hyde, *Australia: The Asia Connection*, Malmsbury, Victoria: Kibble Books, 1978.

50   Burke, *Fear of Security*, pp. 128-131, 134-136.

Although Whitlam never advocated abandoning the alliance, only making it work better in Australia's interests, this proved almost too much to bear for Washington, which was accustomed "to the client-patron relationship that earlier Liberal-Country Party governments had maintained".[51] In response to Australia's desire for greater self-reliance, Henry Kissinger commissioned a national security memorandum in July 1974 to explore the options of relocating key US military installations in Australia to other nations and putting an effective end to the alliance. The memorandum also included the possible option of attenuating certain ties in the relationship, including reducing intelligence flows and military exercises and placing restrictions on trade and capital flows, with the hope of forcing Whitlam to reverse major elements of Australia's foreign policy. Ultimately, this option was deemed too high a risk, and, in any case, Washington's anxieties about the future of the alliance under the Whitlam government soon came to an end.[52]

There has existed a considerable level of bipartisanship with respect to the alliance and national security more generally since the end of the Whitlam government in the mid-1970s and particularly since the 1980s.[53] The persistence of strong bipartisanship on the question of the alliance, and a belief in the notion of a special relationship, has fostered an exaggerated sense of self-importance among Australian political leaders who are often overcome by their connection to, and admiration for, American power.[54] After having accompanied numerous Australian prime ministers to the US as a senior Australian diplomat, Richard Woolcott reflects that many risked "suffering the delusion that Australia is more important to the United States than is really the case".[55]

The added danger is that Australian political and bureaucratic elites, after having internalised the narrative of the special relationship, assume

---

51 These were the words Brent Scowcroft used when he advised US President Gerald Ford on the newly elected Australian Prime Minister, Malcolm Fraser. See Curran, *Unholy Fury*, Kindle Locations 5512-5517.

52 Curran, Kindle Locations 5024-5137.

53 Andrew Carr, Is Bipartisanship on National Security Beneficial? Australia's Politics of Defence and Security, *Australian Journal of Politics and History*, vol. 63, no. 2, 2017.

54 MacDonald and O'Connor, *Australia and New Zealand*; James Ingram, A Time for Change - The Alliance and Australian Foreign Policy, address to the Australian Institute of International Affairs, 9 June 2011, <http://www.internationalaffairs.org.au/media_library/a-time-for-change-the-us-alliance-and-australian-foreign-policy-by-james-ingram-ao-faiia/>, accessed 1 April 2018.

55 Richard Woolcott, *The Hot Seat: Reflections on Diplomacy from Stalin's Death to the Bali Bombings*, Sydney: Harper Collins, 2003, pp. 250-1.

the national interests of both countries have always converged and will continue to do so in the future.[56] When asked by a Senate Committee in August 1999 how future conflicts of interest between Australia and the United States might be resolved, former defence official Paul Dibb stated:

> I find it hard to imagine situations, given the ANZUS alliance, given our shared values and interests and given the closeness that we have, where there would be dramatic differences in the national interest.[57]

In more recent times, specifically after Trump's ascendency to the White House, a number of foreign policy experts have called on Australian leaders to ditch the romantic view of the alliance that emphasises shared values. In the view of historian James Curran, "Australian leaders are going to have to come up with a fresh approach. The language of sentiment and shared values will not work".[58]

The inability or unwillingness to understand that America's interests as a global power do not always align with those of Australia may have significant repercussions in the future as Canberra finds that its most important strategic relationship with the US, and its primary trading partnership with China, are at risk of clashing with one another over strategic imperatives. A major conflict erupting between the US and China remains unlikely. However, as a number of experts on the topic have warned, tensions have been increasing in the past several years and war is

---

56 Iain Henry, Bipartisanship on the US-Australia Alliance Inhibits Serious Debate About the Benefits and Risks, *Canberra Times*, 31 May 2015, <http://www.canberratimes.com.au/comment/bipartisanship-on-the-usaustralia-alliance-inhibits-serious-debate-about-the-benefits-and-risks-20150529-ghcw84.html>, accessed 1 April 2018.

57 Dibb was speaking specifically with respect to potential conflicts over joint intelligence gathering. Paul Dibb, remarks to the Joint Standing Committee on Treaties, Parliament of the Commonwealth of Australia, Canberra, 9 August 1999, <http://nautilus.org/wp-content/uploads/2015/10/Ball-Dibb-testimony-to-JSCOT-Inquiry-into-An-Agreement-to-extend-the-period-of-operation-of-the-Joint-Defence-Facility-at-Pine-Gap.-Report-26-1999.pdf>, accessed 1 April 2018.

58 Daniel Flitton, From Pragmatic to Pugnacious: How Donald Trump Deals with Malcolm Turnbull, *Sydney Morning Herald*, 2 February 2017, <http://www.smh.com.au/federal-politics/political-news/from-pragmatic-to-pugnacious-how-donald-trump-deals-with-malcolm-turnbull-20170202-gu444b.html>, accessed 1 April 2018. Also see Alan Dupont, Values-Based Foreign Policy is Flawed Thinking, *The Australian*, 20 December 2016, <http://www.theaustralian.com.au/opinion/valuesbased-foreign-policy-is-flawed-thinking/news-story/8f3aac905b47f74bd2cb8f064401e097>, accessed 1 April 2018; Iain Henry, Shared Interests, Shared Values? The US-Australian Alliance in the Age of Trump, *Lawfare*, 7 February 2017, <https://lawfareblog.com/shared-interests-shared-values-us-australian-alliance-age-trump>, accessed 1 April 2018.

no longer in the realm of fantasy as it once was.[59] As discussed later in the following chapter, Canberra's current trajectory is entangling Australia in Washington's plans for preserving its leadership status in Asia, a strategy that could drive a wedge between Canberra and Beijing, and potentially drag Australia into a US–Sino war.

---

59   See, for example, Bonnie S. Glasser, Armed Clash in the South China Sea, Contingency Planning Memorandum No. 14, Council on Foreign Relations, April 2012, <https://www.cfr.org/report/armed-clash-south-china-sea>, accessed 1 April 2018.

Chapter Three

BENEVOLENT HEGEMONY

American exceptionalism

The second part of the "special relationship" narrative, and a central tenet of the alliance orthodoxy, lies in the notion that Australia and the US are bound together by their joint commitment to promote liberal values abroad. One of the central objectives of the alliance, it is officially stated, is to "advance and support human rights, democracy, the rule of law and fundamental freedoms around the world".[1] The joint statement by President Trump and Prime Minister Turnbull in February 2018 provides a recent iteration of this mantra:

> The American-Australian alliance is rock solid and based on a common purpose: to promote peace and prosperity. Our friendship is under-pinned by a deep alignment of interests and our societies' shared commitment to the values of freedom, democracy, and the rule of law.[2]

While Australian foreign policy is generally less self-consciously idealistic than in the US, it is still conventional to adopt America's depiction of itself as an exceptional nation, driven by an enlightened foreign policy and a special historical sense of mission to spread freedom and democracy globally.[3]

---

1   Australia-United States Ministerial (AUSMIN) Consultations, 2011 Joint Communique, 15 September 2011, <http://dfat.gov.au/geo/united-states-of-america/ausmin/Pages/ausmin-joint-communique-2011.aspx>, accessed 1 April 2018.

2   Joint Statement by United States President Donald J. Trump and Australian Prime Minister Malcolm Turnbull, US Embassy and Consulate in Australia, 23 February, 2018, <https://au.usembassy.gov/joint-statement-united-states-president-donald-j-trump-australian-prime-minister-malcolm-turnbull/>, accessed 1 April 2018.

3   See, for example, Paul Dibb, "America and the Asia–Pacific" in Robert Ayson and Desmond Ball (eds), *Strategy and Security in the Asia–Pacific*, Crows Nest, Sydney: Allen & Unwin, 2006, p. 176. On the roots of American exceptionalism, which dates

Relatedly, it has been "an article of faith" in both Australian and American scholarly and policy circles that the US is a "benign hegemon", responsible for maintaining international peace and stability, particularly in the Asia–Pacific, since the end of World War Two.[4] The typical formulation among leading Australian defence experts is that "for the past sixty years, the security and stability of the Asia–Pacific have been underwritten by the benign hegemony of the US", which has "allowed countries in the region to prosper and grow at a prodigious rate".[5] Moreover, it is insisted, "What keeps the US engaged in the region today is its peculiar sense of mission to lead the free world, a sense borne of the notion of *exceptionalism*".[6]

This chapter provides only a cursory critical account of the exercise of American political, military and economic power – primarily in the Asia–Pacific region – and Australia's role in supporting that power. However, even this brief review strongly undermines the notion of a joint commitment on the part of both nations to promoting enlightened self-interests or lofty liberal values. Rather, what is revealed is an overriding joint commitment to the maintenance of American hegemony and the favourable strategic and economic order it presides over; even as this has often come at the expense of regional peace and stability and undermined the apparent shared commitment to freedom, human rights and the other so-called foundational values of the alliance.

The losers of American hegemony

US foreign policy, perhaps especially in the Asia–Pacific, has not been fundamentally different to that of the imperial powers that preceded it.[7] In

---

back to the early 17th century, see Howard Zinn, The Power and the Glory, *Boston Review*, 1 June 2005, <http://www.bostonreview.net/zinn-power-glory>, accessed 1 April 2018.

4   Nick Bisley, Enhancing America's Alliances in a Changing Asia–Pacific: The Case of Japan and Australia, *The Journal of East Asian Affairs*, vol. 20. no. 1, 2006, p. 47-8; Mark Beeson, Invasion by Invitation: The Role of Alliances in the Asia–Pacific, *Australian Journal of International Affairs*, vol. 69, no. 3, 2015, p. 310.

5   Andrew Davies and Mark Thompson, *Known Unknowns: Uncertainty About the Future of the Asia–Pacific*, Australian Strategic Policy Institute (ASPI), Canberra, Issue 35, October 2010, p. 6, <https://www.aspi.org.au/report/special-report-issue-35-known-unknowns-uncertainty-about-future-Asia–Pacific>, accessed 1 April 2018.

6   Davies and Thompson, p. 11. Emphasis in original.

7   For a comparison between the American Empire and the British, Roman and Greek empires that came before it, see Alfred W. McCoy, *In the Shadows of the American Century: The Rise and Decline of US Global Power*, Chicago: Haymarket Books, 2017.

the decades prior to the outbreak of World War Two, the US had emerged, like Japan, as an expansionist Pacific imperial power.[8] By the end of World War Two, Washington had assumed effective control in the Philippines, Japan, South Korea and across the entire Pacific Ocean. While rhetorically supporting the process of decolonisation, Washington's objective was to dismantle the exclusive trading blocs of the European imperial powers that obstructed its plans for an integrated global economic order that facilitated American corporate interests. The US also eventually moved to assist European colonial powers in their attempts to regain their former colonial possessions as it became clear this was necessary to ensure the rapid reconstruction of Europe.[9]

America's support for reinstating European colonialism dovetailed with Australia's own vision for the post-war regional order. Like the US, Australia spoke of liberating Asia during World War Two. After the Japanese attack on Pearl Harbor, Australian Prime Minister John Curtin declared, "We are at war with Japan ... because our vital interests are imperilled and because the rights of free people in the whole Pacific are assailed". [10] However, Canberra was only seriously interested in liberating Asia from Japanese imperialism, not Western colonialism, which was not fundamentally different in its nature and objectives. As one noted historian of the Asia–Pacific region writes, "In both lofty rhetoric of empire and the brutality of the conquest and subjugation of Asian peoples ... Japan shared much in common with Western colonial powers".[11]

As a proud member of the British Empire, Australia was a strong supporter of British imperialism and the European imperial order more generally, as well as being a colonial power in its own right with no

8   Gerhard Krebs, World War Zero? Reassessing the Global Impact of the Russo-Japanese War 1904-05, *The Asia–Pacific Journal*, vol. 10, issue 21, no. 2, 2012, <http://apjjf.org/2012/10/21/Gerhard-Krebs/3755/article.html>, accessed 1 April 2018.

9   John W. Dower, *Cultures of War: Pearl Harbor, Hiroshima, 9-11, Iraq*, New York: W. W. Norton & Company Inc, 2010, pp. 377-393; Gabriel Kolko, *Confronting the Third World: United States Foreign Policy 1945 – 1980*, New York: Pantheon Books, 1980, p. 18.

10   Tom O'Lincoln, *Australia's Pacific War: Challenging a National Myth*, Australia: Interventions Publishers, 2011, p. 34.

11   Incidentally, Japan's imperial order in Asia had a more positive impact on economic development than that of American or European colonialism. Mark Selden, East Asian Regionalism and its Enemies in Three Epochs: Political Economy and Geopolitics, 16th to 21st Centuries, *The Asia–Pacific Journal*, vol. 7, issue 9, no. 4, 25 February 2009, <http://apjjf.org/-Mark-Selden/3061/article.html>, accessed 1 April 2018.

intention of relinquishing control of its territorial possessions.[12] With respect to Dutch rule in Indonesia, Minister for External Affairs H. V. Evatt stated frankly in October 1943 that "We visualise the restoration of the former sovereignty".[13] Accordingly, when World War Two ended, Australian troops provided assistance for the restoration of Dutch control in Indonesia. Later, Australia played a more constructive role in supporting the Indonesian liberation struggle. However, this was largely because it saw independence as an inevitable outcome that it could better shape in a direction conducive to its interests.[14]

Australian support for European colonialism was most forcefully expressed in the conservative Liberal-Country Coalition led by Robert Menzies. From opposition during the mid-to-late 1940s, Menzies had supported the European imperial powers in their struggles to quash Asian independence movements – the British in Southeast Asia, the French in Indochina and the Dutch in the East Indies – and he continued to endorse the virtues of empire throughout the 1950s and 1960s.[15] Australia's primary military commitments in Malaya and Vietnam, initiated by the Menzies government, contributed to the broader efforts of British and American power to crush the anti-colonial movements that were then sweeping across Asia.[16]

American and Australian opposition to independence movements in the decades following World War Two stands against the popular rhetoric today that generations of Americans and Australians died in Asia to defend freedom and democracy.[17] Equally tendentious is the claim that American military engagement in the Asia–Pacific has been responsible for underpinning regional peace and stability. The US, after all, was the principle protagonist in Asia's two bloodiest international conflicts, in North Korea and

---

12   Australia's major colony being Papua/New Guinea.

13   O'Lincoln, *Australia's Pacific War*, p. 53.

14   O'Lincoln, pp. 48-49, 52-53.

15   David Goldsworthy, Australian External Policy and the End of Britain's Empire, *Australian Journal of Politics and History*, vol. 51, no. 1, 2005, pp. 17-29; David Goldsworthy, *Losing the Blanket: Australia and the End of Britain's Empire*, Melbourne: Melbourne University Press, 2002; Christopher Waters, After Decolonisation: Australia and the Emergence of the Non-aligned Movement in Asia, 1954-55, *Diplomacy and Statecraft*, vol. 12, no. 2, 2001, p. 156.

16   Greg Lockhart, *The Minefield: An Australian Tragedy in Vietnam*, Crows Nest, Sydney: Allen & Unwin, 2007.

17   Barack Obama, speech to the Australian Parliament in Canberra, Sydney Morning Herald, 17 November 2011, <https://www.smh.com.au/national/text-of-obamas-speech-to-parliament-20111117-1nkcw.html>, accessed 1 April 2018.

Vietnam, wars that were prosecuted with a litany of human rights abuses and war crimes.[18] Since World War Two, US air power in Asia alone has been responsible for millions of deaths and the vast destruction of civilian infrastructure in Korea, Vietnam, Laos, Cambodia, Iraq, Afghanistan and Pakistan.[19] Australian International Relations scholar Mark Beeson has frequently made the point that the notion of American hegemony coinciding with stability in the Asia–Pacific is "noticeably at odds with the historical record".[20]

Throughout the Cold War, the US used the pretext of maintaining stability to support and enhance the repressive capacities of authoritarian regimes that maintained pro-Western loyalties and interests. A direct line can be drawn between US military assistance and the extreme repression that emerged in much of the Third World during the Cold War. As historian Alfred W. McCoy observes:

> Much of the abuse synonymous with the era of authoritarian rule in Asia and Latin America seems to have originated with the United States. While dictatorships in those regions would no doubt have tortured on their own, US training programs provided sophisticated techniques, up-to-date equipment, and moral legitimacy for the practice, producing a clear correlation between US Cold War policy and the extreme state violence of the authoritarian age.[21]

Under the guise of defeating communism, Washington propped up countless "national security states" throughout the Third World, particularly in Asia and Central and South America, overthrowing democratically elected governments and undermining progressively-based mass social movements.[22] Quoting the *Cambridge History of the Cold War*, historian John W.

---

18   Bruce Cumings, *The Korean War: A History*, New York: The Modern Library, 2011; Nick Turse, *Kill Anything That Moves: The Real American War in Vietnam*, New York: Metropolitan Books/Henry Holt and Co, 2013.

19   Jeremy Kuzmarov, Bomb After Bomb: US Air Power and Crimes of War From World War II to the Present, *The Asia–Pacific Journal*, vol. 10, issue 47, no. 3, 19 November 2012, <http://apjjf.org/2012/10/47/Jeremy-Kuzmarov/3855/article.html>, accessed 1 April 2018.

20   See, for example, Beeson, Invasion by Invitation, p. 310.

21   Alfred W. McCoy, *A Question of Torture: CIA Interrogation, from the Cold War to the War on Terror*, New York: Metropolitan Books, 2006, p 11.

22   Noam Chomsky and Edward S. Herman, *The Washington Connection and Third World Fascism: The Political Economy of Human Rights, Volume 1*, Montreal: Black Rose Books, 1980; Noam Chomsky and Edward S. Herman, *After the Cataclysm: Postwar Indochina and the Reconstruction of Imperial Ideology: The Political Economy of Human*

Dower places the fate of America's client regimes in Latin America into context by comparing them to the more publicised experiences of violence and oppression in the Soviet bloc:

> Between 1960, by which time the Soviets had dismantled Stalin's gulags, and the Soviet collapse of 1990, the numbers of political prisoners, torture victims, and executions of nonviolent political dissenters in Latin America vastly exceeded those in the Soviet Union and its East European satellites. In other words, from 1960 to 1990, the Soviet bloc as a whole was less repressive measured in terms of human victims, than many individual Latin American countries.[23]

Where the US did support democratic reform in the Third World, it was in the form of "polyarchy" rather than genuine democracy, ensuring decision making was confined to a small group of elites who preserved US strategic and economic interests. Where the US had formerly supported dictatorship in places such as Marcos's Philippines, Pinochet's Chile and Duvalier's Haiti, it later shifted to supporting quasi democratic reforms as a means to stave off mass-based, popular democratic movements.[24]

With few exceptions, Australia enthusiastically defended the actions of the US during the Cold War, apologising for American-allied dictators that were pro-Western and stable, including the Shah in Iran, Marcos in the Philippines, Suharto in Indonesia and a string of dictators in South Vietnam and South Korea.[25] The portrayal of Marcos in official circles as "the last hope for democracy" just months before martial law was declared in September 1972 was typical of Canberra's approach to Western-allied dictators generally.[26] Three years and 50,000 political prisoners later, the

---

Rights, Volume 2, Cambridge, Massachusetts: South End Press, 1979; Chalmers Johnson, *Blowback: The Costs and Consequences of American Empire*, New York: Henry Holt and Company, 2004. For a useful summary of global US interventions undermining democracy since World War Two, see William Blum, *Killing Hope: US Military and C.I.A. Interventions Since World War II*, Monroe, US: Common Courage Press, 2004.

23   John W. Downer, *The Violent American Century: War and Terror Since World War II*, Kindle Edition, Chicago: Haymarket Books, 2017, Kindle Locations 1124-1129.

24   William I. Robinson, *Promoting Polyarchy: Globalisation, US Intervention, and Hegemony*, Cambridge: Cambridge University Press, 1996.

25   For numerous examples, see George J. Munster and Richard Walsh, *Secrets of State: A Detailed Assessment of the Book They Banned*, Sydney: Angus & Robertson, 1982.

26   This was the characterisation made at the time by Ambassador James Ingram, quoted in Brian Toohey and William Pinwill, *Oyster: The Story of the Australian Secret Intelligence Service*, Melbourne: William Heinemann Australia, 1989, p. 125.

Australian foreign affairs department continued to downplay the repression of the Marcos regime, arguing that "'martial law' in the Philippines is of a different, milder variety from its European archetype", and that there was no serious political opposition to the government.[27] Australia continued to take a soft stand on human rights abuses in Southeast Asia after the end of the Cold War in the 1990s, often under the guise of "cultural relativism" and the need to maintain political stability and economic growth.[28]

Australia did more than just provide diplomatic cover to odious regimes. Along with directly participating in America's two major wars in Asia,[29] Canberra provided direct economic and military assistance for Southeast Asian military regimes such as those in South Vietnam, Thailand, the Philippines and Indonesia, much of it under the guise of the Colombo Plan. Ostensibly a humanitarian program, the Colombo Plan was ultimately employed by Canberra as a psychological warfare campaign to prevent revolutionary political change in Asia and extend Western influence in the region. It included the Australian Security Intelligence Organisation (ASIO) training military regimes throughout Asia in police and security methods, and intelligence officers in counter-subversion techniques.[30]

The Australian Secret Intelligence Service (ASIS) also cooperated closely with its Anglo-American counterparts in several parts of the Third World during the Cold War, particularly Southeast and Northeast Asia, engaging in covert operations to support numerous pro-Western regimes and undermine their political opponents. ASIS aided the CIA's covert operations in Indonesia in support of Sukarno's political opponents in the late 1950s and 1960s, maintained a close working relationship with the secret police in the Philippines when that country was under martial law in the 1970s, and participated, to an unknown extent, in the CIA's efforts to overthrow Prince

---

27   Munster and Walsh, *Secrets of State*, pp. 111-116.

28   Erik Paul, Australia and Southeast Asia: Regionalisation, Democracy and Conflict, *Journal of Contemporary Asia*, vol. 29, no. 3, 1999, pp. 285-308.

29   For a rare examination of Australian atrocities during the Vietnam War, see Alex Carey, *Australian Atrocities in Vietnam*, Sydney: Comment Publishing Company, 1968.

30   Daniel Oakman, The Politics of Foreign Aid: Counter-Subversion and the Colombo Plan, 1950–1970, *Pacifica Review*, vol. 13, no. 3, 2001; Daniel Oakman, *Facing Asia: A History of the Colombo Plan*, Canberra: Pandanus Books, 2004; Christopher Waters, A Failure of Imagination: R.G. Casey and Australian Plans for Counter-Subversion in Asia, 1954-1956, *Australian Journal of Politics and History*, vol. 45, no. 3, 1999, pp. 347-361; St John Kettle, *Australia's Arms Exports: Keeping them out of Repressive Hands*, Peace Research Centre, Research School of Pacific Studies, Australian National University, Canberra, 1989.

Norodom Sihanouk in Cambodia in 1970 and Salvador Allende in Chile in 1973.[31]

The most egregious example of Australian and American cooperation in undermining human rights and democracy in the name of upholding regional "stability" was the support both countries provided for Suharto's 1965 coup in Indonesia, which killed up to one million people, followed by Indonesia's invasion and occupation of East Timor (1975–1999), which killed a further 200,000 people. The scale of the 1965–66 massacres was received with admiration by Australian policy-makers and opinion leaders who were relieved to see the Communist Party of Indonesia (PKI) extinguished.[32] Washington not only watched and cheered the slaughter from the sidelines but directly helped to arm the killers with the equipment necessary to increase their efficiency.[33]

When Suharto launched the invasion of East Timor in 1975 he did so after receiving an unofficial green light from US President Gerald Ford.[34] The Whitlam government also made clear to Indonesia that it would do nothing to obstruct the invasion. In a strong demonstration of bi-partisanship, sub-sequent Fraser, Hawke and Keating governments continued to fully support Suharto's extreme repression, both domestically and as part of the occupation of the East Timorese. It was only in the midst of an unprecedented campaign of civil resistance and public outrage in Australia that the Howard government – which had done everything in its power to provide diplomatic cover for Indonesian atrocities in the lead up to the 1999 vote for independence – reversed Australia's long-standing policy and fully supported the deployment of peacekeeping forces to protect East Timorese independence.[35]

---

31   At one time or another during the Cold War, ASIS had operatives in Singapore, Malaysia, Indonesia, Thailand, the Philippines, Japan, Vietnam, Cambodia, Chile and China. For details, see Joseph Camilleri, *Australian-American Relations: The Web of Dependence*, South Melbourne: Macmillan, 1980, pp. 123-126; Toohey and Pinwill, *Oyster*; Toohey and Wilkinson, *The Book of Leaks*.

32   Anthony Burke, *Fear of Security: Australia's Invasion Anxiety*, Cambridge: Cambridge University Press, 2008, pp. 122-123; Clinton Fernandes, *Reluctant Saviour: Australia, Indonesia and the independence of East Twesimor*, Carlton North, Victoria: Scribe Publications, 2004, pp. 9-11.

33   Carmel Budiardo, "Indonesia: Mass Extermination and the Consolidation of Authoritarian Power" in Alexander George (ed), *Western State Terrorism*, Cambridge: Polity Press, 1991, pp. 194-196.

34   Ben Kiernan, "War, Genocide, and Resistance in East Timor, 1975-99: Comparative Reflections on Cambodia" in Mark Selden and Alvin Y. So (eds), *War & State Terrorism: The United States, Japan, & the Asia–Pacific in the Long Twentieth Century*, Oxford: Rowman and Littlefield Publishers, 2004, p. 212.

35   Fernandes, *Reluctant Saviour*.

State terror and the "Washington consensus"

In response to the 9/11 terrorist attacks against America in 2001, the United States prosecuted its indefinite "war on terror" with enthusiastic Australian participation. The subsequent intervention into the Middle East, still ongoing, has been widely recognised as a catastrophic strategic failure and a human rights disaster, resulting in mass civilian casualties and the destabilisation of the wider Middle East and North African regions. America's long history of intervention in both Afghanistan and Iraq has been a major factor in generating the political, economic and social chaos that plagues these countries today.[36] The rapid rise and success of international jihadi terrorism can be explained, to a significant degree, by the actions of the US and its allies, particularly the 2003 invasion and occupation of Iraq.[37] Australia's participation in the war on terror, although small in military terms, nonetheless helped to undermine the rule of law as well as implicate leading Australian political and military leaders in potential war crimes.[38]

The hypocrisy of the US-led "war on terror" is obscured in mainstream international relations accounts that employ a narrow definition of terrorism that excludes the actions of states. During the Cold War, the term "terrorism" was rarely applied to the atrocities committed by America's extreme right-wing satellites in Central and South America.[39] Today, America's global drone-strike assassination program, crucially supported by US intelligence and communications bases on Australian soil, is a classic example of the modern use of state terror.[40] If state terrorism was not excluded from

---

36   Drew Cottle, "Diggers for Democracy? The Australians in Occupied Afghanistan and Iraq" in Christine De Matos and Robin Gerster (eds), *Occupying the "Other": Australia and Military Occupations From Japan to Iraq*, Cambridge Scholars Publishing: Newcastle upon Tyne, UK, 2009, pp. 18-25.

37   Patrick Cockburn, *The Rise of Islamic State: ISIS and the New Sunni Revolution*, London: Verso, 2015; Charles Glass, *Syria Burning: ISIS and the Death of the Arab Spring*, New York: OR Books, 2015.

38   On the illegality of the invasion and occupation of Iraq, see Ronald C. Kramer and Raymond J. Michalowski, War, Aggression and State Crime: A Criminological Analysis of the Invasion and Occupation of Iraq, *The British Journal of Criminology*, vol. 45, no. 4, July 2005, pp. 446-469. On potential Australian war crimes in Iraq, see Chris Doran and Tim Anderson, Iraq and the Case for Australian War Crimes Trials, *Crime, Law and Social Change*, vol. 56, 2011, pp. 283-299.

39   Edward S. Herman, *The Real Terror Network: Terrorism in Fact and Propaganda*, Boston: South End Press, 1982.

40   For details on the rise and expansion of America's global assassination program, see Jeremy Scahill, *Dirty Wars: The World is a Battlefield*, New York: Nation Books, 2013; and also Nick Turse and Tom Engelhardt, *Terminator Planet: The First History*

the international relations literature, the US would be recognised as one of the most consistent perpetrators and supporters of terrorism since World War Two.[41]

Like terrorism, the term "stability" confers a narrow meaning that ignores the fate of those who fell afoul of American power. Victims of US wars and repressive regimes propped up by American military and economic aid are conveniently whitewashed from history. It is conventional in realist international relations and strategic studies accounts of Asia–Pacific regional affairs to equate stability and the "balance of power" with the prevailing distribution of power or the status quo; an interpretation that conveniently translates into support for US hegemony.[42] American military capacity clearly dwarfs that of any other regional power, but identifying the US role as providing "balance" offers a way of presenting the status quo in palatable terms.[43]

Believers in the benevolence of American hegemony are quick to attribute credit to the US for the phenomenal economic growth in Asia, largely on account of the strategic stability and economic liberalisation policies sustained by American "leadership" since World War Two.[44] What

---

of Drone Warfare 2001-2050, Dispatch Books, 25 May 2012. For a detailed study on how US drone strikes terrorise civilian populations, see James Cavallaro, Stephan Sonnenberg, and Sarah Knuckey, *Living Under Drones: Death, Injury, and Trauma to Civilians from US Drone Practices in Pakistan*, a report by the International Human Rights and Conflict Resolution Clinic at Stanford Law School, Stanford, and the Global Justice Clinic at NYU School of Law, New York, 2012. On Australian participation in American extra-judicial killings through the hosting of US bases, see Richard Tanter, The US Military Presence in Australia: Asymmetrical Alliance Cooperation and its Alternatives, *The Asia–Pacific Journal*, vol. 11, issue 45, no. 1, 11 November 2013, <http://apjjf.org/2013/11/45/Richard-Tanter/4025/article.html>, accessed 1 April 2018.

41   Alexander George (ed), *Western State Terrorism*, Cambridge: Polity Press, 1991; Noam Chomsky, *Pirates and Emperors, Old and New: International Terrorism in the Real World*, London: Pluto Press, 2002; Mark Selden and Alvin Y. So (eds), *War & State Terrorism: The United States, Japan, & the Asia–Pacific in the Long Twentieth Century*, Oxford: Rowman and Littlefield Publishers, 2004; Richard Jackson, Eamon Murphey and Scott Poynting (eds), *Contemporary State Terrorism: Theory and Practice*, London: Routledge, 2010; Cihan Aksan and Jon Bailes (eds), *Weapon of the Strong: Conversations on US State Terrorism*, London: Pluto Press, 2013; Noam Chomsky and Andre Vltchek, *On Western Terrorism: From Hiroshima to Drone Warfare*, London: Pluto Press, 2013.

42   Robert Ayson, Regional Stability in the Asia–Pacific: Towards a Conceptual Understanding, *Asian Security*, vol. 1, no. 2, 2005, pp. 196-198.

43   Natasha Hamilton-Hart, *Hard Interests, Soft Illusions*: Southeast Asia and American Power, New York: Cornell University Press, 2012, p. 148.

44   For two illustrations of this conventional view see Michael Wesley, *There Goes the Neighbourhood: Australia and the Rise of Asia*, Sydney: New South, 2011; and Andrew

is not stated is that the patterns of economic growth supported by the US have concentrated wealth in a small minority, particularly in Southeast Asia, where the data shows that:

> The economic benefits from participation in an expanding regional and global economy under US hegemony have been concentrated in the hands of state elites and their key political constituencies, mainly owners of large private firms and the middle class, a group that remains a minority.[45]

Meanwhile, the rapid economic growth in East Asia during the "miracle years" – variously seen as occurring from the 1950s to the 1990s – was achieved by development models that were otherwise vehemently opposed by the US. As economist Ha-Joon Chang states:

> Despite some lingering disagreements, there is now a broad consensus that the spectacular growth of [post-war Japan and the East Asian Newly Industrialised Countries], with the exception of Hong Kong, is fundamentally due to activist, industrial, trade and technology (ITT) policies by the state.[46]

It was not happenstance that while East Asia continued to boom under various forms of the "infant industry" development model that defied the orthodox economic theories advocated by Washington, America's poster-child neoliberal economies in Latin America crashed spectacularly during the "lost decade" of the 1980s.[47]

As with America's Marshall Plan for Europe in the aftermath of World War Two, Washington's tolerance for the alternative development models adopted by its Asian allies was driven by the long-term objective of thwarting indigenous communist and left-socialist political forces that threatened America's global economic dominance.[48] Access to the massive domestic

Shearer, *Unchartered Waters: The US Alliance and Australia's New Era of Strategic Uncertainty*, Lowy Institute Perspectives, Lowy Institute for International Policy, Sydney, August 2011, <http://www.lowyinstitute.org/publications/uncharted-waters-us-alliance-and-australias-new-era-strategic-uncertainty>, accessed 1 April 2018.

45   Hamilton-Hart, *Hard Interests, Soft Illusions*, p. 85.

46   Ha-Joon Chang, *Kicking Away the Ladder: Development Strategy in Historical Perspective*, London: Anthem Press, 2003, p. 49.

47   Songok Han Thornton and William H. Thornton, *Development Without Freedom: The Politics of Asian Globalization*, UK: Ashgate Publishing, 2008, p. 76.

48   Leo Panitch and Sam Gindin, *The Making of Global Capitalism: The Political Economy of American Empire*, London: Verso, 2012, pp. 94-95.

American market, provision of foreign aid and corporate penetration were used by Washington across the Third World as a means to moderate radical nationalism in a strategy of "developmental containment".[49] In return for America's apparent economic largesse, Third World elites were required to pledge political obedience to Washington's Cold War strategic objectives. Unsurprisingly, the rapid national economic growth of the peripheral capitalist states of East and Southeast Asia was accompanied by pronounced political repression – a kind of "repressive developmentalism" – justified under the guise of maintaining stability and in accordance with traditional "Asian values".[50]

When the geopolitical value of America's Asian allies lapsed at the end of the Cold War, they came under increasing pressure from the US to adopt the prevailing economic orthodoxy or "Washington consensus". Australia was at the forefront of promoting the neoliberal model of development in the region that proved so beneficial for Australian and Western business interests and local Asian elites but severely damaging to the poor, the environment, and political and economic stability in the region. The rapid trade and capital market liberalisation policies that were the hallmark of the neoliberal project – pushed through multilateral economic forums such as the Australian-initiated APEC – led to instability and economic collapse, epitomised by the 1997 Asian Financial Crisis and exacerbated by the economic prescriptions imposed by the US-controlled IMF in its aftermath.[51]

According to one prominent economist, the countries of Southeast Asia would likely be far richer today had they been allowed to continue on the "textbook development path of growth". Indonesia, South Korea, Malaysia and Thailand would be twice as rich, and Vietnam would be almost 50 per cent richer, if the growth paths prior to Washington's neoliberal assault

---

49   James Peck, *Washington's China: The National Security World, the Cold War, and the Origins of Globalism*, Amherst: University of Massachusetts Press, 2006, p. 212.

50   Richard Tanter, Trends in Asia, *Alternatives*, vol. 10, 1984, pp. 164-5; Thornton and Thornton, *Development without Freedom*; Camilleri, *Australian–American Relations*, pp. 78-85.

51   Joseph E. Stiglitz, *Globalization and its Discontents*, New York: W. W. Norton & Company, 2003; Johnson, *Blowback*, pp. 193-215; Ian Taylor, APEC, Globalisation, and 9/11, *Critical Asian Studies*, vol. 36, no. 3, 2004, pp. 463-478; Mark Beeson and Andre Broome, Hegemonic Instability and East Asia: Contradictions, Crises and US Power, *Globalisations*, vol. 7, No. 4, 2010, pp. 507-523; James George and Rodd McGibbon, Dangerous Liaisons: Neoliberal Foreign Policy and Australia's Regional Engagement, *Australian Journal of Political Science*, vol. 33, no. 3, 1998, pp. 399-420.

were maintained.[52] Significantly, had China also succumbed to America's neoliberal economic dictates during the 1990s, the consequences for the global economy and international stability would have been catastrophic.

Playing by the rules

The need to prevent the emergence of a regional hegemonic power that might threaten US security is commonly portrayed as the overriding strategic objective of the US in Asia since World War Two. However, more important and relevant has been the desire to establish regional compliance and continued American leadership. The bilateral "hub-and-spokes" system of alliances served this dual geopolitical objective of preventing the emergence of a "peer competitor" and an indigenous regional grouping that might exclude the US.[53] This system of alliances would ensure Washington could "exert maximum control over [its] smaller ally's actions" and "amplify US control and minimise any collusion among its alliance partners".[54]

One of the rarely acknowledged consequences of unconstrained US power has been the way in which it has continued to undermine regional integration. Astute observers have long noted that accommodation between some or all of the great powers of Asia would undermine the Western alliance system. "Although an accommodation between Japan and China would clearly be preferable", wrote former defence official Paul Dibb, at the turn of the 21st century, "it would not be to the benefit of the Western alliance system if it involved a strategic partnership between Asia's two greatest powers". The same would be true, Dibb continues, if a "triple entente" emerged between China, Russia and India.[55]

Mark Beeson points out that American strategic involvement in the region "is expressly designed to keep East Asia divided and its security

52   Dean Baker, *Rigged: How Globalisation and the Rules of the Modern Economy Were Structured to Make the Rich Richer*, Washington, DC: Centre for Economic and Policy Research, 2016, pp. 4-5.

53   Chengxin Pan, The "Indo-Pacific" and Geopolitical Anxieties About China's Rise in the Asian Regional Order, *Australian Journal of International Affairs*, vol. 68, no. 4, 2014, p. 458; Jae Jeok Park, The US-led Alliances in the Asia–Pacific: Hedge Against Potential Threats or an Undesirable Multilateral Security Order, *The Pacific Review*, vol. 24, no. 2, 2011, pp. 137-158.

54   Victor Cha, senior official in the George W. Bush administration, quoted in Justin Logan, *China, America and the Pivot to Asia*, CATO Institute, Policy Analysis No. 717, 8 January 2013, p. 6, <http://www.cato.org/publications/policy-analysis/china-america-pivot-asia>, accessed 1 April 2018.

55   Paul Dibb, "The Strategic Environment in the Asia–Pacific Region" in Robert D. Blackwell and Paul Dibb (eds), *America's Asian Alliances*, 2000, pp. 6-7.

orientation firmly oriented towards Washington".[56] Quoting international relations expert Michael Mastanduno, Beeson argues that keeping the region divided has been a key element of America's overall grand strategy:

> Since the United States does not want to encourage a balancing coalition against its dominant position, it is not clear that it has a strategic interest in the full resolution of differences between, say, Japan and China or Russia and China. Some level of tension among these states reinforces their individual need for a special relationship with the United States.[57]

Contrary to maintaining stability, the hundreds of US military bases sprawled across Asia give Washington a vested interest in the continuation of multiple regional disputes that keep Japan, South Korea and other US allies dependent on America. As Gavan McCormack writes:

> If relations between Japan and North Korea, or even between North and South Korea, were ever normalised, the tension would drain from them and the comprehensive incorporation of Japan within the American hegemonic project would become correspondingly more difficult to justify. In other words, if peace broke out in East Asia, the justification for the sprawling US military base presence in South Korea and Japan would disappear.[58]

It has now become patently clear, even within mainstream political and scholarly circles, that US primacy may not be the anchor of regional stability it once claimed to be.[59] The rapid rise of China and its increasing ability and willingness to challenge Washington's insistence on dictating the "rules" of the regional order undermines the fundamental premise of orthodox accounts of regional stability that claim US primacy is critical for

---

56   Mark Beeson, East Asian Regionalism and the End of the Asia–Pacific: After American Hegemony, *The Asia–Pacific Journal*, vol. 7, issue 2, no. 2, 8 January 2009, <http://apjjf.org/-Mark-Beeson/3008/article.html>, accessed 1 April 2018.

57   Beeson. Also see Mark Selden, Economic Nationalism and Regionalism in Contemporary East Asia, *The Asia–Pacific Journal*, vol. 10, issue 43, no. 2, 29 October 2012, <http://apjjf.org/2012/10/43/Mark-Selden/3848/article.html>, accessed 1 April 2018.

58   Gavan McCormack, *Target North Korea: Pushing North Korea to the Brink of Nuclear Catastrophe*, Sydney: Random House Australia, 2004, pp. 144-5.

59   Hugh White, Power Shift: Australia's Future Between Washington and Beijing, *Quarterly Essay*, vol. 39, 2010; Hugh White, *The China Choice: Why We Should Share Power*, Oxford: Oxford University Press, 2012; Fraser with Roberts, *Dangerous Allies*.

suppressing conflict between the great powers. America's refusal to cede any strategic space to the PRC despite China's growing national power is steadily increasing the risk of a major destabilising regional conflict.

While China poses no serious conventional threat to the continental United States, the Chinese homeland is vulnerable to extensive damage by forward deployed American forces in the Pacific. China has attempted to redress this historic vulnerability by developing a high-tech 'Anti Access-Area Denial' (A2/AD) capacity in order to keep the military forces of the United States at bay. The US still maintains the overall military edge in the South China Sea but Beijing is increasingly capable of challenging the ability of US forces to operate close to the Chinese mainland.

China has also engaged in controversial and large scale land reclamation efforts and the construction of military installations on various islands in the South China Sea. However, the utility of these military installations in the event of conflict is severely limited, given the US retains "the capability to destroy them at will."[60] Although holding some military relevance they "are more important as a political claim to waterways and undersea resources."[61] A recent RAND report concludes: "China currently lacks the support structure necessary to sustain significant combat forces at a distance from its coast, and its current land reclamation efforts and the construction of new infrastructure on the islands would be of only modest benefit in a high-intensity war."[62]

The Pentagon's current strategic doctrine, initially dubbed "AirSea Battle" but later renamed JAM-GC (Joint Concept for Access and Manoeuvre in the Global Commons), is specifically designed to undermine China's emerging A2/AD capabilities for preventing an attack via China's air and maritime approaches. The strategy "relies on credibly threatening to strike critical military targets deep within Chinese territory from afar and on defeating PLA [People's Liberation Army] air and sea forces in a sustained conventional campaign." It also proposes the US and its allies,

---

60   Mark J. Valencia, Revelations of China's Construction in the South China Sea: Hype Not Helpful, *IPP Review*, 5 April 2017, <http://ippreview.com/index.php/Home/Blog/single/id/391.html>, accessed 1 April 2018.

61   Robert Farley, How Defensible Are China's Island Bases? *War is Boring*, 19 February 2018, <https://warisboring.com/how-defensible-are-chinas-island-bases/>, accessed 1 April 2018.

62   Eric Heginbotham, et.al, *The US-China Military Scorecard: Forces, Geography and the Evolving Balance of Power 1996-2017*, RAND Corporation, 2015, p. 326, <https://www.rand.org/content/dam/rand/pubs/research_reports/RR300/RR392/RAND_RR392.pdf>, accessed 1 April 2018.

particularly Japan and Australia, "impose a distant blockade on China in the event of war."[63]

A common refrain among Australian and American defence commentators is that US military domination in the South China Sea is necessary to protect freedom of navigation in the event that a hostile China disrupts or blocks regional and international trade. The unstated flipside of this equation is that America's foot remains on China's throat, able at any time to choke off the resources and products necessary for Chinese industry and ultimately the PRC's survival. Current US war plans for blockading China would have devastating consequences. A 2016 RAND report evaluating the consequences of a US–China conflict out to the year 2025 concluded it "would produce a shock to Chinese global trade", whereas only US bilateral trade with China would be affected. The damage to China's economy "could be catastrophic and lasting", with a 25–35% reduction in GDP after one year of conflict, compared with a 5–10% reduction in GDP for the US, equivalent to a severe recession.[64]

It is highly unlikely that China would attempt to shut down the free flow of trade in peacetime given it would irreparably damage Beijing's interests. A significant proportion of the trade that passes through the South China Sea goes to and from China, and Beijing clearly has no interest in blocking its own trade.[65] It is the freedom of US military activities, not commercial shipping, that's at stake. As former Australian foreign minister Gareth Evans makes clear, America's primary motivation is not to protect freedom of navigation, which it regularly "talks up". Rather, "its overwhelming preoccupation [is] with the right to engage in military surveillance unhindered, as close inshore as it can" to China.[66]

63   Andrew Davies and Benjamin Schreer, Whither US forces? US Military Presence in the Asia–Pacific and the Implications for Australia, Australian Strategic Policy Institute, 8 September 2011, p. 4, <http://www.aspi.org.au/publications/publication_details.aspx?ContentID=307>.

64   David C. Gompert, et. al. (eds), *War With China: Thinking Through The Unthinkable*, RAND Corporation, Santa Monica, California, 2016, <http://www.rand.org/pubs/research_reports/RR1140.html>.

65   James Laurenceson, Economics and Freedom of Navigation in East Asia, *Australian Journal of International Affairs*, vol. 71, no. 5, 2017, pp. 461-473; Ralf Emmers, "The US Rebalancing Strategy: Impact on the South China Sea" in Leszek Buszynski and Christopher Roberts (eds), *The South China Sea and Australia's Regional Security Environment*, National Security College Occasional Paper, no. 5, September 2013, pp. 41-42.

66   Gareth Evans, The South China Sea and Australia's Regional Security Environment, speech to the launch of the Australian National University's National Security College Occasional Paper No 5, 2 October 2013, p. 2, <http://news.anu.edu.au/files/2013/10/South-China-Sea_G-Evans.pdf>.

Although classified, US surveillance activities in China's Exclusive Economic Zone (EEZ) have probably included military objectives such as the active "tickling" of China's coastal defences, interference with naval communications, "preparation of the battlefield" and the tracking of China's nuclear submarines for potential targeting. "These are not passive intelligence collection operations commonly undertaken and usually tolerated by most states," writes maritime policy analyst Mark J. Valencia, "but intrusive and controversial practices that China regards not only as a violation of the 1982 UN Convention on the Law of the Sea but tantamount to a threat to use force" and therefore "a violation of the UN Charter."[67]

America's insistence on continuing to conduct provocative military surveillance activities in China's near seas has led to a number of dangerous clashes between US and Chinese aircraft and naval vessels since 2001. The Council on Foreign Relations has warned that the "risk of conflict in the South China Sea is significant" and that "the most likely and dangerous contingency is a clash stemming from US military operations within China's EEZ that provokes an armed Chinese response."[68]

As the preeminent power, the United States could play a constructive role in balancing the rise of China vis-à-vis its regional neighbours if Washington was willing to treat Beijing as an "equal." The US frequently asserts that it welcomes China's rise as a major regional player as long as it "plays by the rules." But that is hardly a genuine formula for power sharing given it ignores the fact that the rules of the regional and international order were largely crafted by the US, ensuring the benefits primarily accrue to itself and that of its allies.[69] It also conveniently ignores the fact that the United States regularly violates the rules when it suits its interests. The PRC is often berated by both Washington and Canberra for failing to abide by the United Nations Law of the Sea Convention (UNCLOS), an international treaty that the United States itself refuses to ratify.

America's grand strategy with respect to the PRC has always been to prevent its emergence as a "powerful, autonomous, self-determining nation

67   Mark J. Valencia, The South China Sea: Back to the Future?, *Global Asia*, vol. 5, no. 4, 2010, <http://www.globalasia.org/Issue/Detail/11/troubled-waters.html>, accessed 1 April 2018.

68   Bonnie S. Glaser, Armed Clash in the South China Sea, Contingency Planning Memorandum No. 14, *Council on Foreign Relations*, 2012, <https://www.cfr.org/report/armed-clash-south-china-sea>, accessed 1 April 2018.

69   Michael Beckley, China's Century? Why America's Edge will Endure, *International Security*, vol. 36, no. 3, 2011, pp. 48-50.

asserting its right to formulate the rules along with other great powers".[70] During the Cold War, Washington's strategy was to contain and isolate China until the rest of Asia was sufficiently brought under US influence. Recognition and normalisation of relations occurred only after the threat of regional national liberation movements were defeated, requiring China to adapt to the new Asia that had painfully emerged after the end of the Vietnam War.[71] US foreign policy has since oscillated between "constructive engagement" and containment, but with the same objective of ensuring China remains incorporated into the "norms" and "rules" of the US-led international strategic and economic order.[72]

Australia has similarly long echoed the empty gesture of recognising China's "legitimate interests" while insisting Beijing secures them within the "current regional framework," failing to acknowledge that same framework undermines China's security.[73] Beijing's growing capacity to deny the US or any other hostile power access to its local waters is portrayed by Canberra as a destabilising challenge to the existing order. Incidentally, as Andrew Davies and Mark Thompson of the Australian Strategic Policy Institute point out, Australia has long pursued control of its air and maritime approaches, a strategy which is "as fundamental to China's self-defence as it is to ours."[74]

While Australia continues to insist that regional stability is of the utmost importance, it is simultaneously positioning itself as a central part of America's strategy to contain or "dissuade" the rise of China,[75] risking a major confrontation that could cross the nuclear threshold and drag Australia into a US–Sino war.[76] Over the past several years, Canberra has

---

70 James Peck, *Ideal Illusions: How the US Government Co-opted Human Rights*, New York: Metropolitan Books, 2010, p. 139.

71 Peck, *Washington's China*.

72 Peck, *Ideal Illusions*, pp. 133-139.

73 Commonwealth of Australia, Australia's Strategic Policy: 1997 Strategic Review, Canberra: Department of Defence, 1997, p. 14.

74 Davies and Thompson, Known Unknowns, p. 10.

75 US strategy toward China is perhaps more accurately described as "dissuasion" rather than containment. The goal is not to slow the rate of growth of China's military power but match it, and thereby preserve America's military advantage. Together with strengthening its web of defence relationships in Asia, the US aims to shape Beijing's choices and discourage it from challenging US primacy. Nina Silove, The Pivot before the Pivot: US Strategy to Preserve the Power Balance in Asia, *International Security*, vol. 40, no. 4, Spring 2016, pp. 45-88.

76 Robert Ayson and Desmond Ball, Can a Sino-Japanese War be Controlled?, *Survival: Global Politics and Strategy*, vol. 56, issue 6, 2014, pp. 135-166; Bisley and Taylor, *Conflict in the East China Sea*.

intensified Australia's politico-military integration into the US alliance and into America's geopolitical strategy for maintaining its dominance in the Asia–Pacific, not least through its enthusiastic support for Obama's "Pivot to Asia".[77] The dramatic expansion in size and scope of US military bases – or "joint facilities" – in Australia makes it difficult, if not impossible, for Canberra to disentangle itself from any future US conflicts. The result of increased Australian military and intelligence cooperation with the US and other policy and force structure changes may well mean, "from a Chinese perspective, that Australia is not so much hosting US military bases, but is becoming a virtual American base in its own right".[78]

A number of leading Australian strategic experts – notably Hugh White – and former Australian Prime Ministers – notably Malcolm Fraser – have cautioned leaders in Canberra against aligning with the United States' quest to retain primacy in Asia. These warnings have fallen on deaf ears. The prospect of China providing a potential countervailing force to partially balance the preponderant power of the US is reflexively interpreted by Canberra as a threat that must be contained.[79] For decision makers in Canberra, it appears as though the risks of instability and war, remote though they may be, are more desirable than the prospect of a regional order where the US and its allies have to share power with China.

---

77   Vince Scappatura, The US "Pivot" to Asia, the China Spectre and the Australian-American Alliance, *The Asia–Pacific Journal*, vol. 12, issue 36, no. 3, 9 September 2014, <http://apjjf.org/2014/12/36/Vince-Scappatura/4178/article.html>, accessed 1 April 2018; Hamish McDonald, The Wired Seas of Asia: China, Japan, the US and Australia, *The Asia–Pacific Journal*, vol. 13, issue 15, no. 2, 20 April 2015, <http://apjjf.org/2015/13/15/Hamish-McDonald/4309.html>, accessed 1 April 2018.

78   Richard Tanter, *After Obama – The New Joint Facilities*, Nautilus Institute for Security and Sustainability, 18 April 2012, p. 6, <http://nautilus.org/wp-content/uploads/2011/12/After-Obama-Back-to-the-Bases-footnoted-version-18-April-1500.pdf>, accessed 1 April 2018.

79   As Hardy writes, "By associating regional stability with … unchallenged US primacy, Australia perceives the possible rise of a multipolar Asia as a threat". John Hardy, Ending Ambivalence: Australian Perspectives on Stability in Asia, *18th Biennial Conference of the Asian Studies Association of Australia*, Adelaide, 5-8 July 2010, p. 2.

PART II:

The Australia–US Alliance

Reinterpreted

Chapter Four

PRESERVING WESTERN DOMINANCE

Insecure, dependent, militaristic

What explains the apparent disjunction between Australia's relatively benign security environment and its apparent dependence on "great and powerful friends" to ensure its security? As pointed out already, mutual security interests and shared values do not adequately account for the centrality of the alliance in Australia's defence and foreign policies. One would expect that a historically benign security environment would result in a global outlook marked by national confidence, self-assurance and a fiercely independent and peaceful foreign policy. Yet Australia's defence and foreign policy tradition has ostensibly reflected that of an insecure, dependent and militaristic nation.

Critics of the alliance have typically focused on Australia's traditional security anxieties and other ideological and psychological predispositions to explain the contradiction between the remoteness of actual threats to Australia and the inability of elites in Canberra to kick the habit of dependency on "great and powerful friends". Following from Australia's dependence on Britain, this line of reasoning has frequently been employed as a means to explain Australia's enthusiastic but misguided support for failed US military interventions during the Cold War – notably in Vietnam – and reiterated by supporters and critical observers since to explain the endurance of the alliance in the post-Cold War era.[1] The notion of

---

1   For two critical reviews of the theme of Australian dependence and subservience to the US, see Lloyd Cox and Brendon O'Connor, Australia, the US, and the Vietnam and Iraq Wars: "Hound Dog not Lapdog", *Australian Journal of Political Science*, vol. 47, No. 2, 2012, pp. 173-187; David McLean, Australia in the Cold War: A Historiographical Review, *The International History Review*, vol. 23, no. 2, 2001, pp. 299-321.

Australian dependence, and even subservience, to the US was injected with new life during the intimate relations that developed during the years of the John Howard and George W. Bush administrations and, in particular, in the years following Australia's participation in America's bungled invasion of Iraq.[2]

The origins and nature of Australia's enduring fear of invasion are explored in the next section. However, while undoubtedly playing a significant role, irrational fears and cultural attachments alone do not provide an adequate explanation for the endurance of Australia's alliance with the US. The notion that policy-makers have consistently overlooked Australia's unthreatening strategic environment in their alliance management calculations for over sixty years warrants scrutiny. As one discerning scholar points out:

> When policies such as the ANZUS alliance have been pursued for so long (and at times at great cost) they cannot be considered as simply the result of mistaken perceptions of the world or personal failings of political will. They point to structural determinants of policy not enunciated in liberal or postmodern approaches.[3]

Australia's security anxieties cannot be separated from the fact that Australia's prosperity has always been tied to a global and regional order sustained by Anglo-American power. Australia's early economic growth and industrialisation was made possible by its imperial connection to the British Empire. Australia continued to rely on the British Empire into the 1950s and 1960s, even as it was increasingly integrated into a US-led regional order tied to American global capitalism. The international politico-economic dimension to Australia's reliance on "great and powerful friends" is explored later in this chapter.

Security perceptions aside, as a status quo power Australia's primary foreign policy objective in the two decades after 1945 was, with crucial

---

2   Alison Broinowski, *Allied and Addicted*, Melbourne: Scribe, 2007; Alison Broinowski, *Howard's War*, Melbourne: Scribe, 2003; Anthony Burke, *Fear of Security: Australia's Invasion Anxiety*, Cambridge: Cambridge University Press, 2008; Joseph Camilleri, The Howard Years: Cultural Ambivalence and Political Dogma, *Borderlands E-Journal*, Special Issue: Cultural Ambivalence, Cultural Politics: National Mythologies of Australia, Asia and the Past, vol. 3, no. 3, 2004; Robert Garran, *True Believer: John Howard, George Bush and the American Alliance*, Sydney: Allen and Unwin, 2004; Erik Paul, *Little America: Australia, the 51st State*, London: Pluto Press, 2006.

3   Sam Pietsch, *Australia's Military Intervention in East Timor, 1999*, PhD Thesis, The Australian National University, Canberra, February 2009, pp. 17-18.

American support, the restoration of British influence and the wider European imperial order in the Far East, after it was disrupted by the Japanese. The major threats to this objective were the communist movements resisting colonialism across Southeast Asia. Although taken in large sections of the West to be part of a wider conspiracy of Soviet/Chinese aggression, these communist movements were indigenous, nationalist and mostly benign to Australian security.

It is perhaps not surprising that in the international political climate of the 1950s and 1960s, during the height of the Cold War, and in the context of historically racialised fears of Asia, Australian policy-makers would readily assume a threatening strategic outlook which was also aligned with that of its major allies. However, it is also important to recognise that this was a self-serving belief. As I argue below, the unwillingness of Australian policy-makers to recognise the fallacy of the notion of "international communism", despite abundant evidence to the contrary, must be understood within the context of Australia's vested interests in preserving a pro-Western capitalist order in Asia.

Australian strategic culture

One way to evaluate Australia's defence and foreign policy tradition is through the prism of strategic culture, that is, the salient and enduring beliefs, values and habits of Australia's approach to international affairs. There is a broad consensus among defence and foreign policy analysts that Australia's strategic culture consists of an elevated sense of vulnerability and insecurity and a resort to militarism and alliances to ensure its security.[4] Although there are a number of strategic sub-cultures that place primacy on Australia providing for its own security, the overwhelmingly dominant strain has been reliance on a great power.[5]

---

4   David McCraw, Change and Continuity in Strategic Culture: the Cases of Australia and New Zealand, *Australian Journal of International Affairs*, vol. 65, no. 2, 2011, pp. 169-174; Alan Bloomfield and Kim Richard Nossal, Towards an *Explicative Understanding* of Strategic Culture: The Cases of Australia and Canada, *Contemporary Security Policy*, vol. 28, no. 2, August 2007, pp. 286-90; William Cannon, How Will Australia's Strategic Culture Inform its Engagement in the Indo-Pacific region?, *Culture Mandala: The Bulletin of the Centre for East-West Cultural and Economic Studies*, vol. 11, issue 1, article 3, 2014; Graeme Cheeseman, "Back to 'Forward Defence' and the Australian National Style" in Graeme Cheeseman and Robert Bruce (eds), *Discourses of Danger & Dread Frontiers: Australian Defence and Security Thinking After the Cold War*, Sydney: Allen & Unwin, 1996, pp. 258-271.

5   Peter J. Dean, "The Alliance, Australia's Strategic Culture and Way of War" in Peter J. Dean, Stephan Fruling and Brendan Taylor (eds), *Australia's American Alliance:*

Australia's strategic culture is both a logical consequence of, and reinforcement for, the realist paradigm that has historically dominated the mindset of Australian policy-makers and strategic thinkers.[6] From the perspective of realism, Australia's pursuit of great power allies is understood as the solution to an enduring security dilemma derived from Australia's relative powerlessness and geographic isolation from cultural and strategic partners in Europe and North America. Fearful of their defencelessness against an attack by a large and hostile power – irrespective of how remote that threat may be – Australians have traditionally sought alliances with "great and powerful friends" to guarantee their security.[7]

Australia's enthusiastic support for its Anglo-American allies can be partly explained by its historic apprehension of being abandoned in a time of need.[8] According to orthodox alliance theory, asymmetrical alliances are afflicted by the dual fears of abandonment and entrapment. As Glenn Snyder formulates:

> [If] a state feels highly dependent on its ally, directly or indirectly, if it perceives the ally as less dependent, if the alliance commitment is vague, and if the ally's recent behaviour suggests doubtful loyalty, the state will fear abandonment more than entrapment. It will therefore tend to reassure the ally of its commitment, support him in specific confrontations with the opponent, and avoid conciliating the opponent. The reverse conditions will tend to induce opposite strategies.[9]

Australia's traditional fear of abandonment has been accompanied by an enthusiasm for waging war far from its borders and in support of its Anglo-American allies. Prior to World War Two, defending the British Empire

---

Towards a New Era?, Kindle Edition, Melbourne: Melbourne University Publishing Digital, 2016.

6   Wesley writes that concerns about powerlessness, isolation and cultural difference have produced a particular variant of realism in Australia that has dominated International Relations scholarship since the 1920s. Michael Wesley, The Rich Tradition of Australian Realism, *Australian Journal of Politics and History*, vol. 55, no. 3, 2009, pp. 324-334.

7   Norman Harper, *A Great and Powerful Friend: A Study of Australian American Relations Between 1900 and 1975*, St Lucia, Queensland: University of Queensland Press, 1987; Cannon, Australia's Strategic Culture, p. 12.

8   Andrew O'Neill, Australia's Asia White Paper Review and the Dilemmas of Engagement, *Security Challenges*, vol. 8, no. 1, 2012, p. 17.

9   Glenn H. Snyder, The Security Dilemma in Alliance Politics, *World Politics*, vol. 36, no. 4, 1984, p. 475.

consisted of helping to thwart attempts by rival imperial powers to acquire British colonial possessions and quashing popular indigenous movements seeking freedom and democracy from colonialism.[10] The "loss" of any imperial possessions, it was reasoned – either by conquest or revolt – "would mean the denial of a source of British power which could be marshalled to defend Australia either directly or on a distant perimeter".[11]

As a number of historians have noted, one the ironies of the historical fear of invasion is that Australia has remained virtually untouched by foreign invaders while successive governments have "displayed a bloodthirsty enthusiasm for despatching troops to invade the territory of others, at the behest of either Britain or America".[12] Significantly, the colonies in Australia were founded by British military officers, a succession of whom became governors. When Britain chose to go to war, the Australian colonies enthusiastically obliged. The colonists also waged their own Frontier Wars against Indigenous people, of whom more than 30 000 – perhaps more than 60 000 – were killed. As one noted Australian academic and former public servant articulates, "Settler Australia had war in its genes".[13]

Since 1885, Australia's "alliance reliance" mentality has led it to invade "the Sudan, South Africa, Somaliland, Egypt, Palestine, Turkey, various European countries, several Pacific islands, Korea and Vietnam".[14] Afghanistan, Iraq (thrice) and Syria have since been added to that impressive list. Launching wars in support of its great and powerful allies is now a mythologised source of Australia's national identity.[15] Concerns

---

10   For an insightful account of how Australian forces were used in the service of
      British imperialism to crush a popular uprising in Egypt in 1919, and the atrocities
      committed by Australian soldiers in both Egypt and Syria during WWI, see
      Suzanne Brugger, *Australians and Egypt, 1914-1919*, Carlton, VIC: Melbourne
      University Press, 1980.

11   D. S. Meakin, Australian Attitudes to Indian Independence, *The Australian
      Quarterly*, vol. 40, no. 1, March 1968, p. 83.

12   Alistair Thompson, Marilyn Lake and Drew Cottle, "Australians at War" in Verity
      Burgmann and Jenny Lee (eds), *A Most Suitable Acquisition: A People's History of
      Australia since 1788*, Melbourne: McPhee Gribble Publishers, 1988, p. 189.

13   Alison Broinowski, "Australia's Tug of War: Militarism Versus Independence"
      in David Stephens and Alison Broinowski (eds), *The Honest History Book*, Kindle
      Edition, Sydney: NewSouth Publishing, 2017, Kindle Location 3656.

14   Thompson, Lake and Cottle, "Australians at War", p. 189.

15   Judy Hemming and Michael McKinley, Major Wars and Regional Responses in
      Australia and New Zealand: International Relations as Apologetics and Exegesis
      (and Inadequate), paper presented to the Panel WC76 Memorialisation, Public
      Grieving and War in the Configuring of Political Community: Regional and Local

about the militarisation of Australian history motivated a number of distinguished historians and other eminent Australians to establish a group in 2013 to challenge the popular narrative of war in the development of Australia's national culture.[16]

The roots of Australia's security anxieties and great power dependence can be traced to the time of European colonisation, when these became deeply embedded in the national psyche. For Australia's early white colonisers, who were relatively small in number and far from their cultural homelands in Europe, densely populated Asia was perceived and depicted as a dire security threat to the sparsely populated continent they came to occupy. The perceived threats to Australia's security were mostly illusory and, particularly in the case of Asia, entirely racial. The whole of white Australia during the course of the nineteenth and early-twentieth centuries was effectively seized by the blind determination to create a nation of the "higher" races, eliciting extreme and irrational fears of the "lower" oriental races who it appeared were determined, and perhaps destined, to inundate the more advanced white race they outnumbered.[17]

Race fears were inseparable from prevailing sentiments of British race patriotism. Australians felt part of the British whole, and together with the rising power of the US, were hopeful that the "Anglosphere" could retain its dominance in world affairs. This sentiment was captured by the "Father of Australian Federation", Sir Henry Parkes, when he declared that:

> [These] great states that are forming here will hold out their hands to the states of America and these two great countries will stretch out their hands again to the mother country and will unite one and all in one great empire to govern the world.[18]

It is not an unrelated fact that during the late-nineteenth century, when race-based fears of foreign invasion were arguably at their peak, the internal

---

Perspectives, 56th Annual Convention of the International Studies Association, New Orleans, LA, 18 February 2015; Marilyn Lake and Henry Reynolds (eds), *The Militarisation of Australian History*, Sydney: UNSW Press, 2010.

16 Honest History: Supporting Balanced and Honest History, <http://www.honesthistory.net.au>, accessed 1 April 2018.

17 David Walker, *Anxious Nation: Australia and the Rise of Asia 1850-1939*, St Lucia, Queensland: University of Queensland Press, 1999; Marilyn Lake and Henry Reynolds, *Drawing the Global Colour Line: White Men's Countries and the International Challenge of Racial Equality*, Cambridge: Cambridge University Press, 2008.

18 Philip Bell and Roger Bell, *Implicated: The United States in Australia*, Melbourne: Oxford University Press, 1993, p. 56.

"threat" posed by Aboriginal peoples was considered an even greater concern, at least in the areas where Aboriginal resistance persisted. In 1879, a correspondent to *The Queenslander* argued that the community had "not grudged a large outlay on national defence with but a very doubtful prospect of foreign attack", but asked why was the government not willing to spend as much for the "repression of the enemy within our gates".[19] On another occasion in 1887, a writer to *The Queenslander* observed:

> [T]here are thousands, that can be spent in Defence Forces, to protect the inhabitants of this country from the invisible, perhaps imaginary, but for certain distant enemies; but we cannot afford to keep an efficient body of police to keep in check the enemy we have at our door, the enemy of everyday, the one that slowly but surely robs and impoverishes us.[20]

Concerns about threats to Australia from abroad were inextricably linked to the Frontier Wars white colonisers were waging against the Aboriginal population at home. Widespread fears in the early-twentieth century of the "empty north" being invaded by a populous Asian nation arose from the experience of European colonisers who, after having dispossessed the Aborigines, now feared they too might be "aboriginalised".[21] In a speech at the laying of the foundation stone for Parliament House in Canberra in 1913, the then Attorney General Billy Hughes made the link between the two explicit, exhorting that Australia and America were:

> [Two] nations that have always had their way, for they killed everybody else to get it. I declare to you that in no other way shall we be able to come to our own except by preparing to hold that which we have now. [Cheers.] We are here as visible signs of a continent. We have a great future before us ... The first historic event in the history of the Commonwealth we are engaged in today [is being taken] without the slightest trace of that race we have banished from the face of the earth. We must not be too proud lest we should, too, in time disappear. We must take steps to safeguard that foothold we now have. [Cheers.][22]

---

19   Henry Reynolds, *Forgotten War*, Sydney: NewSouth Publishing, 2013, p. 79.
20   Reynolds, p. 79.
21   Walker, *Anxious Nation*, pp. 113-126.
22   Greg Lockhart, "Absenting Asia" in David Walker and Agnieszka Sobocinska (eds), *Australia's Asia, From Yellow Peril to Asian Century*, Perth: University of Western Australia Publishing, 2012, p. 275.

Such race fears constituted a major driving force behind Australia's defence preparations in the lead up to World War One. A force of 100,000 men was envisioned by Australian policy-makers to defend the continent against an aggressive Japan who, it was thought, would launch a racial war against Australia to forcibly allow its citizens to freely enter the country and overturn the "white Australia policy". Germany, on the other hand, was a secondary concern, viewed primarily as a threat to Great Britain and its colonial possessions. The British skilfully played on the irrational fear of Japan as a means to encourage Australians to mobilise for war, all the while correctly anticipating that Australians would rush to serve British interests anywhere in the world once war came.[23]

Much of the fear of Japan leading up to World War Two was similarly based not on sound strategic assessments but an "almost racially-based dogma" that saw Japan as a threat to "white Australia".[24] When Japanese militarism did emerge as a genuine security threat between 1941 and 1945, it appeared to vindicate Australia's fears of Asia and reinforced its alliance reliance mentality, even as Britain proved incapable of coming to Australia's aid.[25] When Japanese expansion toppled the British garrison at Singapore and most Western colonial governments in Asia by 1942, the experience became burned into Australia's strategic memory, influencing defence policy for at least the next three decades, particularly as the advent of the Cold War merged old fears about Asia with new fears about "international communism".[26]

---

23   Douglas Newton, *Hell-Bent: Australia's Leap into the Great War*, Melbourne: Scribe Publications, 2014; Greg Lockhart, Race Fear, Dangerous Denial: Japan and the Great Deception in Australian History, *Griffith Review Edition 32: Wicked Problems, Exquisite Dilemmas*, 2011, pp. 58-96.

24   Neville Meaney, "E.L Pearce and the Problem of Japan" in Carl Bridge and Bernard Attard (eds), *Between Empire and Nation: Australia's External Relations from Federation to the Second World War*, Melbourne: Australian Scholarly Publishing, 2000.

25   Despite the early warning signals, most Australian government officials and defence experts in the 1920s and 1930s believed British assurances that necessary reinforcements to defend Singapore against an expansionist Japan would be forthcoming. Malcolm Murfett, "The Singapore Strategy" in Carl Bridge and Bernard Attard (eds), *Between Empire and Nation*.

26   Greg Lockhart, *The Minefield: An Australian Tragedy in Vietnam*, Crows Nest, Sydney: Allen & Unwin, 2007, pp. 8-15.

Vested interests

While Canberra's security perceptions were built on deep-seated race fears of Asia, Australia's dependence on and enthusiastic support for its great power ally cannot be separated from the fact that the nation's prosperity relied on the continuation of the British imperial project both at home and abroad. As Goldsworthy writes, "Having material stakes in Britain's empire helped to create in Australia a mindset that was strongly supportive of the imperial status quo".[27]

Fear of the "other" was a key ideological construct utilised by European empires as a rationalisation for imperialism.[28] In the case of the British Empire, concerns about race survival and belief in popular theories of racial hierarchy provided a form of ideological legitimisation for Britain's awesome power and control over vast swathes of the world's population:

> The physical, political and to some extent cultural usurpation of so many people demanded justification. Many indigenous people were exploited, oppressed and even killed in the process of colonisation, and conscientious Britons needed to rationalise this profitable, but morally ambiguous conduct.[29]

Similarly, race fears served to legitimise Australia's support for the British Empire and the colonial project to which it owed significant economic benefits.[30] The abundance of natural resources that were the source of Australia's wealth and economic development were acquired by displacing and dispossessing the Indigenous population. The extraction, development

---

27 David Goldsworthy, *Losing the Blanket: Australia and the End of Britain's Empire*, Melbourne: Melbourne University Press, 2002, p. 5.

28 For the classic text on western depictions of the "other" as a derivative of and justification for the will to dominate, see Edward Said, *Orientalism*, New York: Pantheon Books, 1978.

29 Nicholas Clements, *The Black War: Fear, Sex and Resistance in Tasmania*, St Lucia, Queensland: University of Queensland Press, 2014, p. 14.

30 The following is largely based on a reading of Ray Broomhill, "From Lucky Country to Banana Republic? The Political Economy of Australian Development in a Long-Run Perspective" in Paul Bowes, Ray Broomhill, Teresa Gutierrez-Haces and Stephen McBride (eds), *International Trade and Neoliberal Globalism: Towards Re-peripheralisation in Australia, Canada and Mexico?*, London: Routledge, 2008; Peter Cochrane, *Industrialisation and Dependence: Australia's Road to Economic Development, 1870-1939*, St. Lucia, Queensland: University of Queensland Press, 1980; Barrie Dyster and David Meredith, *Australia in the International Economy in the Twentieth Century*, Cambridge: Cambridge University Press, 1990; Ian W. McLean, *Why Australia Prospered: The Shifting Sources of Economic Growth*, Princeton: Princeton University Press, 2013.

and export of those natural resources were highly dependent on British investment and the global trading system, underpinned to a substantial degree by UK naval power.[31] Australia's economic prosperity was thus inextricably tied to the fate of the British Empire and the continued exploitation of those colonised countries which, under significant duress, were made to restructure their economies in ways that complemented the industrial needs of the West.

In some ways, Australia's status as a colony of Britain served as a hindrance to economic development, particularly given the national economy was dependent on British investors who were reluctant to provide capital for investment in industries and technology other than those that satisfied the needs of the British market. Eventually, however, in accord with Australia's status as a white-settler nation, and its privileged position within the Empire's division of labour, the City of London came to sanction Australia's industrial development. Permitted, however reluctantly, to develop behind protectionist trade barriers and engage in massive state-funded infrastructure projects, Australia managed to break into the ranks of the industrialised world. Other non-white settler colonies of European powers, by contrast, were brutally forced into becoming sources of cheap raw materials and foodstuffs, the imposition of "free trade" policies effectively "kicking away the ladder" to development that Australia and other industrialised states had used to climb to prosperity.[32]

Australian foreign policy after World War Two continued to lend itself to the waning global imperial order, particularly in Southeast Asia, where Australia held direct and indirect economic interests.[33] The continued subordination of the region to the old colonial powers was considered necessary to safeguard the economic strength of Europe and the imperial preferential trading system which Australia remained heavily dependent on. The paramount importance of Malaya's economy to the Commonwealth, for example, provided the incentive on the part of Britain, and arguably

---

31   Membership in the British Empire had perhaps doubled Australian trade by World War I. Mclean, pp. 165-170.

32   Ha-Joon Chang, *Kicking Away the Ladder: Development Strategy in Historical Perspective*, London: Anthem Press, 2003; Ha-Joon Chang, *Bad Samaritans: The Myth of Free Trade and the Secret History of Capitalism*, New York: Bloomsbury Press, 2008.

33   For a summary of Australia's direct economic interests in the Southwest Pacific and Southeast Asia during the 1950s and 1960s, see Goldsworthy, *Losing the Blanket*, pp. 29-30. Of course, these interests were far less important to Australia's prosperity than existing trade and investment links with the UK and Europe.

Australia, to crush the revolutionary nationalist-communist movement that gained strength there in the years after World War Two.[34]

Canberra's plans for the post-World War Two regional economic order aligned, more or less, with that of its allies in London and Washington. This was made evident by Spender's Colombo Plan that hinged on the objective of restoring and developing Southeast Asia's capacity for exporting food and raw materials to the UK and continental Europe. Southeast Asia was also deemed important as an outlet for Australia's secondary products and for supplying Australia with desperately needed dollar earnings. The Colombo Plan could only succeed, however, with massive American economic investment and other forms of support. Significantly, this dovetailed with Washington's own agenda for defeating revolutionary movements in Asia.[35]

As British power continued to decline in the two decades after 1945, Australia was gradually integrated into America's neo-imperial order that came to replace the old colonial powers in Asia. This shift required both the growing influence of American corporations over the Australian economy[36] and a regional division of labour that saw Australia play an important second-tier role in the subordination of Southeast Asia to joint American-Japanese economic domination – otherwise known as the "Pacific Basin Strategy".[37] In a process largely completed by the mid-1960s, Australian trade policy was reoriented away from dependence on Britain and Western Europe towards economic integration with the Asia–Pacific region and within the broader framework of the US-led multilateral global trading

---

34   Malaya's rubber and tin mining industries were the biggest dollar earners in the Commonwealth. Malaya was thus described by a British Lord in 1952 as the "greatest material prize in South-East Asia". Mark Curtis, *Web of Deceit: Britain's Real Role in the World*, London: Vintage Press, 2003, p. 335.

35   Gregory Pemberton, *All the Way: Australia's Road to Vietnam*, Sydney: Allen & Unwin, 1987, pp. 1-3, 13-15.

36   Greg Crough and Ted Wheelwright, *Australia: A Client State*, Melbourne: Penguin Books, 1982; Joseph Camilleri, *Australian-American Relations: The Web of Dependence*, South Melbourne: Macmillan, 1980, pp. 16-19, 44-48.

37   See Henry S. Albinski, *ANZUS: The United States and Pacific Security*, Lanham, MD: University Press of America, 1987, p. 12; Camilleri, pp. 48-54; Robert Catley and Bruce McFarlance, *From Tweedledum to Tweedledee: The New Labor Government in Australia. A Critique of its Social Model*, Sydney: Australia and New Zealand Book Company, 1974; Crough and Wheelwright, pp. 58-81; Nitish K. Dutt, The United States and the Asian Development Bank, *Journal of Contemporary Asia*, vol. 27, no. 1, 1997, pp. 71-84; Jim Hyde, *Australia: The Asia Connection*, Malmsbury, Victoria: Kibble Books, 1978; Bruce McFarlane, "Australian Post-War Economic Policy" in Ann Curthoys and John Merritt (eds), *Australia's First Cold War 1945-1953, Vol 1, Society, Communism and Culture*, Sydney: Allen and Unwin, 1984.

system.[38] Australia's traditional defence of the British Empire was thus superseded by its support for America's "informal empire", with the US's unique capacity to maintain and extend a global strategic and economic order favourable to Western capitalist interests.[39]

Strategic dependence

The peak period of strategic dependence on the United States is widely regarded to be the 1950s and 1960s, when Australia was governed by conservative governments. During World War Two, Australia unmistakably surrendered its sovereignty to the US, partly out of strategic necessity, but to an extent that was probably unnecessary.[40] After the war, Australia emerged as more or less an independent nation, although it retained substantial political, economic and cultural links to the British Empire. Under the direction of Minister of External Affairs, H. V. Evatt, Australia assumed an unprecedented degree of independence from the major powers, evidenced by Evatt's advocacy on behalf of smaller nations at the San Francisco Conference in 1945, and Australia's early independent position on the first major dispute in the Cold War, concerning the Korean peninsula.[41]

In the case of Korea, the Australian Labor government was initially firmly opposed to supporting any action that might further divide the country. Despite intense lobbying from Washington, Australia opposed separate elections in the South as this ran contrary to the goal of a unified peninsula. Australia also privately condemned the American occupation in South Korea for entrenching power in the hands of extreme rightists, for labelling all opponents of Syngman Rhee's regime as "communist" and suppressing dissent through "police state" machinery. By late 1948,

---

38   Ann Capling, *Australia and the Global Trade System: From Havana to Seattle*, Cambridge: Cambridge University Press, 2001.

39   On the nature of America's "informal empire" and its role in protecting and extending global capitalism, see Leo Panitch and Sam Gindin, *The Making of Global Capitalism: The Political Economy of American Empire*, London: Verso, 2012. On the links between Australia and the neoliberal order sustained by US regional hegemony see Erik Paul, *Neoliberal Australia and US Imperialism in East Asia*, London: Palgrave Macmillan, 2012.

40   Peter Edwards, Curtin, MacArthur and the "Surrender of Sovereignty": A Historiographical Assessment, *Australian Journal of International Affairs*, vol. 55, no. 2, 2001, pp. 175-185.

41   On Evatt's advocacy at the San Francisco Conference, formally the United Nations Conference on International Organisation, see Roger J. Bell, *Unequal Allies: Australian-American Relations and the Pacific War*, Melbourne: Melbourne University Press, 1977, pp. 183-6.

however, with the deepening Cold War atmosphere and external pressure from Western intelligence and security agencies, the ALP shifted its position in full support of the US.[42]

Nevertheless, Evatt was committed to securing an equal partnership with the US as far as possible, including full consultation on all matters of common interest. In May 1949 the US chargé in Canberra, Andrew B. Foster, expressed his belief that the Labor government on the whole was "extremely jealous of the independent position of Australia, suspicious of what it regards as American economic imperialism, and determined not to be pushed around".[43]

The Liberal-Country opposition, on the other hand, was far more predisposed to ensuring the interests of the "Anglosphere" were front and centre in Australia's foreign policy. In December 1949 the US State Department warmly welcomed Menzies' electoral victory, advising that while Evatt tended to "subordinate" United States-Australian relations to the United Nations, the Menzies administration made them "a cardinal point of Australian foreign policy".[44] Menzies readily accepted America's Cold War perceptions of the communist threat at home and abroad. Post-war conservatives in Australia as a whole held disparaging views of communists, considering them to be "human vermin", "the scourge of Satan", a "fifth column" and "un-Australian".[45] Any communist association or participation in any peace organisation in Australia was taken to be evidence of communist subversion, influence and control.[46]

Like their US counterparts, Australian conservative leaders took communist movements worldwide to be part of a monolithic bloc, headquartered in Moscow and Beijing, whose purpose was global domination. For two decades, Eisenhower's 1954 "domino theory" laid the basis for both American and Australian security policies. Menzies' rationale for sending military forces into Malaya in 1955, as part of the Commonwealth Strategic

42   Gavan McCormack, *Cold War Hot War: An Australian Perspective of the Korean War*, Sydney: Hale & Iremonger, 1983, pp. 19-21, 40-58.

43   Joseph M. Siracusa, *The ANZUS Treaty Revisited*, *Security Challenges*, vol. 1, no. 1, 2005, p. 95.

44   Pemberton, *All the Way*, p. 7.

45   Stephen Alomes, Mark Dober and Donna Hellier, "The Social Context of Postwar Conservatism" in Ann Curthoys and John Merritt (eds), *Australia's First Cold War 1945-1953, Vol 1, Society, Communism and Culture*, Sydney: Allen and Unwin, 1984.

46   Phillip Deery, Menzies, the Cold War and the 1953 Convention on Peace and War, *Australian Historical Studies*, vol. 34, no. 122, 2003, pp. 248-269.

Reserve, was in case "of an overt Chinese offensive into the region".[47] Ten years later, Menzies provided the following justification for sending a combat battalion to Vietnam in April 1965:

> The takeover of South Vietnam would be a direct military threat to Australia and all the countries of South and South East Asia. It must be seen as part of a thrust by Communist China between the Indian and Pacific Oceans.[48]

Communist movements in Southeast Asia were not satellites of the Soviet Union or Red China. The communist guerrilla movement in Malaya, which sparked the Malayan "Emergency" in 1948, was a revolt against colonial rule arising primarily from domestic political, industrial and communal grievances; "international communism" had little to do with it.[49] In Vietnam, the conflict was not a case of the Sino-Soviet controlled communist North instigating war against the South, as commonly depicted at the time. After 1954, the conflict "was essentially a struggle between a radicalised Vietnamese patriotism, embodied in the Communist Party, and the United States and its wholly dependent local allies".[50]

While assuming the mantle of communism, the radical social movements that swept across Southeast Asia and much of the Third World from 1945 to the 1960s were first and foremost revolutionary nationalist movements seeking to free their countries from European colonisation and American domination. Distinction between the two was critical for accurately assessing any potential security threat; and yet, "Western colonial powers often described anti-colonial movements as 'communist', whether they were in fact directed by communists or non-communists". For Western policy-makers, including in Australia, it was "almost inconceivable" that

---

47   Christopher Waters, After Decolonisation: Australia and the Emergence of the Non-aligned Movement in Asia, 1954-55, *Diplomacy and Statecraft*, vol. 12, no. 2, 2001, p. 157.

48   Lockhart, *The Minefield*, p. 13.

49   Peter Edwards with Gregory Pemberton, *Crises and Commitments: The Politics and Diplomacy of Australia's Involvement in Southeast Asian Conflicts 1948-1965*, Sydney: Allen & Unwin, 1992, pp. 26-30. Chin Peng, long-time leader of the Malayan Communist Party, including the period of the Emergency, writes, "We were never aided financially by the USSR; neither did Moscow ever order us which path to take. Medical aid for our TB [Tuberculosis] patients was all we got from China until 1961 when the struggle took another form in line with Mao's reading of world revolution". Chin Peng, *Alias Chin Peng: My Side of History*, Singapore, Media Master, 2003, pp. 115-116.

50   Gabriel Kolko, *Anatomy of a War: Vietnam, the United States, and the Modern Historical Experience*, New York: Pantheon Books, p. 107.

revolutionary movements could be both communist and nationalist: "it was assumed they had to be one or the other".[51]

Throughout the period when Canberra's Vietnam policy was being decided, numerous Western observers called attention to the extensive and freely available evidence contrary to Australia's perception of events; and yet, this evidence was persistently ignored and no serious attempt was made to ascertain the facts. The ignorance was so great that "Canberra could, as late as 1963, convince itself and state openly that the regime of Ngo Dinh Diem enjoyed popular support" and that it was *impossible* for the South Vietnamese to support the pro-communist South Vietnamese National Liberation Front rather than the Government in Saigon".[52]

Despite the unreality of these beliefs, it has long been maintained that the fear of Chinese communist "aggression" and domination over Southeast Asia, and the apparent direct security threat this posed to Australia, must be assumed to be the primary driving factor behind Australian defence and foreign policies during this period. As Gregory Clarke posed the question in 1967, how can "the claim to believe in such a threat be genuine ... when it appears to be based on such a distorted interpretation of China's behaviour?"[53] The answer, Clarke believed, lay in the "ideological and psychological outlook" of Australian policy-makers. A fervent belief in the inherent evil of Soviet communism and, above all, the traditional fear of the threat to Australia as a European outpost on the edge of Asia, sufficiently explained the inability of policy-makers to accurately interpret the behaviour of communist China or even conceive of China as a normal state.[54]

In a similar vein Alan Renouf argued, over a decade later in 1979, that ideology and deeply embedded irrational fears of invasion best explained the inability of Australian policy-makers to distinguish between national liberation movements and communist aggression, which led for example to Australia's strategic blunder in Vietnam. "Had Australian governments not been blinded by political ideology and misled by fear", writes Renouf, "they would not have made such a bad error".[55] Australia's "baffling irrational

---

51   Edwards with Pemberton, *Crises and Commitments*, p. 37.

52   Gregory Clark, *In Fear of China*, Melbourne: Lansdowne Press, 1967, pp. 173-74, quote p. 174. Emphasis in original.

53   Clark, p. 172.

54   Clark, pp. 184-191.

55   Alan Renouf, *The Frightened Country*, South Melbourne: MacMillan, 1979, p. 275.

consistency" in seeing the threat of communism everywhere was the result of the "traditional fear of invasion to the North".[56]

Later accounts have broadly followed this line of argument, stressing Australia's "strategic dependence" on the US as an explanation for Canberra's enthusiastic support of America's Cold War objectives. At one extreme, Australia's distorted view of the communist threat is explained as the result of Canberra's uncritical embrace of the American alliance and a wholehearted adoption of Washington's characterisation of regional events.[57] A more nuanced position is articulated by McLean, who argues that although Australia's distorted view of the communist threat was the result of "cultural predispositions", Canberra's polices and perceptions were not formed in Washington or London but rather locally derived from a combination of traditional fears of Asia and Australia's particular regional circumstances.[58]

Certainly, the desire for security – rooted in deeply embedded themes of fear and dependence – played a role in driving Australia's threat perceptions. However, recognising the fact of Australia's rather benign security environment is important because, as Lockhart points out, "while reality is the historian's hedge against fantasy, beliefs are subject to political manipulation".[59] It would be unwise to discount the actual remoteness of threats to Australia's security and focus solely on the beliefs of policy-makers as a means to understand their actions. Beliefs, even when held with conviction, do not always convey underlying interest-based motivations. There is ample evidence by now that "what we see and what we believe can be influenced by what we want".[60] The leaders of imperial Japan, after all, viewed their mission to conquer Asia as deriving from a similar set of sincere beliefs to bring liberty, stability and prosperity to the region. As historian John W. Dower writes, "They were, in their own eyes, moral and rational men. That the nation's actions, and their own, so often belied their words did not trouble them or even register upon them".[61]

---

56   Renouf, pp. 276-277.

57   See, for example, Camilleri, *Australian-American Relations*; Bell and Bell, *Implicated*.

58   McLean, Australia in the Cold War.

59   Greg Lockhart, Mugged at Oxford: Or, "Little Point in Defending the Periphery"!, *Australian Historical Studies*, vol. 35, no. 123, 2004, p. 151.

60   Natasha Hamilton-Hart, *Hard Interests, Soft Illusions*: Southeast Asia and American Power, New York: Cornell University Press, 2012, p. 29.

61   John W. Dower, *Cultures of War: Pearl Harbor, Hiroshima, 9-11, Iraq*, New York: W. W. Norton & Company Inc, 2010, pp. 99-100. Elsewhere, Dower writes that even after Japan's defeat, none of the war crimes trials defendants accepted that they had

What's missing from conventional accounts of Australian policies and perceptions during the 1950s and 1960s is the fact that revolutionary nationalist movements, while posing little threat to Australian security, did pose a real and significant threat to the European imperial order in Asia and, in the long-term, to Washington's vision of a US-led capitalist global order. As a status quo power heavily invested in the continuation of the British Empire, and increasingly integrated into America's regional political and economic order, Australia had clear interests in the defeat of revolutionary nationalism and the preservation of Anglo-American dominance in Asia. It is only prudent to assume these interests may have been paramount when evaluating the actions of Australian foreign policy-makers during this period.

Defenders of the imperial order

The conventional view that, during the Cold War, Australia's security was bound to the outcome of a global conflict between Western democracy and communist totalitarianism, is deeply flawed. The decolonisation movement that swept across Southeast Asia in the 1950s and 1960s posed little actual threat to the security of Australia and this must be contextualised in terms of the broader UK and US imperialist agendas of the time.

Australia's Cold War perceptions, rooted in the concepts of the "domino theory" and "monolithic communism", were certainly shared throughout the Western world to a greater or lesser extent. Unlike in Australia, however, there has been extensive critical scholarship, particularly with respect to US foreign policy, that challenges the notion that misperceptions led to unwise policies and erroneous doctrines. According to this scholarship, rather than misjudging the communist threat, the tendency of US planners to see communist aggression everywhere was necessitated by the challenge that decolonisation and revolutionary movements posed to US global strategy – already largely formulated before the conclusion of World War Two – to expand and restructure the international capitalist system under US leadership.[62]

---

been engaged in a conspiracy to wage wars of aggression. "On the contrary, they believed to the end with all apparent sincerity that their policies, however disastrous in outcome, had been motivated by legitimate concerns for Japan's essential rights and interests on the Asian continent". John Dower, *Embracing Defeat: Japan in the Aftermath of World War II*, London: Allen Lane, The Penguin Press, 1999, p. 468.

62   William Blum, *Killing Hope: US Military and C.I.A. Interventions Since World War II*, Monroe, US: Common Courage Press, 2004, pp. 12, 18-20; Noam Chomsky, *For*

The US emerged from World War Two determined to sustain its position of unprecedented global wealth and power in a world devastated by war. This point is aptly illustrated by the 1948 memorandum of George Kennan, Head of the US State Department Policy Planning Staff:

> We have about 50 per cent of the world's wealth, but only 6.3 per cent of its population ... In this situation, we cannot fail to be the object of envy and resentment. Our real task in the coming period is to devise a pattern of relationships which will permit us to maintain this position of disparity without positive detriment to our national security. To do so, we will have to dispense with all sentimentality and day-dreaming ... We should cease to talk about vague and – for the Far East – unreal objectives such as human rights, the raising of living standards, and democratisation. The day is not far off when we are going to have to deal in straight power concepts. The less we are then hampered by idealistic slogans, the better".[63]

In order to preserve its leadership position, US national security planners sought to eradicate the existing system of closed trading blocs and develop in their place a global economy open to US capital, just as the UK had sustained an open world trading system during its period of ascendancy in the mid-to-late-nineteenth century. While initially intending to displace the existing system of European imperialism with American globalism, the US later helped to reconstruct parts of the colonial order as a temporary measure for funding the rapid reconstruction of Europe and supporting European governments in their efforts to quash Third World revolutionary

---

Reasons of State, London: Penguin Books, 2003 [1973], pp. 34-35, 51-55; Gabriel Kolko, *Confronting the Third World: United States Foreign Policy 1945 – 1980*, New York: Pantheon Books, 1980, pp. 117-118, 130; James Peck, *Washington's China: The National Security World, the Cold War, and the Origins of Globalism*, Amherst: University of Massachusetts Press, 2006, pp. 1-45, 169, 234; James Peck, *Ideal Illusions: How the US Government Co-opted Human Rights*, New York: Metropolitan Books, 2010, pp. 12-36; Panitch and Gindin, *The Making of Global Capitalism*, p. 11; Bruce Cumings, *The Korean War: A History*, New York: The Modern Library, 2011, pp. 215-216; William I. Robinson, *Promoting Polyarchy: Globalisation, US Intervention, and Hegemony*, Cambridge: Cambridge University Press, 1996. For a similar account from the perspective of the UK, see Mark Curtis, *The Great Deception: Anglo-American Power and World Order*, London: Pluto Press, 1998; Mark Curtis, *Web of Deceit: Britain's Real Role in the World*, London: Vintage Press, 2003. The following section is largely based on a reading of these texts.

63   George Kennan, Review of Current Trends, US Foreign Policy, Policy Planning Staff, PPS No. 23, 28 February 1948.

movements that sought an independent path to political and economic development.

The military power of the Soviet Union and Communist China posed the only serious obstacles to Washington's plans for the creation of a new world economic order. While the Soviet Union checked American penetration into Eastern Europe, it was independent nationalism that posed the greatest threat to Washington's plans to reduce the Third World to a part of its own economic system. That the primary consideration was American dominance and not Soviet containment was made clear in the 1950 National Security Council master document on the strategy of containment, NSC-68, which stated that the "overall policy at the present time may be described as one designed to foster a world environment in which the American system can survive and flourish ... a policy which we would probably pursue even if there were no Soviet threat".[64]

Much like the French *Mission Civilisatrice*, the US needed a persuasive ideological ethos of worldwide significance to provide a context for their actions and justification for their means. Anti-communism was the perfect fit because "seeing the dangers of Communism everywhere was a way of seeing American global interests everywhere".[65] While the conventional wisdom, including in Australia, is that institutionalised paranoia and ignorance largely explain the persistence of American officials in mistakenly viewing wars for national liberation as part of a Red Chinese or Soviet orchestrated conspiracy, this does not account for the consistency of this error across time and place. As Chomsky explains:

> Why were policy makers always subject to the same form of igno-rance and irrationality? Why was there such systematic error in the delusional systems constructed by post-war ideologists? Mere ignorance or foolishness would lead to random error, not to regular and systematic distortion: unwavering adherence to the principle that whatever the facts may be, the cause of international conflict is the behaviour of the Communist powers, and all revolutionary movements within the United States system are sponsored by the Soviet Union, China or both ... Ignorance and stupidity can surely lead to error, but hardly to such systematic error or such certainty in error.[66]

---

64   Quoted in Panitch and Gindin, *The Making of Global Capitalism*, p. 95.

65   Peck, *Ideal Illusions*, p. 23.

66   Chomsky, *For Reasons of State*, p. 53.

Chomsky does not suggest that US policy-makers did not believe their doctrines. What they may have believed, rather, is less relevant for understanding US foreign policy than the functions of those beliefs. He writes:

> The fact that policy makers may be caught up in the fantasies they spin to disguise imperial intervention, and may sometimes even find themselves trapped by them, should not prevent us from asking what function these ideological constructions fulfil – why *this* particular system of mystification is consistently expounded in place of some alternative. Similarly, one should not be misled by the fact that the delusional system presents a faint reflection of reality. It must, after all, carry some conviction. But this should not prevent us from proceeding to disentangle motive from myth.[67]

Australian policy-makers are said to have "shared the mistakes made by their counterparts in Washington", carrying out the same fundamental error with respect to the threat of "international communism" despite clear evidence to the contrary.[68] However, as is the case with the US, the "baffling irrational consistency" of Australian policy-makers to view anti-colonial movements everywhere in Asia as a security threat raises important questions that are insufficiently accounted for by resort to psychological explanations of fear and ignorance.

If Australia's persistent eagerness to participate in foolhardy US foreign wars was driven by irrational fears, why were Australia's military contributions consistently calculated to ensure the minimal contribution required to secure American goodwill? If the basis of such mistaken policies were genuine and deeply held but erroneous security anxieties, would not successive Australian governments have been eager to militarily contribute to a degree that matched the dreaded threat? In the case of Vietnam, Renouf points out:

> There was an inconsistency in Australia's attitude that was not lost to the US. While Australia continually *talked* of the tremendous historical, world-wide significance of Vietnam, her governments never *acted* as if they believed their own statements. If they did believe this, why was it so difficult to get anything from them for South Vietnam except words and money? This inconsistency was obvious to [senior

---

67   Chomsky, pp. 54-55. Emphasis in original.
68   Renouf, *The Frightened Country*, p. 274.

US presidential advisor] Clark Clifford when he visited Canberra in 1967. Talking with the Government he realised that the forward defence strategy meant that it was principally the US which should defend Australia in Asia, not Australia herself.[69]

The reluctance on the part of Canberra to commit to a military effort that matched its rhetoric during the Vietnam War is not an isolated occurrence. When it comes to Australian support for US military interventions abroad, "Australia's alliance habit is towards big rhetoric while sending a small force ... minimising the military and political burden".[70] The "US alliance management equation" of announcing firm loyalty to Washington while making as small a military contribution as possible is one "that Canberra has followed with remarkable consistency through five wars since World War II – Korea, Vietnam, Kuwait, Iraq and Afghanistan".[71]

Contrary to theories of dependence, which stressed Australia's subordination to US interests, later scholarship confirms that Australia was less a follower of the US than an enthusiastic partner; and policy-makers in Canberra were often more hawkish in their advocacy for defeating communism, or other equally dubious threats, than their American counterparts.[72] Australian governments have not displayed helpless dependence and irrationality but have shrewdly paid the minimum premium required to "lock the US into the region" against the possibility of a future threat.[73]

The nature of that threat throughout the 1950s and 1960s, however, could not have been in the form of a direct attack. High-level strategic assessments stated at the time that Australia was not under serious threat of external aggression in the foreseeable future, communist or otherwise. The "threat" of national independence on the other hand, was an accurately identified concern because those liberation movements pertained to British

---

69   Renouf, *The Frightened Country*, p. 278. Emphasis in original.

70   Graeme Dobell, The Alliance Echoes and Portents of Australia's Longest War, *Australian Journal of International Affairs*, vol. 6, no. 4, 2014, p. 391.

71   Dobal, p. 392. For similar arguments along these lines, see Cox and O'Connor, Australia, the US, and the Vietnam and Iraq Wars; Albert Palazzo, The Making of Strategy and the Junior Coalition Partner: Australia and the 2003 Iraq War, *Infinity Journal*, vol. 2, no. 4, 2012, pp. 26-30.

72   Cox and O'Connor; Pemberton, *All the* Way; Michael Sexton, *War for the Asking: Australia's Vietnam Secret*, Ringwood, Victoria: Penguin Books, 1981.

73   Peter Edwards, *Permanent Friends? Historical Reflections on the Australian-American Alliance*, Lowy Institute Paper 8, Lowy Institute for International Policy, Sydney, 13 December 2005, <http://www.lowyinstitute.org/publications/permanent-friends-historical-reflections-australian-american-alliance>, accessed 1 April 2018.

colonial interests in Asia, to which Australia was still aligned. Moreover, as previously outlined, Australia held vested economic interests in the continuation of Anglo-American domination in Asia.

In the context of the actual threat that nationalist liberation movements posed to colonialism, Australia's otherwise "baffling irrational consistency" in mistaking communism in Asia as a security threat to Australia can be seen as a rationalisation for propping up the imperial order in Asia. As Lockhart explains:

> By building on an apparition of earlier Japanese expansion, Menzies had constructed the threat to the imperial position in Malaya as an imagined Chinese invasion. Arguably, this move better enabled him to manage politically and psychologically what he really feared: the threat that the local forces of radical Asian nationalism did pose to the British Empire in Asia after the Japanese interregnum.[74]

The suppression of radical Asian nationalism and the preservation of the British Empire could only succeed with the full support of Washington, which shared both of these objectives, albeit for slightly different reasons. Australia's strategic dependence on the US and its enthusiastic support for American intervention in Southeast Asia, including the small and mostly symbolic force sent to Vietnam, can thus be explained as a political strategy to lock the US into the region as a means to preserve Western dominance in Asia.

---

74   Lockhart, p. 11.

Chapter Five

AUSTRALIA AS AN ASIA–PACIFIC REGIONAL POWER

Middle power dreams

While firmly committed to the restoration and preservation of the British Empire in Southeast Asia in the two decades after World War Two, it was also evident to Australian policy-makers that British power in the Far East was in rapid decline. Concomitantly, Australia willingly integrated into America's neo-imperial regional order that replaced the old colonial powers; henceforth developing an interest in the preservation and extension of American global capitalism. While in the past, Australia's strategic outlook was shaped primarily by Empire interests, by the mid-1960s it was clear to those inside the US State Department that Australia had increasingly come to view "the world in much the same terms as does the US. She seeks the same general objectives and would fashion her role in Asia as a microcosm of the American role around the world".[1]

This new strategic outlook was not the result of simply replacing strategic dependence on Britain with that of the US. Rather, it came about because of a general alignment of interests, particularly with respect to preserving Western dominance in Asia and extending Australia's regional influence. Although Australia relied on its "great and powerful friends" to ensure its security in the 1950s and 1960s – no matter how distant the threat – thereafter Australia began to take greater responsibility for its own direct security and wider regional interests as a strategically independent power.

---

1   Tracy H. Wilder and Robert F. Packard, *Australia in Mid-Passage: A Study of Her Role in the Indian Ocean-Southeast Asia Area*, Foreign Service Institute, US Department of State, 11 April 1966, p. 7, <http://nautilus.org/wp-content/uploads/2012/09/711-Tracy-H.-Wilder-and-Robert-F.-Packard.pdf>, accessed 1 April 2018.

However, it remained dependent on the US to preserve the "stability" of the wider regional and global order.

Beginning in the 1970s, and in accordance with Australia's newfound independence, the primary purpose of the US alliance underwent a gradual transformation from guaranteeing Australia's security to bolstering its military and intelligence capabilities for defending the nation independently, despite the persistence of Australia's non-threatening security environment. However, the new Defence of Australia (DOA) and "self-reliance" doctrines, as they were called, quickly evolved from a focus on defending the continent and its immediate surrounds to promoting Australia's wider interests abroad as a significant regional power.

Australia's expansionist defence policy has roots in its strategic culture. In the previous chapter, the influence of historical and racialised security anxieties within Australia's wider strategic culture was noted. In this chapter I highlight the existence of an equally influential "imperialist spirit" that is connected to, but nevertheless distinct from, the traditional fear of invasion. Australians harboured fervently expansionist ambitions in the Southwest Pacific during the nineteenth and early-twentieth centuries – albeit a kind of sub-imperialism within the British Empire – founded on a mix of strategic, economic and nationalist motivations.

This imperialist spirit continued into the post-World War Two period under the guise of Australia's "special responsibilities" as a "metropolitan power" and a custodian of the British Empire in the Asia–Pacific. It manifested prominently in Australia's ruling conservative parties in the 1950s and 1960s that were firmly opposed to self-determination for the peoples of Asia.[2] Today, Australia's neo-imperial mindset can be seen in its self-identification as a leading "middle power" holding obligations on behalf of the Western-security community.

It is in this context that the current US alliance can be understood as bolstering Australia's capacity for regional influence and control rather than as defending the Australian continent. Although allying with the global hegemonic power undoubtedly provides some security benefits, in the face of a persistently benign security environment and Australia's enduring "middle power" ambitions, the alliance has far greater relevance as a means for power projection. Significantly, official accounts and realist arguments

---

2   Christopher Waters, After Decolonisation: Australia and the Emergence of the Non-aligned Movement in Asia, 1954-55, *Diplomacy and Statecraft*, vol. 12, no. 2, 2001, p. 156.

in favour of the alliance frequently emphasise its utility in enhancing Australia's status as an "Asia–Pacific power".

Independent and expansionist

By the early 1970s, a major shift in Australia's strategic environment and defence relationships had already taken place. The old colonial system in Southeast Asia, which Australia fought hard to preserve in the 1950s and 1960s, collapsed far earlier than expected. Divergent influences remained, where even as the "threat" of communist and radical nationalist movements was, for the most part, successfully thwarted, British interests were largely preserved for some time thereafter. The US largely replaced the old colonial system in Asia with its own form of neo-imperialism, reorienting the political and economic life of the region according to its global agenda of an integrated world trading system open to American corporate interests.

With the threat of radical nationalism in Southeast Asia effectively "inoculated" by the Vietnam War, Australia was empowered to take greater responsibility for its own security as a more strategically independent nation, even as it remained dependent on the US to maintain overall "stability" in East Asia.[3] Beginning in the early to mid-1970s, forward defence gradually receded as the basis of Australia's defence policy in favour of the DOA and "self-reliance" doctrines, although these concepts were not entirely new and continued to remain "conceptually and operationally inchoate" until the mid-to-late 1980s.[4]

The notion that Australia needed to develop an independent force to defend itself first arose in the early 1960s as policy-makers began to acknowledge that Australia's security interests would not always coincide with that of the US, particularly over Indonesia. However, it was not until the 1970s and the advent of the Whitlam government that the idea of operations independent from allies transformed from a credible contingency

---

3   As Edwards writes, "It remains the case that the strongest argument to be raised in favour of the commitment by the United States and its allies is that it delayed the communist victory in South Vietnam by ten years, from 1965 to 1975, thereby giving several potential Southeast Asian 'dominoes', such as Thailand, Malaysia and Singapore, time to strengthen themselves economically, politically and socially". Peter Edwards, *Permanent Friends? Historical Reflections on the Australian-American Alliance*, Lowy Institute Paper 8, Lowy Institute for International Policy, Sydney, 13 December 2005, p. 21, <http://www.lowyinstitute.org/publications/permanent-friends-historical-reflections-australian-american-alliance>, accessed 1 April 2018.

4   Desmond Ball, The Strategic Essence, *Australian Journal of International Affairs*, vol. 55, no. 2, 2001, p. 235.

to deliberate policy.[5] Still, while the Whitlam government had entered office with the determination to implement a more self-reliant approach to defence, the overall structure of Australia's defence forces and defence equipment acquisition programs continued to reflect earlier decisions and priorities to project Australian military strength beyond the continental boundaries in order to support the security of its neighbours in Southeast Asia and the Southwest Pacific.[6]

When the DOA and self-reliance doctrines finally matured, reflected in the 1986 Dibb report, they immediately provoked criticism from American officials, the Australian military and conservative commentators. These critics charged that the report proposed a defence posture that was too isolationist and failed to take into consideration Australia's responsibilities for maintaining regional security in accordance with the US alliance. Significantly, the criticism impelled a change in the 1987 White Paper which made a point of stressing Australia's regional responsibilities and alliance obligations.[7]

While Dibb did prioritise the defence of the continent, Australia's "direct" and "primary" spheres of military interest were deemed to be ten per cent and twenty per cent of the earth's surface respectively – hardly isolationist – and expeditionary combat in support of Australia's allies was to continue, albeit with a reduced focus.[8] In any case, if there were any hint of a "fortress Australia" mentality in defence thinking, it was well and truly abandoned by the Department of Defence's November 1989 report, *Australia's Strategic Planning in the 1990s*. That report unambiguously declared Australia's defence strategy "goes beyond the defence of the nation against direct attack to include the promotion of our security interests".[9]

---

5   Stephan Fruhling, *A History of Australian Strategic Policy Since 1945*, Canberra: Defence Publishing Service, Department of Defence, 2009, p. 44.

6   Graeme Cheeseman, From Forward Defence to Self-Reliance: Changes and Continuities in Australian Defence Policy 1965-90, *Australian Journal of Political Science*, vol. 26, no. 3, 1991, p. 433.

7   Frank P. Donnini, *ANZUS in Revision: Changing Defence Features of Australia and New Zealand in the Mid-1980s*, Alabama: Air University Press, February 1991, pp. 68-74.

8   Paul Dibb, *Review of Australia's Defence Capabilities*, Report to the Minister for Defence, Canberra: Australian Government Publishing Service, March 1986, pp. 3-4, 37, 50-51. Also see, Commonwealth of Australia, *The Defence of Australia 1987*, Canberra: Department of Defence, 1987, pp. 2-3.

9   Commonwealth of Australia, *Australia's Strategic Planning in the 1990s*, Canberra: Department of Defence, 27 November 1989, p. 2.

The planning document summarised how Australia's strategic policy evolved from dependence on allies to defending the homeland independently and finally "to a positive acceptance of both self-reliance and our need to help shape our regional strategic environment, in which we are a substantial power".[10] Under the heading "Promoting Our Strategic Interests", the document argued that Australia "should see itself as a substantial regional power exerting considerable influence on the rate, direction and outcomes of strategic change". Among the reasons cited was "the fact that we are a substantial regional military power" and "our alliance with the US".[11]

Australia's new strategic doctrine of prioritising the defence of the continent and its immediate surrounds thus faded almost as soon as it was announced, overcome by Australia's deeply embedded expeditionary mindset and desire to establish its own "Pax-Australiana".[12] As a number of scholars argued throughout the 1990s, the post-Dibb defence strategy reflected a "new Australian militarism" that conceived of Australia's substantial regional military power as a diplomatic instrument to further the nation's interests abroad and enhance Australia's international status.[13] In the words of former Foreign Minister Gareth Evans, the more self-reliant defence posture that had emerged since the 1980s "liberated" Australia so that it could pursue a much broader security agenda in line with the nation's "middle power" status.[14]

As in previous decades, the post-Cold War era saw Australia continue to support America's efforts at maintaining its global hegemony and contribute to major US military interventions around the world. However, the difficulty in balancing these two objectives – to advance Australia's ability to shape its own regional strategic environment and support its ally globally – proved to be significantly contentious. This became particularly evident

---

10   *Australia's Strategic Planning in the 1990s*, p. 3.

11   *Australia's Strategic Planning in the 1990s*, pp. 42–43.

12   Graeme Cheeseman and Michael McKinley, Moments Lost: Promise, Disappointment and Contradictions in the Australian-United States Defence Relationship, *Australian Journal of International Affairs*, vol. 46, no. 2, 1992, p. 203.

13   Grame Cheeseman and St John Kettle (eds), *The New Australian Militarism: Undermining Our Future Security*, Sydney: Pluto Press, 1990; Gary Smith and St John Kettle (eds), *Threats Without Enemies: Rethinking Australia's Security*, Sydney: Pluto Press, 1992; Graeme Cheeseman and Robert Bruce (eds), *Discourses of Danger & Dread Frontiers: Australian Defence and Security Thinking After the Cold War*, Sydney: Allen & Unwin, 1996.

14   Graeme Cheeseman, "Back to 'Forward Defence' and the Australian National Style" in Graeme Cheeseman and Robert Bruce (eds), *Discourses of Danger*, p. 269.

during the conservative government of Prime Minister John Howard, especially after the terrorist attacks on 11 September 2001, which had the effect of rallying Australian political opinion in support of the US-led "war on terror".

Although the Howard government continued to place importance on the notion of Australia as a "middle power" or, more confidently, a "pivotal", "considerable" and "significant" power, it advocated moving beyond regionalism to advancing Australia's interests on the global stage in concert with its major ally.[15] The decision by the Howard government to focus the ADF on distant operations in support of the US, as well as regional operations in Southeast Asia and the South Pacific, was characterised by critics of the alliance, such as Joseph Camilleri, as being "as clear a statement as any could be that Australia had officially returned to a policy of forward defence".[16]

Concerned that Australia's priorities under the Howard government had tilted too far in favour of expeditionary combat missions in support of allies, noted strategic commentators urged Australia to concentrate on developing Australia's capacity to defend the continent and project credible force into the region, with the focus on the latter.[17] Professor Hugh White, for example, argued Australia should "build and sustain military capabilities that will give it strategic weight as a regional power", capable of independently protecting its interests as far offshore as possible.[18] Similarly, former US ambassador Michael Thawley argued Australia should not be content to become "progressively more of a strategic price-taker as others around us grow", but instead work towards becoming more of a "strategic price-setter". Thawley advocated that Australia increase "the size of our defence force and develop more significant force projection capabilities" so

---

15   Alexander Downer, Should Australia Think Big or Small in Foreign Policy, speech to the Centre for Independent Studies: The Policymakers Forum, 10 July 2006.

16   Joseph Camilleri, A Leap Into the Past - In the Name of the "National Interest", *Australian Journal of International Affairs*, vol. 57, no. 3, 2003, p. 447.

17   Paul Dibb, "Australia-United States" in Brendan Taylor (ed), *Australia as an Asia Pacific Regional Power: Friendship in Flux*, London: Routledge, 2007, pp. 38-9; Paul Dibb, "The Self-Reliant Defence of Australia: The History of an Idea" in Ron Huisken and Meredith Thatcher (eds), *History as Policy: Framing the Debate on the Future of Australia's Defence Policy*, Canberra: Australian National University E Press, 2007, p. 22; Hugh White, *Beyond the Defence of Australia: Finding a New Balance in Australian Strategic Policy*, Lowy Institute for International Policy, Sydney, 2006, <http://www.lowyinstitute.org/publications/beyond-defence-australia>, accessed 1 April 2018.

18   White, pp. ix-x, 56.

that the nation could aim to "shift the balance in any potential conflict in our region".[19]

The advent of Kevin Rudd's Labor government brought new hopes for realising these ambitious goals. The 2009 Defence White Paper proposed the acquisition of major force projection capabilities well out of proportion to Australia's security needs, including doubling the size of the submarine fleet to twelve, acquiring three Air Warfare Destroyers, a new class of eight frigates, one hundred fifth-generation combat aircraft and around 1,100 armoured combat vehicles.[20] The intention was to acquire the necessary military capabilities for making a significant contribution to the "balance of power" in the region; an objective that was recognised as an evolution, not a revolution, in Australian strategic thinking. As Robert Ayson put it in a review of the 2009 White Paper, "Residing deep within the Australian strategic consciousness ... is a desire that it be a dominant influence in its own part of the wider Asian strategic balance".[21] Controversially, the Rudd government appeared to be preparing the ADF to support the US in a major regional war, China being the obvious target.[22]

By the end of Rudd's term in office, Australia had undergone a significant expansion in military power. Over the two decades to the year 2010, successive defence funding increases saw Australia achieve the tenth largest military expenditure in the world, all the while continuing to outspend all of its Southeast Asian neighbours by a considerable margin.[23] Construction had begun on two new Landing Helicopter Docks, first envisioned by the Howard government in 2000, capable of deploying over 2,000 troops and associated weapons, vehicles and aircraft. Altogether, in the words of White, the ADF had acquired key air and naval assets that

---

19   Michael Thawley, More Power to Australia, address to the Sir Robert Menzies Lecture Trust, Melbourne, Parliament House, 4 November 2005.

20   Commonwealth of Australia, *Defending Australia in the Asia–Pacific Century: Force 2030*, Defence White Paper 2009, Canberra: Department of Defence, 2009.

21   Robert Ayson, Australia's Defence Policy: Medium Power, Even Bigger Ambitions?, *The Korean Journal of Defence Analysis*, vol. 22, no. 2, 2010, p.192.

22   An allegedly secret chapter in the 2009 white paper detailed plans to fight China by using the Australian Navy's submarines to help blockade key trade routes, raising the prospect of China firing missiles at targets in Australia in retaliation. Brendan Nicholson, Secret "War" With China Uncovered, *The Australian*, 2 June 2012, <http://www.theaustralian.com.au/national-affairs/policy/secret-war-with-china-uncovered/story-fn59nm2j-1226381002984>, accessed 1 April 2018.

23   Mark Thompson, *The Cost of Defence: ASPI Defence Budget Brief 2012-2013*, Australian Strategic Policy Institute (ASPI), Canberra, May 2012, p. 167, <https://www.aspi.org.au/report/cost-defence-aspi-defence-budget-brief-2012-2013>, accessed 1 April 2018.

reinforced Australia's status as "the most significant air and naval power in the region south of China and east of India".[24]

The notion of Australia as an influential actor requiring high-end military capabilities to bolster its regional influence continued to be advocated by Rudd's successor, Julia Gillard. In 2013, the Gillard government published Australia's first National Security Strategy, declaring that one of Australia's central objectives or "ends" was "to influence and shape our regional and global environment to be conducive to advancing Australia's interests and values".[25] In particular, "strengthening our position as an influential regional actor" was deemed "a focus of our foreign policy".[26] The maintenance of "credible high-end capabilities" was considered necessary to "act decisively when required", deter potential threats, and "strengthen our regional influence".[27]

The Gillard government released a new Defence White Paper in 2013, reaffirming the intention to deliver the "core capabilities" identified in Rudd's 2009 White Paper.[28] However, plans for a large military build-up in the short term were effectively deferred due to "fiscal realities" and subsequent cuts to defence spending, a decision that evoked hysterical commentary in Australia and from key officials in Washington despite the fact that the US had also planned future defence cuts.[29] Australia maintained its rank as the 10th largest defence spender in the world in 2013 and continued its significant lead in defence spending in Southeast Asia.[30]

---

24 Quoted in Michael Wesley, *There Goes the Neighbourhood: Australia and the Rise of Asia*, Sydney: New South, 2011, p. 26.

25 Commonwealth of Australia, *Strong and Secure: A Strategy for Australia's National Security*, Canberra: Department of the Prime Minister and Cabinet, 2013, p. 4.

26 *Strong and Secure*, p. 23.

27 *Strong and Secure*, p. 17.

28 Commonwealth of Australia, *Defence White Paper 2013*, Canberra: Department of Defence, 2013, pp. 3, 23.

29 Geoffrey Barker, Time For A Balanced Debate on Defence, *Australian Financial Review*, 21 June 2012, <http://www.afr.com/news/policy/defence/time-for-balanced-debate-on-defence-20120620-j2jck>, accessed 1 April 2018; Andrew Carr, FactCheck: Is Defence Spending Down to 1938 Level? *The Conversation*, 3 September 2013, <https://theconversation.com/factcheck-is-defence-spending-down-to-1938-levels-17427>, accessed 1 April 2018; Mark Thompson, How Much Is Too Little? Learning to Live With a Smaller Force, *The Strategist*, Australian Strategic Policy Institute (ASPI), 15 August 2012, <http://www.aspistrategist.org.au/how-much-is-too-little-learning-to-live-with-a-smaller-force/>, accessed 1 April 2018.

30 Mark Thompson with Karl Claxton and Tom Muir, *The Cost of Defence: ASPI Defence Budget Brief 2014-2015*, Australian Strategic Policy Institute (ASPI), Canberra, May 2014, pp. 39, 168, 181, <https://www.aspi.org.au/report/cost-defence-aspi-defence-budget-brief-2014-2015>, accessed 1 April 2018.

Although the 2013 Defence White Paper toned down the alarmist rhetoric towards Beijing, the identification of China as a potential threat continued as a major theme.[31] The decision taken by the subsequent conservative Abbott government to purchase a large number of fifth-generation fighter jets, and the intention to spend up to $40 billion on twelve new submarines, added real impetus to the objective of preparing Australia for a future war with China.[32] As defence experts have noted, the only significant strategic function for purchasing the submarines is their "symbolic political contribution to maintaining alliance credit through a niche role in US naval operations against China".[33] Similarly, the unique capability of the F-35 Joint Strike Fighter "to conduct deep strike missions against a sophisticated integrated air defence system on Day 1 of a conflict" only has relevance in a US-led war against China.[34]

Meanwhile, strategic elites advocated Australia boost its "hard" and "soft" power, including "a more capable military", so as to "protect the full breadth of our interests".[35] For example, Rory Medcalf argued in 2015 that current realities:

[Compel] us to think about security interests in broad terms. The expansive version of national security today includes maintaining the kind of international, transnational and domestic order that serves our interests as a middle power.[36]

---

31   Benjamin Schreer, Business as Usual? The 2013 Defence White Paper and the US Alliance, *Security Challenges*, vol. 9, no. 2, 2013, pp. 38-39; Brendan Taylor, The Defence White Paper 2013 and Australia's Strategic Environment, *Security Challenges*, vol. 9, no. 2, 2013, pp. 15-16.

32   The Abbott government committed Australia to purchasing 58 F-35 Joint Strike Fighter jets, bringing Australia's total to 72.

33   Richard Tanter, *The $40 Billion Submarine Pathway to Australian Strategic Confusion*, NAPSNet Policy Forum, Nautilus Institute for Security and Sustainability, 20 April 2015, <http://nautilus.org/napsnet/napsnet-policy-forum/the-40-billion-submarine-pathway-to-australian-strategic-confusion/>, accessed 1 April 2018.

34   Andrew Davies and Harry White, *Taking Wing: Time to Decide on the F-35 Joint Strike Fighter*, Australian Strategic Policy Institute (ASPI), Canberra, March 2014, p. 5, <https://www.aspi.org.au/report/taking-wing-time-decide-f-35-joint-strike-fighter>, accessed 1 April 2018.

35   Michael Fullilove, The Birthplace of the Fortunate, 2015 Boyer Lectures, 18 October 2015, <http://www.abc.net.au/radionational/programs/boyerlectures/2015-10-18/6689512#transcript>, accessed 1 April 2018.

36   Rory Medcalf, Don't "Contain" China, but Australia Must Push for Rules-Based Security Order, *Australian Financial Review*, 11 September 2015, <http://www.afr.com/opinion/dont-contain-china-but-australia-must-push-for-rulesbased-security-order-20150910-gjjp0v>, accessed 1 April 2018.

At the very minimum, as a "top 20 nation", Australia was urged to "seek the capacity to substantially shape the security environment of the South Pacific and Southeast Asia" while playing a more limited role in wider East Asia, "where it can matter", such as imposing a "distant blockade" on China in any future US-Sino war.[37] Others insisted that Australia go further, aiming to play a decisive role in East Asia and equipping the ADF with the military capabilities to inflict serious damage in any potential future conflict with China.[38]

It fell upon the government of Malcolm Turnbull to act on these hawkish aspirations and deliver the significant military build-up first envisioned by Rudd, but never properly funded. Turnbull's 2016 Defence White Paper boasted that it was the first to be "fully costed" in order to "match our strategy and capability plans with appropriate resources", pledging to lift defence spending to 2 per cent of GDP by 2020-2021, and invest an unprecedented $195 billion into the military over ten years.[39] The 2016 White Paper put credibility behind previous plans to acquire twelve new "regionally superior" submarines and a fleet of new fifth-generation fighter jets to conduct offensive strike operations "as far from Australia as possible".[40] Other big ticket items reaffirmed in the 2016 White Paper included twelve new major surface vessels (three AWDs and nine frigates) that can "project force into the region and beyond".[41]

The three core priorities identified by the 2016 Defence White Paper are defending Australia, securing Southeast Asia and the Southwest Pacific and ensuring a stable Indo-Pacific and a "rules-based global order".[42] In a departure from previous white papers, all three are accorded equal weight in the design and development of the ADF.[43] Peter Jennings, who led the

---

37   Andrew Carr, "Learning to Act Like a Major Power – Australia as a Top 20 Nation" in Australian Strategic Policy Institute (ASPI), *Are We A Top 20 Nation or a Middle Power? Views on Australia's Position in the World*, 18 December 2014, p. 4, <https://www.aspi.org.au/report/are-we-top-20-nation-or-middle-power-views-australias-position-world>, accessed 1 April 2018.

38   Ross Babbage, Australia's Strategic Edge in 2030, *Kokoda Papers*, no. 15, February 2011, <http://www.regionalsecurity.org.au/Resources/Documents/KP15StrategicEdge.pdf>, accessed 1 April 2018.

39   Commonwealth of Australia, *2016 Defence White Paper*, p. 9.

40   *2016 Defence White Paper*, pp. 90, 94.

41   *2016 Defence White Paper*, p. 92.

42   Otherwise referred to as Australia's "Strategic Defence Interests" and "Strategic Defence Objectives". *2016 Defence White Paper*, p. 68.

43   Ross Babbage, DWP 2016: Five Key Questions, *The Strategist*, Australian Strategic Policy Institute (ASPI), 29 February 2016, <http://www.aspistrategist.org.au/dwp-2016-five-key-questions/>, accessed 1 April 2018; Kim Beazley, DWP 2016:

expert panel advising the government's white paper, has written that the most important strategic defence interest identified in the White Paper is to secure Australia's wider regional interests, the new design of the ADF ensuring Australia can "take the fight into maritime Southeast Asia".[44] Elsewhere, Jennings observes that the 2016 White Paper can "be seen as the concluding verse to the generation-long saga of the Defence of Australia (DOA) strategy. 'DOA' is now fully effected in a maritime strategy focused on Southeast Asia and the Pacific".[45]

A player of significance

Since the emergence of the self-reliance and DOA doctrines, there has been a clear expansionist evolution in Australia's defence strategy. An increasingly central objective of the ADF has been to project force as a substantial regional power and promote Australia's "national interests", right up to and including the global level. "In a more contested and competitive world", the 2017 Foreign Policy White Paper declares, Australia must "maximise our national power and international influence."[46] Simultaneously, Australia has gradually stepped back from the concept of self-reliance, returning to an earlier assumption that Australia will always be fighting alongside the US and that the key role of the ADF is to support its ally's actions.[47] Australia's evolving strategic doctrine is a reflection of its long-standing ambition to be a "middle power" in international affairs, capable of influencing its regional and global environment.

At the elite level, as Andrew Carr relates, "being a middle power has been at the heart of how Australian politicians have framed and conceived of their nation's role in international affairs, and they have done so with

---

A Throwback to a Harder Era, *The Strategist*, Australian Strategic Policy Institute (ASPI), 2 March 2016, <http://www.aspistrategist.org.au/dwp-2016-a-throwback-to-a-harder-era/>, accessed 1 April 2018.

44   Peter Jennings, Defence White Paper: Battlefront Pitched Beyond "Sea Air Gap", *The Australian*, 27 February 2016, <http://www.theaustralian.com.au/opinion/defence-white-paper-battlefront-pitched-beyond-sea-air-gap/news-story/f518f3a25fa9d0d06a798f58e48b4624>, accessed 1 April 2018.

45   Peter Jennings, The 2016 Defence White Paper: Good Posture, *The Strategist*, Australian Strategic Policy Institute (ASPI), 25 February 2016, <http://www.aspistrategist.org.au/the-2016-defence-white-paper-good-posture/>, accessed 1 April 2018.

46   Commonwealth of Australia, *2017 Foreign Policy White Paper*, 2017, p. 2.

47   Hugh White, DWP 2016 and Self-Reliance, *The Strategist*, Australian Strategic Policy Institute (ASPI), 8 March 2016, <http://www.aspistrategist.org.au/dwp-2016-and-self-reliance/>, accessed 1 April 2018.

an enthusiasm beyond any other comparable country".[48] Although there is no consensus on the definition of a "middle power", Australia by and large fulfils the criteria by any of the typical measures, including possessing substantial military and economic power, a history of diplomatic activism on the regional and global stage and self-identification.[49] For Australian elites, since as far back as the 1940s, the employment of the term middle power has reflected the desire to be a "player of significance".[50]

Australia's middle power imaginings can be traced back to the nation's settler-colonial origins. To the degree that the colonies and, later, a federated Australia, had a foreign policy towards surrounding Pacific neighbours during the nineteenth and early-twentieth centuries, it was shaped by enthusiasm for imperialist expansion.[51] This "imperialist spirit" was linked to, but distinct from, traditional security anxieties. Australia's "Monroe Doctrine" of preventing nearby territories falling into the hands of rival European imperial powers often underpinned the drive for colonial conquest.[52] Nevertheless, security concerns did not always dominate. For example, Australia's desire for expansion was driven in no small part by the interests of Australian capital and the substantial economic benefits derived from dominating trade and investment in the region.[53]

From as early as the 1820s, when the desire for imperialist expansion into the Southwest Pacific first emerged in the colonies, there was little or no concern that claims to surrounding Pacific territories from foreign imperial powers might threaten Australia's security. For over a half century the desire for expansion was primarily justified by the objective of

48   Andrew Carr, *Winning the Peace: Australia's Campaign to Change the Asia–Pacific*, Melbourne: Melbourne University Publishing, 2015, p. 52.

49   Andrew Carr, Is Australia a Middle Power? A Systemic Impact Approach, *Australian Journal of International Affairs*, vol. 68, no. 1, 2014.

50   Andrew Carr, "ANZUS and Australia's Role in the World Affairs" in Peter J. Dean, Stephan Fruling and Brendan Taylor (eds), *Australia's American Alliance: Towards a New Era?*, Kindle Edition, Melbourne: Melbourne University Publishing Digital, 2016., Kindle Location 1623.

51   Note that the following discussion is largely based on a reading of Roger C. Thompson, *Australian Imperialism in the Pacific: The Expansionist Era 1820-1920*, Melbourne: Melbourne University Press, 1980.

52   Anthony Burke, *Fear of Security: Australia's Invasion Anxiety*, Cambridge: Cambridge University Press, 2008, p. 25.

53   Stuart Rosewarne, "Ruling the Region" in Verity Burgmann and Jenny Lee (eds), *A Most Suitable Acquisition*; Stuart Rosewarne, Australia's Changing Role in the South Pacific: Global Restructuring and the Assertion of Metropolitan State Authority, *Journal of Australian Political Economy*, no. 40, December 1997, pp. 80-116.

securing commercial and Christian missionary interests.[54] From the 1880s onwards, fears of expansionist European powers were presented as the primary, although not only, justification for colonial conquest. Queensland's attempt to annex East New Guinea in 1883 was largely motivated by the desire to preserve it as a labour recruiting ground for Queensland's sugar industry, but in order to justify his actions and present it as a *fait accompli*, Queensland Premier Thomas McIlwraith fabricated a threat of imminent German annexation.[55]

After federation, nationalist pride in the nascent power of the new nation injected great fervour into Australia's ambition for its own colonial project in the Southwest Pacific. The liberal *Adelaide Advertiser* reflected the hopes of a unified nation when it declared that, in contrast to the 1880s, now "we have the machinery for bringing the concentrated opinion of Australia to bear upon matters affecting our continental interests". The "numberless islands" that surround Australia's waters, "whatever allegiance they may now own – we still regard as ... preordained, at however remote a date, to be our heritage".[56]

Informed by a belief in racial superiority and the imperial sentiment of the day, linked to national status, hegemony in the Southwest Pacific was widely viewed as part of Australia's destiny as a white power.[57] This pro-imperial spirit was most notably expressed with respect to Australia's sustained desire to annex the New Hebrides (modern day Vanuatu). There were no conceivable security threats to justify Australia's pursuit of annexation. Since 1903, when Britain offered and, in 1904, secretly drafted a convention to establish a joint Anglo-French protectorate over the New Hebrides, thereby preserving its non-militarisation, any possibility of a threat to Australia was effectively neutralised. Nevertheless, successive Australian leaders continued to push for annexation as a matter of "national honour" and prestige.[58]

---

54 East New Guinea, due to its closeness to Australia, was an exception. Still, when moves to annex it first emerged in the 1870s, defence and economic benefits were considered equally important.

55 In the end, Britain disallowed Queensland's attempt at annexation. Thompson, *Australian Imperialism*, pp. 51-65.

56 Thompson, p. 158.

57 Significantly, even intervention in regional public health was envisioned as a means to fulfil Australian dreams of hegemony in the Pacific Islands. Alexander Cameron-Smith, Australian Imperialism and International Health in the Pacific Islands, *Australian Historical Studies*, vol. 41, no. 1, 2010, pp. 57-74.

58 Thompson, *Australian Imperialism*, pp. 173-203.

Australia's imperialist spirit was on full display in the lead up to World War One, when secret preparations were undertaken for an expeditionary force of 20,000 men to engage in colonial conquest in the Pacific and for wider use in service of the British Empire. The plans for offensive action were stunningly broad. It was proposed that the colonies of Germany, Holland, Portugal and France in the East Indian Archipelago and the Pacific would be seized. "There were few places within four thousand miles of Australia", notes Douglas Newton, "for which a case for conquest could not be made".[59]

Although race fears featured significantly in Australia's desire for expansion, the outbreak of World War One also presented an opportunity for Australia to extend its political sovereignty in the Pacific. The successful takeover of New Guinea from the Germans was advocated by *The Age* with the following justification on 12 August 1914:

> We have long since realised that we have a Pacific Ocean destiny ...
> By virtue of the European war an unexpected path has been opened
> to the furtherance of our ambition [to lay down] the foundations of a
> solid Australian sub-empire in the Pacific Ocean.[60]

For most parliamentarians, the territory of New Guinea was "rightfully" Australian; it belonged to Australia "as Tasmania does".[61] At the war's conclusion, Prime Minister Hughes argued at the League of Nations for outright annexation of New Guinea. Although security grounds were presented as the primary concern, the desire to exploit its natural resources also featured prominently in parliamentary debates. When it came to the push for control over Nauru, there was no doubting the desire to exploit its considerable phosphate deposits.[62]

Australia's expansionist stance continued into World War Two. At the 1944 ANZAC Conference, Australian Minister for External Affairs H. V. Evatt looked to secure Australian control over wide areas of the Pacific, including sovereignty over the Solomon Islands, the New Hebrides and Fiji.[63] Washington reacted to the Australia-New Zealand

---

59   Douglas Newton, *Hell-Bent: Australia's Leap into the Great War*, Melbourne: Scribe Publications, 2014, p. 47.

60   Tom O'Lincoln, *Australia's Pacific War: Challenging a National Myth*, Australia: Interventions Publishers, 2011, p. 22.

61   Patricia O'Brien, Remaking Australia's Colonial Culture?: White Australia and its Papuan Frontier 1901-1940, *Australian Historical Studies*, vol. 40, no. 1, 2009, p. 97.

62   Thompson, *Australian Imperialism*, pp. 211-12.

63   O'Lincoln, *Australia's Pacific War*, p. 59.

Agreement (ANZAC Pact) by claiming Australia was attempting to establish a "Monroe Doctrine" and a "co-prosperity sphere" covering most of the Pacific islands south of the equator; a policy dubbed "ANZAC imperialism".[64] That policy would, Harper notes, "of course be a revival of Australian Pacific ambitions more than half a century earlier".[65]

After World War Two, Australian elites continued to envision their country as an "outpost", "bastion" and "custodian" of the British Empire in the Asia–Pacific. However, they now viewed themselves on an equal footing with London and as having a new and more independent role in the world. Evatt, Spender, Casey and other prominent post-World War Two planners argued that Australia was a Commonwealth nation as well as a "middle power" and "metropolitan power" with special rights and responsibilities in the region.[66] From the end of World War Two, the Australian Labor government pushed to take leadership of Empire interests in the region and expand Australia's military and political role south of the equator. Crucially, a reassertion of British imperialism was recognised as necessary for Australia to achieve its regional leadership goals.[67] According to Bell, this was the central objective of Australia's foreign policy during this time. He observes that:

> Increased Dominion diplomatic and military independence, combined with active support for a reassertion of British power and influence in the Far East under Australian leadership, was the principal feature of Australian policy during 1944-6.[68]

Conservatives after World War Two carried the flame of Australia's imperialist spirit into the 1950s and 1960s. The Liberal-Country Coalition, led by Prime Minister Robert Menzies, seriously considered the expansion of Australia's empire in the South Pacific throughout the 1950s, while successive conservative governments "stood against the tide" of rapid decolonisation that was occurring in the colonies of European nations

---

64   Norman Harper, *A Great and Powerful Friend: A Study of Australian American Relations Between 1900 and 1975*, St Lucia, Queensland: University of Queensland Press, 1987, p. 127.

65   Harper, p. 127.

66   Srdjan Vucetic, *The Anglosphere: A Genealogy of a Racialised Identity in International Relations*, Stanford: Stanford University Press, 2011, pp. 56-58.

67   Roger J. Bell, *Unequal Allies: Australian-American Relations and the Pacific War*, Melbourne: Melbourne University Press, 1977, pp. 161-164.

68   Bell, p. 171.

during the 1960s.[69] Menzies and his colleagues were strong supporters of the continuation of British prestige and wider European imperialism in the Far East, viewing all of the European powers, with the exception of Russia, "to be worthy of support, since all, in their varying ways, could be seen as bearers of European influence in the non-Western parts of the globe".[70] Accordingly, Menzies had from the late 1940s onwards endorsed the attempts by the British, French and Dutch to crush independence movements in Southeast Asia.

The middle power concept underwent a transformation of sorts during the Hawke and Keating Labor governments during the 1980s and 1990s, refashioned to promote Australia's self-proclaimed status as a "good international citizen". However, this reconceptualisation tended to reinforce the status quo because of the overlap in interests and worldview between Australia and the United States.[71] The association of the middle power concept with the liberal internationalism of Labor leaders such as H. V. Evatt, Gareth Evans and Kevin Rudd masks the fact that Australia's middle power activism has been consistent with classical realist interpretations that emphasise the pursuit of self-interest via the exercise of power and influence.[72] The dominant stream in Australian middle power imagining is grounded in empire and imperialism, not liberal internationalism.[73]

Significantly, Australia's middle power ambitions have always been undertaken within the ambit of its great power alliances. Australia's connection to a "great and powerful friend" was long ago understood to provide it with a larger voice in international diplomacy. Writing on the concept of the Anglosphere in 1929, former Prime Minister Billy Hughes observed that:

The Dominions as part of the Empire are listened to by foreign nations with interest, for the influence of a great world power lends weight to their lightest word ... In themselves, although potentially

69 Christopher Waters, "Against the Tide": Australian Government Attitudes to Decolonisation in the South Pacific, 1962-1972, *The Journal of Pacific History*, vol. 48, no. 2, 2013.

70 David Goldsworthy, Australian External Policy and the End of Britain's Empire, *Australian Journal of Politics and History*, vol. 51, no. 1, 2005, p. 18.

71 Carr, "ANZUS and Australia's Role in the World Affairs", Kindle Locations 1624-1639.

72 Carl Ungerer, The "Middle Power" Concept in Australian Foreign Policy, *Australian Journal of Politics and History*, vol. 53, no. 4, 2007, p. 540.

73 Allan Patience, The Two Streams of Australia's Middle Power Imaginings and their Sources, *Australian Journal of Politics and History*, vol. 60, no. 3, 2014, pp. 449-465.

great nations … they do not count for much; as part of an Empire that has behind it great riches and organised force, the world pays them the tribute it always gives to wealth and power.[74]

In terms of the US alliance, its role in Australian defence and foreign policies evolved with Australia's increasing independence, growing strategic ambitions and changes in the regional distribution of power. As detailed in the previous chapter, while initially conceived of in security terms, the alliance played its most important role as an expression of Australia's interests in restoring and preserving the Western imperial order in Asia. However, as the old colonial order receded, and Australia's strategic independence grew, the alliance took on greater relevance for bolstering Australia's growing middle power ambitions within the US-led global strategic and economic order. Today, the Australia-US alliance is understood to "enhance Australia's standing in the region in a way that would not otherwise be possible".[75]

Influence and credibility

Notwithstanding Australia's growing strategic ambitions, the fundamental role of the US alliance has ostensibly remained the same since the 1970s; namely, to provide regional and global "stability" and ensure Australia has access to the defence technology and intelligence benefits deemed crucial for defending the nation independently. The 2016 Defence White Paper reiterates that Australia's security is underpinned by the ANZUS Treaty and America's regional presence, and that the ADF's persistent technology, intelligence and capability superiority would be beyond Australia's capacity without the US alliance.[76]

However, as illustrated above, the central defence planning concepts of "self-reliance" and DOA are clearly no longer about ensuring the ADF has the capacity to defend the continent without the assistance of major allies. Australia's strategic doctrine now emphasises "the capability for expeditionary warfare—unilaterally within the region and in concert with the United States and other partners globally—in addition to the foundational security provided by the ADF in the Australian theatre".

---

74   Harper, *A Great and Powerful* Friend, p. 38.

75   Jae Jeok Park and Hyun Chung Yoo, The Resilience of the US Australia Alliance: Does a (Potential) China Threat Provide a Rationale for the Alliance?, *The Korean Journal of Defence Analysis*, vol. 27, no. 4, December 2015, p. 425.

76   Commonwealth of Australia, *2016 Defence White Paper*, pp. 49, 121-122.

Consequently, this "has produced a drastic increase in the ADF's ability to project power, with what is now a regionally dominant amphibious capability and a much more flexible and deployable army".[77] The continued use of the terms "self-reliance" and "DOA" thus obscures rather than elucidates Australia's current defence policy and the role of the alliance within it.[78] In the context of Australia's enduring benign security environment and longstanding "middle power" ambitions, the primary purpose of the alliance is to bolster Australia's capacity for regional influence.

The importance of the Australia-US relationship to Australia's middle power status is frequently highlighted by strategic elites and ardent alliance supporters, including political and defence officials. Although the core of the alliance is defined in security terms, its more tangible value to Australia is said to be its "force multiplier" effect – not only militarily but economically and diplomatically – enhancing Australia's "freedom of action" and bolstering its regional status as a "middle power" and an "Asia–Pacific power" that can "punch above its weight" in the region and beyond.[79]

Noted former Australian defence official Paul Dibb is perhaps the most cogent exponent of the argument that the alliance is of central importance for bolstering Australia's status as a significant regional power. In an edited collection published in 2007, dedicated to the theme of "Australia as an Asia–Pacific Regional Power", Dibb argued that:

> Australia's alliance with the United States in many ways underpins its status as an Asia–Pacific power … As it is, Australia's closeness to America and its influence in Washington transforms Australia's

---

77   Timothy J. Blizzard, The PLA, A2/AD and the ADF: Lessons for Future Maritime Strategy, *Security Challenges*, vol. 12, no. 3, 2016, p. 64.

78   Stephan Fruhling, Australian Defence Policy and the Concept of Self-Reliance, *Australian Journal of International Affairs*, vol. 68, no. 5, 2014, pp. 531-547.

79   See, for example, Jae Jeok Park and Hyun Chung Yoo, The Resilience of the US Australia Alliance: Does a (Potential) China Threat Provide a Rationale for the Alliance?, *The Korean Journal of Defence Analysis*, vol. 27, no. 4, December 2015, pp. 417-434; Paul Dibb, "Australia-United States" in Brendan Taylor (ed), *Australia as an Asia Pacific Regional Power*; Greg Sheridan, *The Partnership: The Inside Story of the US-Australian Alliance Under Bush and Howard*, Sydney: UNSW Press, 2006, p. 320; Wesley, *There Goes the Neighbourhood*, p. 165; Ball, The Strategic Essence, pp. 243-244; Thawley, More Power to Australia; Carr, *Winning the Peace*, pp. 7-8; Andrew Shearer, *Unchartered Waters: The US Alliance and Australia's New Era of Strategic Uncertainty*, Lowy Institute Perspectives, Lowy Institute for International Policy, Sydney, August 2011, p. 13, <http://www.lowyinstitute.org/publications/uncharted-waters-us-alliance-and-australias-new-era-strategic-uncertainty>, accessed 1 April 2018.

regional status: it allows Australia to punch above its weight in regional and, indeed, international security organisations.[80]

While Dibb maintains that the "core" of the alliance is the protection of a great and powerful friend, the benefits of the relationship ultimately derive from access to the corridors of power in Washington, irreplaceable US intelligence, cooperation in defence science and technology and advanced US military weapons that together bolster "Australia's strategic influence in regional affairs and its reputation for military strength".[81] Richard Brabin-Smith, another noted former official in the Australian Department of Defence, also emphasises the fact that "Australia has gained immeasurably, over many decades, from its [privileged] access to US-sourced defence capabilities and US defence science and technology".[82]

The post-Cold War strategic context of Australia's middle power status and the US alliance are perhaps best articulated in a seminar Dibb presented on the ANZUS alliance to the Defence Sub-Committee of the Joint Standing Committee on Foreign Affairs, Defence and Trade in 1997.[83] Dibb warned that the growing economic might of ASEAN implied Australia would have to work harder in the future to maintain its position as "the leading middle power in Southeast Asia", remain relevant "in terms of the capacity to defend Australia", "show leadership in the region" and "shape the regional strategic environment to our advantage as an important middle power".[84]

Crucially, Dibb pointed out that threats to Australia in the post-Cold War strategic environment are not primarily about the potential for a direct attack, but rather the threat to Australia's position as a middle power. He argues that recognising "greater strategic complexity and uncertainty" in the region is not about:

---

80   Dibb, "Australia-United States" in Brendan Taylor (ed), *Australia as an Asia Pacific Regional Power*, p. 33.

81   Dibb, p. 37.

82   Richard Brabin-Smith, "Capability Development and Defence Research" in Peter J. Dean, Stephan Fruling and Brendan Taylor (eds), *Australia's American Alliance: Towards a New Era?*, Kindle Edition, Melbourne: Melbourne University Publishing Digital, 2016, Kindle Locations 3964-3965.

83   Paul Dibb, The Asia–Pacific Region Post Cold War, seminar presented to the Defence Sub-Committee of the Joint Standing Committee on Foreign Affairs, Defence and Trade on the ANZUS Alliance, Canberra, 11 August 1997.

84   Dibb.

[Defining] a clear and imminent direct military threat ... it is about the balance of power and balance of influence and our survival as an independent middle power strongly allied with the United States and not subordinate to some external—or externally lodged—Asian great power.[85]

In an argument that has taken on greater relevance today in light of China's rise, Dibb presciently warned that the major concern for Australia in the future is the end of the "Vasco da Gama period" – or the end of Western dominance in the region for the first time in 500 years – as great Asian powers increase their ability to shape the regional strategic environment.[86] That will not occur, Dibb predicts reassuringly, as long as the US stays engaged so that the "balance of influence" (a more honest term than the conventional "balance of power") remains firmly with the West. Dibb sums up his strategic assessment in the following terms:

> [There] are no clear military threats to Australia, but, increasingly, as a middle power in a shifting balance of power, we will need to shape our own regional strategic environment. As the balance of power changes, which undoubtedly it will, our survival as an independent middle power becomes a first order issue for us. As new powers emerge and as Australia's relative strategic mass declines, then it will become more important— not less important—that we retain our alliance with the United States in good repair and that we do what we can to keep US interests in the region engaged. That may well mean doing more with the United States and carrying more of the alliance burden, not less.[87]

The rapid rise of China and its willingness to test US primacy in recent years, particularly in the East and South China Seas, has brought the issue of Australia's alliance with the US and the changing balance of regional power relations into sharp focus.[88] The 2016 Defence White Paper identifies the relationship between the US and China as fundamental to Australia's

---

85   Dibb.

86   For a more recent discussion on this topic, see Coral Bell, *The End of the Vasco da Gama Era: The Next Landscape of World Politics*, Lowy Institute Paper 21, Lowy Institute for International Policy, Sydney, 2007, <http://www.lowyinstitute.org/publications/end-vasco-da-gama-era>, accessed 1 April 2018.

87   Dibb, The Asia–Pacific Region Post Cold War. Author's emphasis.

88   For details, see Vince Scappatura, The US 'Pivot' to Asia, the China Spectre and the Australian-American Alliance, *The Asia–Pacific Journal*, vol. 12, issue 36, no. 3, 9 September 2014, <http://apjjf.org/2014/12/36/Vince-Scappatura/4178/article.html>, accessed 1 April 2018.

future strategic circumstances.[89] It places strong emphasis on supporting America's regional military presence and the strategic "rebalance" in order to maintain a stable Indo-Pacific and "rules-based global order" – a phrase mentioned 48 times. The potential threats to stability identified include "major powers trying to promote their interests outside of the established rules"[90] – that is, outside of the rules largely crafted by the US to ensure the benefits of the international system accrue primarily to itself and to a lesser extent its allies.[91]

Significantly, there is disagreement about whether Australia's middle power status is enhanced or circumscribed by its alliance with the US. For subscribers to the "idealist" view, which defines middle powers in terms of how they *ought* to act, the US alliance is seen to constrain Australia's independence and therefore its credibility as a middle power, reducing its scope for acting as a "good international citizen". According to this view, Australia's long-standing commitment to employ middle power diplomacy in pursuit of nuclear non-proliferation has been compromised by its alliance obligations to host key US bases integral to America's nuclear war fighting capacity, as well as Australia's unwavering diplomatic support of Israel, despite its status as an undeclared nuclear power.[92]

Similarly, idealists have argued in the past that the middle power "dreams" of both the Rudd and Gillard Labor governments were left unrealised because of a lack of "credibility" in regional and international forums as a result of aligning too closely with the position of the US.[93] Although the fulfilment of Australia's middle power ambitions did not require an abandonment of the alliance, "a greater degree of independence within an alliance framework" was seen to be a necessary condition.[94] Most recently, Canberra's decision to align itself with the US in its strategic rivalry with China is considered evidence that the alliance constrains

---

89   Commonwealth of Australia, *2016 Defence White Paper*, p. 30.

90   *2016 Defence White Paper*, p. 40.

91   Michael Beckley, China's Century? Why America's Edge Will Endure, *International Security*, vol. 36, no. 3, 2011, pp. 48-50.

92   Mark Beeson, Can Australia Save the World? The Limits and Possibilities of Middle Power Diplomacy, *Australian Journal of International Affairs*, vol. 65, no. 5, 2011, p. 567.

93   James Cotton and John Ravenhill, "Middle Power Dreaming: Australian Foreign Policy During the Rudd-Gillard Governments" in James Cotton and John Ravenhill (eds), *Middle Power Dreaming: Australia and the World Affairs 2006-2010*, South Melbourne: Oxford University Press, 2011.

94   Carl Ungerer, Spit and Polish for Middle Power, *Sydney Morning Herald*, 28 March 2008, <http://www.smh.com.au/articles/2008/03/27/1206207302302.html>, accessed 1 April 2018.

Australian foreign policy in an area where one assumes a middle power could exercise greater freedom of action.[95]

But idealists have placed too much emphasis on the "moral" behaviour of middle powers when there is little empirical evidence to support this.[96] While Australia's alliance commitments may constrain its scope for acting as "a good international citizen", this has not been Australia's overriding foreign policy consideration or a central element of its middle power ambitions. Despite the rhetoric, Australia's "default" strategic culture has in fact been to further its interests irrespective of international law or institutions.[97] As one review of Australia's response to repressive military regimes in the Asia–Pacific concluded, Canberra's actions have "ultimately arise[n] from calculations of Australian national security, strategic interests, alliance maintenance and power potential, but tend to be obscured by the universalist rhetoric of promoting democracy and protecting human rights".[98]

It is no surprise that Australian policy-makers have continued to find no contradiction between Australia's middle power ambitions and its alliance obligations. To the contrary, "the Australian government has consistently argued that the country's strong alliance relationship with the United States supports its capacity to be a globally influential middle power", viewing its connection to a large power "as an unqualified benefit to the nation's influence".[99] In this context, the value of the alliance in providing access to advanced US military technology, defence science and intelligence benefits critical for ensuring Australia's regional military superiority, despite the absence of any threats, makes sense. Combined with patronage from Washington in regional and global diplomatic forums, the alliance provides Australia, at least in the eyes of elites in Canberra, with "a military and diplomatic heft it could not afford otherwise" or achieve independently.[100]

Significantly, the bolstering effect of the alliance on Australia's national power has mutual benefits by ensuring Canberra is a more effective and

---

95   Mark Beeson and Richard Higgott, The Changing Architecture of Politics in the Asia–Pacific: Australia's Middle Power Moment? *International Relations of the Asia–Pacific*, vol. 14, 2014, pp. 227-228.

96   Carr, *Winning the Peace*, pp. 22-23, 26.

97   Alan Bloomfield and Kim Richard Nossal, Towards an *Explicative Understanding* of Strategic Culture: The Cases of Australia and Canada, *Contemporary Security Policy*, vol. 28, no. 2, August 2007, p. 294.

98   Stuart Firth, Australia's Policy Towards Coup-Prone and Military Regimes in the Asia–Pacific: Thailand, Fiji and Burma, *Australian Journal of International Affairs*, vol. 67, no. 3, 2013, p.358.

99   Carr, *Winning the Peace*, pp. 7-8.

100   Wesley, *There Goes the Neighbourhood*, p. 165.

credible ally in undertaking its regional "burden sharing" responsibilities on behalf of the US-led Western security community. This is an explicit requirement of the alliance since the US announced the Guam doctrine in 1969, but it has gradually taken on increasing importance as Australia's national power has grown. Australia, wrote Paul Dibb in the mid-2000s, "has a significant role to play in securing American interests, as well as its own, in the Asia–Pacific region", largely as a result of its growing "geopolitical clout in Southeast Asia and the South Pacific".[101] Washington's expectations of Australia in this regard were spelled out by Denis Blair, former commander of US forces in the Pacific region, when he suggested that:

> Washington counts on Canberra to keep close watch on Southeast Asia and Oceania, to develop policy responses to crises that arise, confident they will be policies and responses that the US will share and support.[102]

Conversely, the ability and willingness of Australia to launch successful military interventions in the region, particularly in its own "patch" in the South Pacific, is understood by Canberra as essential for maintaining and bolstering Australia's "credibility" as a middle power in the Asia–Pacific and beyond. Patronage by the US in the regional and global diplomatic arena, critical to Australia's middle power ambitions, is dependent upon Australia meeting its alliance obligations to uphold stability in its own region. Australian interventions in the region spanning over two decades, including in Papua New Guinea (PNG), Fiji and the Solomon Islands, have been undertaken with the primary objective of maintaining Australia's credibility in Washington's eyes.[103]

---

101   Dibb, *US–Australia Alliance Relations*, p. 5.

102   Mark Beeson, Issues in Australian Foreign Policy July to December 2013, *Australian Journal of Politics and History*, vol. 60, no. 2, 2014, p. 272.

103   Firth, Australia's Policy Towards Coup-Prone and Military Regimes, pp. 363, 369; Dan Halvorson, Reputation and Responsibility in Australia's 2003 Intervention in the Solomon Islands, *Australian Journal of International Affairs*, vol. 67, no. 4, 2013, pp. 439-455; Charles Hawksley, Australia's Aid Diplomacy and the Pacific Islands: Change and Continuity in Middle Power Foreign Policy, *Global Change, Peace & Security*, vol. 21, no. 1, 2009, pp. 115-130; Kristian Lasslett, State Crime by Proxy: Australia and the Bougainville Conflict, *British Journal of Criminology*, vol. 52, no. 4, 2012, pp. 717-720; Elsina Wainwright, *Our Failing Neighbour: Australia and the Future of Solomon Islands*, Australian Strategic Policy Institute (ASPI), Canberra, 10 June 2003, pp. 14-15, <https://www.aspi.org.au/report/our-failing-neighbour-australia-and-future-solomon-islands>, accessed 1 April 2018.

Australia's intervention in support of the PNG government to brutally quash a protracted secessionist movement in Bougainville during the late 1980s and 1990s is a particularly egregious example of what maintaining credibility in Washington's eyes entails.[104] Despite official statements denying any direct involvement, the Hawke-Keating governments covertly supplied military equipment, training and logistical support to the PNG armed forces and backed a blockade of the Island that included humanitarian supplies. Without Australian support, the PNG military could not have effectively carried out its war against Bougainville, which targeted civilians on a mass scale, including atrocities such as the shelling of villages, forced displacement, extra-judicial killings of civilians and POWs, torture, rape and the denial of essential humanitarian aid.

Australian officials were well aware of the atrocities being committed but they were publicly rejected or downplayed as it was clear that nothing could be done to prevent them without endangering Australia's strategic aims. While Australian geopolitical and economic interests in PNG (including $1.8 billion of investment), as well as regional security concerns, were compelling ancillary considerations, the core motivation for intervention was to maintain Australia's "credibility" as a functioning middle power. As one senior official from the Department of the Prime Minister and Cabinet explains, "the South Pacific was Australia's patch, and a barometer of its credibility as an international force".[105]

The need to acquire US patronage was viewed as central to the entire Hawke and Keating governments' middle power approach to defence and foreign policy in the Asia Pacific. However, US patronage was not given freely. It "depended upon Australia playing a productive role in the Western alliance" system, including a "willingness to assume its fair share of the global security burden", particularly in the South Pacific or "Australia's patch".[106] The need to maintain credibility in the eyes of the United States during the Bougainville crisis was too important to Australian officials "to risk placing a serious question mark over Australia's competency as a regional power by taking the sort of decisive actions needed to *prevent* further mass atrocities".[107]

Historically, Australia's credibility and utility to the US has come in the form of its geostrategic position as a "suitable piece of real estate" for

---

104   The following account is based on Lasslett, State Crime by Proxy.

105   Lasslett, p. 719.

106   Lasslett, p. 718.

107   Lasslett, p. 720. Emphasis in original.

hosting US intelligence facilities which, in recent years, have undergone the most dramatic expansion in size and scope since the end of the Cold War.[108] In the mid-1960s, according to a declassified study for the US State Department, Australia's value was judged by its potential to become a "credible power" that could exert sufficient regional influence and perhaps "eventually be an alternative to the British".[109] Significantly, that assessment was not only accurate but prescient. Today, the Washington-based strategic community views Australia as a geographic "sweet spot" for basing US forces targeted at China and, like the UK in the twentieth century, as a "means to preserve US influence and military reach across the Indo-Pacific".[110]

---

108 Ball, *A Suitable Piece of Real Estate*. For recent developments on the expansion and evolution of US intelligence facilities in Australia, see the numerous papers located at "The Pine Gap Project". Richard Tanter, *The Pine Gap Project*, Nautilus Institute for Security and Sustainability, 22 February 2016, <https://nautilus.org/briefing-books/australian-defence-facilities/pine-gap/the-pine-gap-project/>, accessed 1 April 2018.

109 Tracy H. Wilder and Robert F. Packard, *Australia in Mid-Passage: A Study of Her Role in the Indian Ocean-Southeast Asia Area*, Foreign Service Institute, US Department of State, 11 April 1966, p. 17, <http://nautilus.org/wp-content/uploads/2012/09/711-Tracy-H.-Wilder-and-Robert-F.-Packard.pdf>, accessed 1 April 2018.

110 Jim Thomas, Zack Cooper and Iskander Rehman, *Gateway to the Indo-Pacific: Australian Defence Strategy and the Future of the Australia-US Alliance*, Centre for Strategic and Budgetary Assessments, November 2013, p. 6, <http://csbaonline.org/publications/2013/11/gateway-to-the-indo-pacific-australian-defense-strategy-and-the-future-of-the-australia-u-s-alliance-2/>, accessed 1 April 2018.

PART III:

The US Lobby and Australian Elite Opinion

Chapter Six

THE AUSTRALIAN AMERICAN LEADERSHIP DIALOGUE

The US Lobby

After establishing that material interests and the quest to advance state power and influence form the basis of elite support for the alliance, Part III of this book turns to the importance of ideational constructs in sustaining that support. As previously noted, the breadth and depth of elite support for the alliance derives from a pro-US security consensus and alliance orthodoxy, rooted in domestic institutions, ideologies and historical legacies that serves to ideologically constrain Australian national security policymakers and prevent them from departing too far from the status quo. Together with prominent voices in the media, academia, defence, think-tanks and non-government organisations that promote the alliance orthodoxy, this loose network of elites and institutional relationships can be broadly described as the "US Lobby" which functions to further entrench Australia's "special relationship" with America.

The objective of the US Lobby is not to hijack and transform Australia's national security policy but to preserve and protect the status quo, instilling and reinforcing the alliance orthodoxy among the public and especially in the minds of the next generation of elite and alliance managers. Although the alliance has enjoyed a high degree of elite and public support, concerns about its strength, and even its existence into the future, have resulted in efforts to see this alliance further institutionalised. The apparent goal has been to insulate the alliance from any serious critical reflection on its costs and benefits, head off any potential opposition and bind Australia to an ever closer relationship with America. In Part III of this book I investigate how the alliance orthodoxy is transmitted and reproduced, using the Australian American Leadership Dialogue as a case study.

A gap has long existed between the Australian public and officialdom when envisaging the role and purpose of the US alliance. As the noted Australian strategic and defence studies expert Desmond Ball has pointed out, "there are significant differences between the positions articulated in official policy statements and public opinion" about the role of the alliance in Australia.[1] Ball highlights that in elite circles:

> Since the 1980s, the important aspects of the alliance have been the preferential access to US defence technology, which has been important in maintaining the high-technology focus of Australian defence strategy; the intelligence cooperation and exchange arrangements; and the access to the most senior strategic councils in Washington.[2]

"On the other hand", Ball continues, "the media and the general public tend to view the importance of the alliance very much in traditional terms – that is, whether or not it provides a US security guarantee in the event of attack on Australia".[3]

The difference in official and popular interpretations of the alliance can be traced to its origins. Australians were understandably anxious about the possibility of attack by a resurgent Japan in the aftermath of World War Two. However, in negotiations with Washington regarding a Pacific defence pact, the primary objective of the then Minister for External Affairs, Percy Spender, was not to gain assurance of US support to defend Australia. Australian policy-makers understood that there were no foreseeable, credible, direct threats to their country. Spender's central objective was to gain access to and influence over high-level strategic planning in Washington. The ANZUS Pact served the political purpose of appeasing unfounded public fears of an invasion, making it possible for the Australian government to justify the deployment of forces in the Middle East in line with Anglo-American war plans.[4]

Incidentally, it was the Howard government that invoked the ANZUS Treaty for the first time in response to the terrorist attacks against America on 11 September 2001, instigating Australia's intervention in the Middle East as part of the "war on terror". Few Australians would know that by

---

1   Desmond Ball, The Strategic Essence, *Australian Journal of International Affairs*, vol. 55, no. 2, 2001, p. 245.

2   Ball, p. 246.

3   Ball, p. 245.

4   Philip Dorling, *The Origins of the ANZUS Treaty: A Reconsideration*, South Australia: Flinders Politics Monographs, Flinders University, 1989.

joining in the American invasion of Iraq in 2003, the Howard government violated the very first article of the ANZUS Treaty. Keeping in mind the invasion of Iraq violated the UN Charter and international humanitarian law,[5] Article I of the ANZUS Treaty states that the parties:

[U]ndertake, as set forth in the Charter of the United Nations, to settle any international disputes in which they may be involved by peaceful means ... and to refrain in their international relations from the threat or use of force in any manner inconsistent with the purposes of the United Nations.[6]

As with the case of the ink-blot designs in the Rorschach test, Australian policymakers have always been quick to see what they wanted to see and to adapt the ANZUS Treaty accordingly.[7]

Among the general public, a deep understanding of the alliance and the full implications for Australian defence and foreign policies remains absent. According to one national survey, of the 61 per cent of Australians who had read or heard of the ANZUS Treaty, 63 per cent did not know the US was a member.[8] Many Australians are ignorant of the fact that the Treaty does not constitute a guarantee the US will come to Australia's aid in the event of an attack, but merely stipulates an obligation for each state to "consult" and act "in accordance with its constitutional processes".[9] While a majority of Australians are in favour of US forces and bases in Australia, few believe Australia should offer support to US military action in Asia were a conflict to develop, for example, between China and Japan,

5   Ronald C. Kramer and Raymond J. Michalowski, War, Aggression and State Crime: A Criminological Analysis of the Invasion and Occupation of Iraq, *The British Journal of Criminology*, vol. 45, no. 4, July 2005, pp. 446-469.

6   1951 Security Treaty between Australia, New Zealand and the United States (ANZUS), reproduced at Australian Politics, ANZUS Treaty, <http://australianpolitics.com/topics/foreign-policy/anzus-treaty-text>, accessed 1 April 2018.

7   Joseph M. Siracusa, The ANZUS Treaty Revisited, *Security Challenges*, vol. 1, no. 1, 2005, p. 103.

8   United States Studies Centre (USSC), Australian Attitudes Towards the United States: Foreign Policy, Security, Economics and Trade, presentation by Professor Murray Goot, 3 October 2007, p. 17, <https://assets.ussc.edu.au/view/be/21/cc/b6/6d/57/0a/65/3c/3a/98/b9/23/2b/f7/44/original/959a3d253927020b0ed1a1bd671e65306f29b4f4/0708_nationalopinionsurvey_part1.pdf>, accessed 1 April 2018.

9   1951 Security Treaty between Australia, New Zealand and the United States (ANZUS), reproduced at Australian Politics, ANZUS Treaty, <http://australianpolitics.com/topics/foreign-policy/anzus-treaty-text>, accessed 1 April 2018.

despite the fact that America's presence is likely to implicate Australia in any future US–Sino war.[10]

Although members of the elite typically express a high degree of confidence about the strength of the Australia-US alliance, it is also recognised that the relationship requires careful management and nurturing to ensure its continued success. In the past, there have been concerns about the possible weakening of both public and elite opinion towards the US, with the suggestion that "measures should be taken with the aim of obviating or minimising threats to the continued health of the alliance".[11] More recently, there have been concerns raised about a potentially worrying trend in public opinion polls regarding the depth of the public commitment to the alliance.[12] As one prominent US national security thinker has observed, "The reality today is that the US alliance remains very popular among Australians in the abstract, but support falls off when the public is queried about concrete policy choices, such as joining the United States in Japan's defence or pushing China from militarised sea features".[13] To head off the lack of deep support for the alliance, Brendan Taylor, former Head of the Strategic and Defence Studies Centre (SDSC) at ANU, advises the following:

> [Alliance] managers might be wise to introduce a series of new
> education programs (conceivably in schools and universities) to ensure

10   71 per cent of Australians are opposed to supporting the US and Japan in any potential conflict with China in the East China Sea. Australia-China Relations Institute (ACRI), East China Sea: What Australians Think, 19 January 2015, <http://www.australiachinarelations.org/content/east-china-sea-what-australians-think>, accessed 1 April 2018.

11   Peter Edwards, *Permanent Friends? Historical Reflections on the Australian-American Alliance*, Lowy Institute Paper 8, Lowy Institute for International Policy, Sydney, 13 December 2005, p. 21, <http://www.lowyinstitute.org/publications/permanent-friends-historical-reflections-australian-american-alliance>, accessed 1 April 2018, pp. 53-61, quote p. 57. Significantly, Edwards cites the AALD as a positive example in redressing this problem, albeit solely focused on elite opinion.

12   Simon Jackman, et. al., *The Asian Research Network: Survey on America's Role in the Asia–Pacific*, United States Studies Centre at the University of Sydney, June 2016, pp. 34-35, <https://www.ussc.edu.au/analysis/the-asian-research-network-survey-on-americas-role-in-the-Asia–Pacific>, accessed 1 April 2018; Brendan Taylor, Unbreakable Alliance? ANZUS in the Asian Century, *Asian Politics and Policy*, vol. 8, no. 1, 2016, pp. 80-81.

13   Richard Fontaine, Against Complacency: Risks and Opportunities for the Australia-US Alliance, United States Studies Centre, October 2016, p. 10, <https://www.ussc.edu.au/analysis/against-complacency-risks-and-opportunities-for-the-australia-us-alliance>, accessed 1 April 2018.

that the public remains well informed as to the benefits (as well as the costs and risks) associated with the ANZUS alliance.[14]

While the Australia-US relationship "is arguably in its best ever shape", with "every prospect that it will continue to both broaden and deepen into the foreseeable future", Taylor cautions that it is always necessary to "guard against complacency".[15]

In response to the uncertainly surrounding the alliance after the election of US President Donald J. Trump, Professor Rory Medcalf, Head of the National Security College (NSC) at ANU, along with a team of his colleagues, published a paper urging Australians: "don't panic, don't relax". According to the authors of this report, the alliance is "broad and deep enough to survive a Trump presidency", but to hedge against US unpredictability, Australia should take the lead in strengthening the US alliance system in Asia to take more of the responsibility for regional security. The report reiterates that Australia's alliance with the US "remains central to our national security. We have no realistic alternative. Our interests are extensive and our capabilities cannot protect them in full".[16]

Following this report, in an address to the National Press Club in Canberra, Medcalf cautioned that "the challenge [for Australia] ahead is how do we preserve and protect the alliance through a difficult phase". He urges Australian politicians, policymakers and opinion leaders "to do more to tell the public precisely why and how the US backed alliance system is in our interests". He goes on to explain how the NSC has contributed to this goal, having trained 3,000 government officials in the past seven years, with many Masters and PhD students going on to serve as future policymakers. As well as contributing to the public debate, the NSC has helped to build partnerships through "forthright and trusted conversations" with American officials, such as former US Director of National Intelligence, Jim Clapper, and Commander of the US Pacific Fleet, Admiral Scott Swift. "Such conversations are a reminder that the alliance is deep, enduring and many-layered – it goes much beyond the President or the politics of the day".[17]

---

14   Taylor, Unbreakable Alliance?, p. 83.

15   Taylor, pp. 75, 82.

16   Rory Medcalf, Ryan Young, Marina Tsirbas, Matt Sussex, The Trump Presidency and Australia's Security: Don't Panic, Don't Relax, National Security College, ANU, Policy Options Paper, no. 1, January 2017, <https://nsc.crawford.anu.edu.au/sites/default/files/publication/nsc_crawford_anu_edu_au/2017-05/policy-options-paper1.pdf>, accessed 1 April 2018.

17   Rory Medcalf, The Future of Australia's Alliance with the United States, Speech at the National Press Club, Canberra, 21 February 2017, <https://crawford.anu.edu.au/

Leading defence academics at ANU have a long history of extolling official policy positions in foreign policy and national security, with a revolving
door often operating between senior government officials and advisors and
senior academics.[18] One notable exception is Professor Hugh White from
the SDSC at ANU, who in recent years has emerged as the most prominent
critic of the Australia-US alliance within the national security elite. While
representing an important dissident voice, White's criticism of the alliance
is narrowly contingent on his belief that China will replace America as the
dominant power in Asia. America's "benign hegemony", White argues,
has kept Asia stable and prosperous, and the "benefits of dependence [for
Australia] have far outweighed the costs". When it comes to the future of
Australia's alliance with the US, "Independence is not an appealing option
to choose, but an unavoidable and uncomfortable fact to be managed".[19]

Pro-alliance boosters in academia who subscribe to the alliance orthodoxy have been joined over the past two decades by the growth of private
institutions that now dominate the public and private space of ideas and
policy advice in foreign affairs and defence. For example, the Australian
Strategic Policy Institute (ASPI), established by the Australian government in 2001, is an "independent" think-tank that produces policy advice
for Australia's strategic and defence leaders but also engages with the wider
public through the media and the Institute's blog *The Strategist*. Historically,
it has received the vast bulk of its funding from the Department of Defence,
but it is also funded by a range of corporate sponsors, including several
major arms producers. Their reports have been downloaded 470,000 times
and *The Strategist* routinely attracts more than 2,000 unique readers a day.[20]

Initially established to provide an alternative source of policy ideas for
government, ASPI has transformed into an active participant in political

news-events/news/9214/future-australias-alliance-united-states>, accessed 1 April
2018.

18   David Sullivan, "Sipping a Thin Gruel: Academic and Policy Closure in Australia's
Defence and Security Discourse" in Graeme Cheeseman and Robert Bruce (eds),
*Discourses of Danger & Dread Frontiers: Australian Defence and Security Thinking After
the Cold War*, Sydney: Allen & Unwin, 1996; David Sullivan, Professionalism and
Australia's Security Intellectuals: Knowledge, Power, Responsibility, Australian
Journal of Political Science, vol. 33, no. 3, 1998, pp. 421-440.

19   Hugh White, Without America: Australia in the New Asia, *Quarterly Essay*, vol. 68,
2017, pp. 58, 76.

20   Australian Strategic Policy Institute (ASPI), Annual Report 2016-2017, pp.
2-5, 19-21, <https://s3-ap-southeast-2.amazonaws.com/ad-aspi/2017-11/ASPI-
AnnualReport_1617.pdf>, accessed 1 April 2018.

debate with a distinctly pro-American viewpoint.[21] ASPI's executive director, Peter Jennings, is a former high-level Australian public servant in defence and national security matters. After Trump was elected US president, Jennings praised his election commitment to undertake a massive military build-up, arguing that Australia stood to benefit from further American militarisation. Jennings also argued Australia should offer a Trump-led America even more than it did in the past, including by sending a Special Forces unit to Iraq and Syria, conducting freedom of navigation operations against China in the South China Sea, providing home porting facilities for the US Navy and offering to be a regional maintenance hub for the Joint Strike Fighter.[22] As one prominent Australian historian notes, Jennings is one of the "resident Archbishops of the Alliance".[23]

Writing in 2004, political and international editor of the *Sydney Morning Herald*, Peter Hartcher, observed that the Australia-US relationship is buttressed by three structures:

The economic structure is the [Australia-US free] trade agreement. The military-industrial structure is the big defence procurement investments and ... the personal contact structure is the Australian American Leadership Dialogue ... which over 10 years has created a new infrastructure of personal relationships between leading figures in the two countries.[24]

Writing several years later, prominent political commentator Paul Kelly pointed out that "through the decade, Australia's institutional bonds with the US surged with ... stronger private networks typified by the [United States] Studies Centre, the Australian American Leadership Dialogue and

21   John Menadue, The Australian Strategic Policy Institute Has Become a "Go To" Organisation For Anti Chinese Commentary, <https://johnmenadue.com/john-menadue-the-australian-strategic-policy-institute-has-become-a-go-to-organisation-for-anti-chinese-commentary/>, accessed 20 September 2018.

22   Peter Jennings, Australia Will Be More Important to the US Under Trump, *The Australian*, 3 December 2016, <https://www.theaustralian.com.au/news/inquirer/australia-will-be-more-important-to-the-us-under-trump/news-story/c4315af1b5b6757cac67c19bbda751c4>, accessed 1 April 2018.

23   James Curran, Fighting with America: Why Australia Needs a More Discerning Ally, The Interpreter, Lowy Institute for International Policy, 9 December 2016, <https://www.lowyinstitute.org/the-interpreter/debate/fighting-america>, accessed 1 April 2018.

24   Peter Hartcher, Dunny Escape to Done Deal, *Sydney Morning Herald*, 19 November 2004, <http://www.smh.com.au/articles/2004/11/18/1100748140918.html>, accessed 1 April 2018.

the Lowy Institute [for International Policy]".[25] Similarly, Professor Nick Bisley has argued that the Australian American Leadership Dialogue (AALD) and the United States Studies Centre (USSC) are "the two most prominent ... non-governmental efforts to reinforce the centrality of the alliance for Australian foreign policy".[26]

Unlike ASPI or the Lowy Institute for International Policy, the USSC and the AALD are solely dedicated to strengthening Australia's relationship with the United States. The USSC was established in 2006 at the University of Sydney with an endowment of $25 million dollars from the Howard government, with additional funding provided by the University of Sydney, the New South Wales government and private and corporate sponsors under the auspices of News Corp CEO Rupert Murdoch and the American Australian Association (AAA). The AAA was established in 1948 by Rupert's father Keith Murdoch "to promote cooperation and understanding between the United States and Australia" by offering scholarships, exchange programs, social and cultural events, corporate and government networking forums and benefit dinners funded by a host of Australian and American corporations.[27]

After a national opinion poll in 2005 revealed that Australians held some less than favourable opinions of America's role in the world after the invasion and occupation of Iraq, Rupert Murdoch blamed left-wing bias in the media and implored that Australians:

> [M]ust resist and reject the facile, reflexive, unthinking anti-Americanism that has gripped much of Europe ... That is why the American-Australian Association is proud to join with the Australian government in founding a new Centre for United States Studies in Australia. The centre will conduct research, raise awareness, dispel myths, groom new leaders ... [28]

The establishment of the USSC immediately raised controversy over its association with the AAA and the degree of influence the pro-US lobby group holds over the appointment of senior staff, research themes and

---

25 Paul Kelly, US Bull Wants to Help in the China Shop, *The Australian*, 8 June 2011.

26 Nick Bisley, An Ally For All The Years To Come: Why Australia Is Not A Conflicted US Ally, *Australian Journal of International Affairs*, vol. 67, no. 4, 2013, p. 412.

27 American Australian Association, About Us, <http://www.americanaustralian.org/?aboutus>, accessed 1 April 2018.

28 Robert Manne, Threats to University Independence: The Case of the Humanities, *The Journal for the Public University*, vol. 4, 2007, p. 18.

the overall agenda of the centre.[29] In 2006, Michael Baume, a former Liberal politician and board member of the centre, warned that "If the centre succumbed to the anti-American prejudice endemic in Australian universities, the AAA would pull the funding".[30] An analysis of the centre's visiting scholars from 2007-2009 revealed an overwhelming pro-US bias, with over a third having worked substantially for the US or Australian governments".[31]

In 2011, Julia Gillard's Labor government announced that it would fund a three-year "Alliance 21 Project" to the tune of $2 million dollars to be led by the USSC. The project enlisted more than 50 prominent strategic thinkers in both Australia and the United States "to identify new challenges and opportunities for the alliance, and to map out policies to reinforce linkages between Australia and the United States".[32] The culmination of the project was a report presented to the Australian government in October 2014 representing the input of over 130 authors and contributors from both the United States and Australia, primarily from academia, private think-tanks, business and government.[33]

The Alliance 21 report is an embodiment of the alliance orthodoxy and the objective of binding Australia to an ever-closer relationship with America. The authors of the report declare a belief in the alliance as a "special relationship", "grounded in shared norms and interests" and working together for over sixty years "in support of human dignity, democracy and adherence to international norms".[34] The "core insight of the Alliance 21 program is that the real strength of the Australia-United States alliance lies in common values and a record of mutual support".[35]

The report identifies three "fundamental strategic guideposts" to guide alliance managers in the future: pursue "an even closer partnership",

---

29   Tim Anderson, Hegemony, Big Money and Academic Independence, *Australian Universities' Review*, vol. 53, no. 2, 2010, pp. 11-17.

30   Bernard Lane, US Centre to be Objective, *The Australian*, 6 February 2008, <https://www.theaustralian.com.au/higher-education/us-centre-to-be-objective/news-story/3d0dc9a17e33c35a40fd8d7ff887f5bd>; accessed 1 April 2018.

31   Anderson, Hegemony, Big Money and Academic Independence, p. 15.

32   United States Studies Centre (USSC), Alliance 21: About, https://www.ussc.edu.au/programs/alliance-21/about, accessed 1 April 2018.

33   USSC, Alliance 21: The Australia-United States Partnership, University of Sydney, 2014, pp. 47-50, <https://assets.ussc.edu.au/view/89/ae/d8/4b/c2/a7/ff/ec/84/e7/9e/1b/87/15/a0/18/original/959a3d253927020b0ed1a1bd671e65306f29b4f4/Alliance21_Report_FINAL.pdf>, accessed 1 April 2018.

34   USSC, pp. 6, 11.

35   USSC, p. 45.

"increasingly work together in Asia" and develop a "far more comprehensive" relationship beyond defence and security.[36] The last guidepost requires a greater effort on the part of both countries to encourage leaders in politics, the media, business and the broader public "to recognise the growing material interest and mutual benefits" of the relationship "and to encourage a clearer understanding of the alliance as a special relationship with few equals anywhere in the world".[37]

The report does acknowledge that there are "costs" to the alliance, namely an increase in the defence burden for Australia. However, "enjoying the benefits" of the alliance also requires "facing up to the costs".[38] Consequently, among the principal recommendations for Australia are "increases in defence spending", "supporting US-led efforts to address global security challenges" and "opening [Australian defence] facilities to a greater US presence".[39]

In 2015, the Australian government and several corporate partners committed to funding the Alliance 21 Project for several more years. The second phase of the project was jointly established by the USSC and its more recently founded "sister centre", the Perth USAsia Centre at the University of Western Australia, which formally opened in 2013 under the auspices of the AAA to "strengthen partnerships and strategic thinking between Australia, the Indo-Pacific and the United States".[40] The second Alliance 21 Project saw the introduction of a fellowship program to support an exchange of senior scholars and policy analysts "to examine shared interests and mutual challenges through policy research and public engagement", and includes a partnership with the US Department of State.[41]

Together, these unashamedly pro-US organisations dominate the public and elite ideas space with research reports, policy advice, conferences, major public addresses and day-to-day commentary and analysis that more or less conforms to the alliance orthodoxy. Their views are amplified by sympathetic opinion makers in the media, some of whom are quoted in the

---

36   USSC, p. 6

37   USSC, p. 14.

38   USSC, p. 33.

39   USSC, p. 8.

40   Perth USAsia Centre, Annual Report: 2016, p. 1, <http://perthusasia.edu.au/getattachment/ce904fde-452a-4247-9385-1eb9233cfe6a/2016-Annual-Report-FINAL.pdf.aspx?lang=en-AU>, accessed 1 April 2018.

41   USSC, Alliance 21: About; Perth USAsia Centre, Alliance 21 Fellowship, <http://perthusasia.edu.au/alliance-21>, accessed 1 April 2018.

following sections and chapters, who regularly seek their perspectives when commenting on contemporary events in the defence and national security space. The list of foreign policy and national security elites, journalists, academics, think-tanks and non-government organisations that promote the alliance orthodoxy are too numerous to cite and critically investigate; they undoubtedly constitute the dominant voice in Australian foreign policy and national security discourse. However, while the views and objectives of much of the pro-US lobby are relatively open to public scrutiny, this is not the case with the Australian American Leadership Dialogue (AALD).

The AALD is widely lauded as "arguably the most valuable private-sector foreign policy initiative ever undertaken in Australia",[42] "a central institution in the US-Australia relationship"[43] and "the most important of all non-government organisations dedicated to the strengthening of the Australia-US alliance in all its manifestations; civil, political and commercial".[44] Veteran Australian diplomat Richard Woolcott says that of all the private diplomatic initiatives he has participated in over the decades, none are comparable to the AALD, which is "far and away the most successful" of them all.[45] Former American diplomat Mel Sembler agrees, stating that the AALD is "admired by many other countries" who aim to replicate its success.[46] Paradoxically, the AALD is also largely unknown beyond a small group of interested participants and observers. Supporters of the AALD concede that it is a "vital but largely invisible part of the alliance infrastructure"[47] and a "semi-secret of the alliance".[48]

While there has been much commentary surrounding the success of the AALD in influencing policy outcomes, there has been no detailed critical analysis of AALD's agenda to preserve and strengthen the Australia-US alliance. The only academic inquiry into the AALD to date is limited to evaluating its success as an exercise in informal diplomacy, failing to question the self-declared objective of the AALD to reinforce and recreate

---

42   Stephen Loosley, Support Grows For Free Trade, *Sunday Telegraph*, 19 August 2001.

43   Greg Sheridan, Financial Shadow On Alliances, *The Australian*, 25 September 2008.

44   Glenn Milne, Rudd's Relevance Deprivation Syndrome, *The Drum, ABC*, 29 September 2010, <http://www.abc.net.au/unleashed/35454.html>, accessed 1 April 2018.

45   Author interview with Richard Woolcott, 22 March 2011.

46   Author interview with Mel Sembler, 21 March 2012.

47   Peter Hartcher, In With The New, And No Hard Feelings, *Sydney Morning Herald*, 26 January 2008, <http://www.smh.com.au/news/opinion/in-with-the-new-and-no-hard-feelings/2008/01/25/1201157663391.html>, accessed 1 April 2018.

48   Greg Sheridan, *The Partnership: The Inside Story of the US-Australian Alliance Under Bush and Howard*, Sydney: UNSW Press, 2007, p. 311.

policy orthodoxies.[49] One of the objectives of this book is to help to redress this gap in the study of Australian-American relations by critically evaluating the AALD's role in managing Australia's alliance with the US.

Anyone wishing to subject the AALD to critical analysis is immediately faced with a number of constraints. Only a select few are invited to attend AALD discussions which are also governed by a strict non-disclosure convention. This prevents any comments from being publicly repeated without the express permission of the participant. The AALD also produces little by way of official publications. My request to the board of the AALD to distribute a questionnaire to participants was rejected, as was permission for me to attend an AALD event.[50]

Instead of citing AALD discussions directly, some 120 interview requests were emailed to current and former participants of the AALD. Of the sixty-five who responded, forty accepted the invitation to be interviewed. The founder of the AALD, Phillip Scanlan, initially agreed to respond to a series of written questions via email. However, answers to the questions were not forthcoming, despite repeated follow-up requests.[51] In-depth face-to-face and phone interviews were conducted by the author in 2011 and 2012. Interviewees were asked to respond to a series of questions relating to the AALD's origins, objectives, organisational structure and management, selection process, personal and institutional value, influence on Australia-US relations, flaws, challenges, success, reputation, relevance and long-term viability. Interviewees were also asked about the nature and degree of their involvement with AALD, their opinion on the diversity of views and the general nature of discussion and debate, and the impact of the AALD on their opinion of the alliance.

Interviewees represent a wide range of participants with varying degrees of experience and involvement with the AALD, including founding members, current and former board members, Liberal and Labor Party MPs, public servants, prominent academics, key journalists and senior representatives from business. Together with material publicly available

49   Elena Douglas and Diane Stone, The Informal Diplomacy of the Australian American Leadership Dialogue, *Australian Journal of International Affairs*, vol. 69, no. 1, 2015, pp. 18-34.

50   Both requests were made in June 2011 to the then chairman of the Australian board of the AALD, Mehrdad Baghai.

51   In May 2011, Scanlan, who was the then Australian Consul-General in New York, agreed via his assistant to respond to my questions. However, answers to the questions were not forthcoming, despite a series of follow-up calls and emails to the Consulate-General in August, September 2011, and March, April, May 2012.

about the AALD, these sources provide the basis for the argument that follows.[52]

The main contention of this book is that the AALD exists to sustain the prevailing orthodoxy, detailed in Part I, that views the Australia-US alliance as a "special relationship" driven by mutual security interests and shared values. The AALD emerged within the context of elite fears about the strength of the alliance into the future and sought to insulate it from potential challenges. The AALD fulfils its central objective to preserve the status quo in three main ways. First, it carefully frames discussion and debate about the value of the alliance to Australia. Second, it facilitates the socialisation of Australian elites into the alliance orthodoxy. Finally, it serves as a "gatekeeper" of the status quo and a litmus test on the alliance loyalty of potential future leaders.[53]

Origins

A spectacular fireworks display over Sydney Harbour welcomed the long-awaited arrival of President George H. W. Bush on New Year's Eve, 1991. It was 25 years since a sitting American president had made a state visit to Australia, the last being Lyndon B. Johnson in October 1966 at the height of the Vietnam War. The visit was secured by then Prime Minister Bob Hawke at a black-tie dinner event in the White House on 27 June 1989. The President had responded immediately to the request from Hawke whom he considered to be a close and personal friend.[54]

The official meeting between the two heads of state, however, was not to be. While Bush had planned to make the trip in early 1991, he was delayed until the end of the year, by which time Paul Keating was Prime Minister. The President's decision to continue as planned was somewhat awkward for Keating, whose strained relationship with Bush was well publicised. In keeping with expectations, Hawke received a warm and friendly embrace

---

52 This includes an analysis of over 1500 news items published about, or with reference to, the AALD, sourced from Dow Jones Factiva and the *Australian Financial Review*.

53 For an earlier version of this argument see Vince Scappatura, The Role of the AALD in Preserving the Australia-US Alliance, *Australian Journal of Political Science*, vol. 49, no. 4, 2014, pp. 596-610.

54 Author interview with Mel Sembler, 21 March 2012. It was Mel Sembler, US ambassador to Australia at the time, who passed on Prime Minister Hawke's request to President Bush.

from Bush upon his arrival, while the President's encounter with Keating was far more formal; the latter noticeably nervous and tense.[55]

The aloofness in the personal relationship between the President and the new Prime Minister reflected broader concerns regarding the strength of the Australia-US relationship. While Keating declared he would be just as committed to the US alliance as Hawke, he also promised more "relative independence".[56] The US had kept a close eye on the possibility of a leadership challenge in Australia because of this attitude and what it indicated about Keating's commitment to US foreign policy interests. However, Keating's comments were more likely for domestic consumption and to placate left-wing members of the ALP.[57] Nonetheless, Keating's rhetoric and the President's visit resurfaced doubts about the utility of the alliance in a post-Cold War world. Specifically, there was significant concern and speculation in Australia regarding the possibility of US disengagement from Asia and a weakening of the "hub-and-spokes" alliance system in the Asia–Pacific.[58] The ALP's attempts at "self-reliance within the alliance" in the late 1980s only heightened these concerns as it implied the possibility of greater detachment from the US.[59]

The Australia-US alliance was considered the cornerstone of Australia's foreign policy but, since the Soviet Union had disappeared, it was feared so too had "the strongest bond holding the US and Australian alliance together, the threat to world peace from Soviet Communism".[60] Furthermore, in the post-Cold War era, as Stephen Mills asked in the *Australian Financial Review* of 3 January 1992, what "does the Australia-United States relationship mean for both countries, for the Asia–Pacific

---

55   Margo Kingston, Loyalty Remembers Yesterday's Man, *The Age*, 3 January 1992; Michael Millett, Keating Gets the Kudos but Hawke Gets the Emotion, *Sydney Morning Herald*, 3 January 1992.

56   Pilta Clark, Keating's US Vision Is Still Cloudy, *Sydney Morning Herald*, 31 December 1991.

57   Clark.

58   Rod Lyon, *Alliance Unleashed: Australia And The US In A New Strategic Age*, Australian Strategic Policy Institute (ASPI), Canberra, June 2005, pp. 5-6, <https://www.aspi.org.au/report/alliance-unleashed-australia-and-us-new-strategic-age>, accessed 1 April 2018; Hugh White, "Four Decades of the Defence of Australia: Reflections on Australian Defence Policy Over the Past 40 Years" in Ron Huisken and Meredith Thatcher (eds), *History as Policy: Framing the Debate on the Future of Australia's Defence Policy*, Canberra: Australian National University E Press, 2007, p. 173.

59   Lyon, p. 5.

60   David Lague, Australia Charts New Course in Asia–Pacific, *Australian Financial Review*, 31 December 1991.

region, and for the broader global community?" While the ANZUS Pact was sure to remain, "what does it mean and what will it do?"[61]

Responding to this apprehension about the role of the US in the new world order, President Bush sought to reassure his Australian friends by declaring that America was "going to stay totally involved in this part of the world ... right up to the very end of eternity".[62] Despite these remarks, doubts lingered about the commitment of future US presidents, particularly given the personal bonds between leaders in both nations were believed to be fading with time. As a veteran of the war in the Pacific, President Bush was recognised as "one of the last of the generation of American leaders with that kind of connection to Australia".[63]

Distinguished business leader Phillip Scanlan, then managing director of Coca-Cola Amatil's global beverages operations, shared these concerns. Scanlan held a particular interest in the US and its relationship to Australia, cultivated in part by the time he had spent as a postgraduate student at the Harvard Kennedy School of Government and, more personally, by his American-born wife. Scanlan would later assume the prestigious diplomatic post of Australian Consul-General in New York from 2009-2012.

Scanlan held a deep-seated fear that he "would wake up one morning and find that the US has declared independence from Australia".[64] Serendipitously, Scanlan was presented with a unique opportunity to express his concerns at a level where it counted. That occurred when he received an invitation from his old friend, Nick Greiner, then premier of New South Wales, to attend a New Year's Day cruise on Sydney Harbour, held in honour of President Bush's visit. Greiner had first met Scanlan in the late 1970s when the latter was chief of staff to New South Wales Liberal opposition leader Peter Coleman. After Scanlan took up his position at Amatil, the former political colleagues remained friends. They were of similar age, held similar attitudes and lived near each other at the time.[65]

Scanlan hoped that, at best, he might have the opportunity to meet Bush and introduce his American-born wife, Julie Scanlan. When the occasion arrived and Scanlan and his wife came to take their seats, both were

---

61 Stephen Mills, US Sends Hugs and Kisses Then We're On Our Own, *Australian Financial Review*, 3 January 1992.

62 Tony Stephens, Blessings from the King George Show, *Sydney Morning Herald*, 2 January 1992.

63 George Bush Comes to Town, *Sydney Morning Herald*, 1 January 1992.

64 Phillip Scanlan, Australian American Leadership Dialogue, *New Observer*, 2 May 2004; Brian Toohey, The Dialogue Box, *Australian Financial Review*, 24 April 2008.

65 Author interview with Nick Greiner, 6 July 2011.

surprised to find themselves sitting at the same table with the President.[66] Along with a number of other Australian and American dignitaries, a conversation inevitably arose about the state of the relationship between the two countries.[67] President Bush eventually turned to Scanlan and asked his thoughts on the matter. Scanlan obliged, expressing his concerns about the forthcoming difficulties in preserving the Australian-American relationship after the shared memories of sacrifice in World War Two passed and a new generation of leaders arose. Scanlan feared that diminishing personal bonds between the leaders of both nations would create a distance neither wanted, but may occur as each nation took the other for granted.[68]

The President listened with approval and was encouraged by Scanlan's idea of forming a new group of Australian and American leaders to cultivate fresh ties and preserve the centrality of the relationship into the future. Two nights later, Brent Scowcroft, the President's national security advisor, told Scanlan "We've spoken to people. We've checked you out. The President wants you to go ahead".[69] Less than eighteen months later, the inaugural Australian American Leadership Dialogue (AALD) took place in Washington in June 1993.

In order to bring the idea of the AALD into being, Scanlan took a break from his corporate career and tapped into his extensive Australian and American political contacts. Scowcroft had agreed to become a chief recruiter on the Republican side of American politics, along with Mel Sembler, who was the then US Ambassador to Australia. Philip Lader, who went on to become President Bill Clinton's Deputy Chief of Staff and US Ambassador to the UK, was enlisted to recruit Democrats; as was Thomas J. Schneider, a close friend of President Clinton and who later

---

66   Note that Greiner did not plan or organise for Scanlan to be seated at the same table with himself and the President. Apparently, it was happenstance that someone in Greiner's office had arranged the seating placements in this way. Author interview with Nick Greiner, 6 July 2011.

67   Others at the table are reported to have included the President's wife, Barbara Bush, Nick Greiner and his wife, Kathryn Greiner, US Secretary of State, James Baker, and US National Security Advisor, Brent Scowcroft.

68   Daniel Flitton, Man of Many Words, *The Age*, 11 August 2007, <http://www.theage.com.au/news/in-depth/man-of-many-words/2007/08/10/1186530610605.html>, accessed 1 April 2018.

69   Paul Kelly, *The March of Patriots: The Struggle for Modern Australia*, Melbourne: Melbourne University Publishing, 2010, p. 163. According to Gerard Henderson, Scanlan had been "speaking about these matters to some people privately" for one or two years before his encounter with President Bush. The visit by Bush "gave him the opportunity to do something about it". Author interview with Gerard Henderson, 7 March 2012.

came to serve on the management board of the AALD. Anne Wexler, one of Washington's most influential lobbyists, and her husband Joe Duffey, Director of the United States Information Agency (USIA) from 1993 to 1999, became important Democratic members of the AALD soon after its establishment. Wexler in particular is credited with being "instrumental" in the establishment and success of the AALD.[70] According to the *Sydney Morning Herald*, Wexler "brought a range of influential Democratic figures" into the AALD, some of whom went on to become "senior officials in the Obama Administration".[71]

The AALD also attracted strong support from the political establishment in Australia. According to the then Labor senator Nick Bolkus, recently ousted Prime Minister Bob Hawke was "fairly intricately involved" in putting the AALD together, a key member in organising the Australian side, and fundamental to "the foundations of the Dialogue".[72] Prime Minister Keating was also in full support of the AALD while his wife, Annita van Iersel, helped to financially support it in her role as General Manager of United Airlines Australia.[73] According to Don Russell, Australia's ambassador to the US at the time, the AALD had the backing of the Australian embassy, with Russell happy to lend his good name to assist in its establishment.[74]

Although the idea for the AALD was Scanlan's alone, he received considerable support for its establishment. Former Australian diplomat Richard Woolcott assisted Scanlan in the early stages of the AALD's development.[75] So did Scanlan's long-time friend and professional business associate Stephen Loosley, who helped to "put a framework around the idea".[76] Loosley supported the AALD for many years, initially as a New South Wales Labor senator and subsequently as a serving member on the Australian board of the AALD from 1999-2010.

---

70   Author interview with Mel Sembler, 21 March 2012.

71   Pacific Alliance Loses a Powerful Friend, *Sydney Morning Herald*, 11 August 2009.

72   Author interview with Nick Bolkus, 6 September 2011. It was Hawke who had personally invited Bolkus to be one of the twenty or so Australian delegates who participated in the inaugural AALD event in Washington in 1993.

73   Keating has since become a critic of the AALD, labelling it "a sort of a cult thing" where the Australian delegation are "bowing and scraping and going on". Keating Says Australia Should Focus Less On US Alliance, 11 November 2016, *7.30 with Leigh Sales, ABC News*, <http://www.abc.net.au/7.30/keating-says-australia-should-focus-less-on-us/8015204>, accessed 1 April 2018.

74   Author interview with Don Russell, 21 December 2012.

75   Author interview with Richard Woolcott, 22 March 2011.

76   Author interview with Stephen Loosley, 11 January 2012.

Scanlan used his political contacts to attract high-level participation from both major political parties in Australia.[77] Then Liberal MP David Kemp, a personal friend of Scanlan's, encouraged ministers of the Coalition shadow ministry to take an interest in the AALD after its establishment.[78] Nick Greiner also helped to gather delegates from the Liberal Party and, although defeated at the 1992 state election, went on to attend the AALD for the next ten years as a private citizen.[79] Kim Beazley, a close personal friend of Scanlan,[80] agreed to become the "standard bearer" for the ALP and subsequently became a long-standing supporter and AALD participant.[81]

Despite these cumulative efforts, the success of the AALD was the result of the personal initiative, sacrifice and determination of its founder, Phillip Scanlan. David Kemp's remarks are representative of many AALD participants I interviewed, when he claims "very few people would either have the motivation or the capacity or the linkages" to achieve the high-level commitment and quality of discussion that is the distinguishing marker of the AALD's success.[82] Scanlan remained chairman of the AALD until April 2009, when he was appointed Australian Consul-General in New York in recognition of his services and commitment to the alliance. Although no longer chairman, Scanlan remains on the board of the AALD and exerts a powerful influence over its operation and objectives.[83]

Relationship management

For 25 years, the AALD has brought together a select group of high-level politicians, government officials, business people, journalists, academics and other influential leaders from both countries for an annual private forum

---

77   According to Sheridan, "Scanlan convinced successive prime ministers Keating and Howard to do private sessions exclusively for the visiting Americans". Sheridan, *The Partnership*, p. 315.

78   Author interview with David Kemp, 31 August 2011.

79   Author interview with Nick Greiner, 6 July 2011.

80   Beazley was best man at Scanlan's wedding.

81   Kelly, *The March of Patriots*, p. 163.

82   Author interview with David Kemp, 31 August 2011.

83   As one former board member, who chose to remain anonymous, confirms, the Australian board is largely responsible for administrative functions, the selection process being "very much in the gift of the chairman". Even after Scanlan formally abdicated his role as chairman in 2009, according to Andrew Robb, "he still keeps a weather eye on all things, including the invitation list". Author interview with Andrew Robb, 15 July 2011.

on designated matters of mutual interest. Alternating between Washington and various Australian cities each year, the AALD takes place between June and August over a 2-3 day period. The forum comprises formal keynote addresses and chaired discussion sessions. The first AALD event on 11-12 June 1993 in Washington was attended by thirty-five prominent but mainly out-of-office political representatives and business leaders.[84] Since that time, the AALD has grown to attract an ever increasing number of delegates, with participation of up to 150 people at each event.[85] Without access to official records, the total number of AALD attendees over its lifetime is impossible to verify.[86]

One estimate, provided by Brian Toohey of the *Australian Financial Review*, was that between 1993 and 2008, approximately 360 delegates had attended the Dialogue's meetings.[87] Toohey names 55 Australian and 11 American participants. Research I conducted, based on public sources, identifies 253 participants from 1993-2011, many of them regular attendees. Of these, 151 (60%) were Australian delegates and 102 (40%) American. Of the Australian delegates over half were politicians, public officials and ex-officials, with an equal share from both major political parties; over a quarter came from the business sector; almost 15 per cent were media representatives and 5 per cent came from academia. While the numbers compiled are incomplete, the data size is significant enough to indicate that the AALD has been at least fairly successful in penetrating both major Australian political parties and, over the years, increasingly engaged a significant number of Australian and American political and business elites and key opinion makers in the media.

The AALD has expanded its operations by establishing numerous other regular dialogue events in addition to the central mid-year forum. These

---

84   Those participants were Richard L. Armitage, Judith Hippler Bello, Sandra Yates, Richard Woolcott, Stephen Bollenback, Dick Cheney, Patricia Ann Turner, Warwick L. Smith, James S. Gorelick, David D. Hale, Gregory Paul Sheridan, Emery Severin, Robert D. Hormats, Philip Lader, Phil Scanlan, Kevin Michael Rudd, Franklin L. Lavin, Jim Leach, Irene Kwong Moss, David Kemp, Winston Lord, Paul London, Steve Howard, Jill L. N. Hickson, Kevin G. Nealer, Douglas H. Paal, Carolyn Hewsen, Nicholas F. Greiner, Karl C. Rove, Thomas J. Schneider, Ros Gregory Garnaut, Robert B. Zoellick, Nick Bolkus, Peter Cook and Paul D. Wolfowitz. Official copy of the list of participants held by the author.

85   Stephen Loosley, The Ties That Bind, *The Australian*, 17 May 2013, <http://www.theaustralian.com.au/business/the-deal-magazine/the-ties-that-bind-story-e6frgabx-1226643018865>, accessed 1 April 2018.

86   I attempted on numerous occasions to secure an interview with Phillip Scanlan – who no doubt has access to these records – to no avail.

87   Toohey, The Dialogue Box.

include the West Coast Leadership Dialogue and the Young Leadership Dialogue, both established in 2007, the Honolulu Leadership Dialogue, which first began in 2008, and the New York Leadership Dialogue established in 2009. The AALD also initiated a Leadership Dialogue Scholar program in 2005. There is far less publicly available information about these additional dialogues. They typically attract smaller numbers of delegates than the central Dialogue and, consequently, less media attention.

Themes discussed at the AALD include economics and trade, defence and security, foreign policy, domestic politics, innovation and technology, energy and climate, education, health and social inclusion. Although the scope for discussion is wide, the focus surrounding each AALD event is often topical. Examples of major issues discussed include the 1997 East Asian financial crisis, the "war on terror" and the 2003 invasion of Iraq, the 2008 Global Financial Crisis, climate change, Australia's National Broadband Network, the ongoing threat posed by Iran and North Korea, the regional implications of the rise of China and the Obama administration's "Pivot" to Asia.

AALD sessions are exclusively for invited guests. Although the AALD is managed by an Australian and American board, by all accounts Scanlan plays the decisive role in the selection of invitees.[88] Discussions at the AALD operate under a strict non-disclosure convention that is often described as the Chatham House Rule but is in fact more narrow.[89] The AALD's rules prevent participants from disclosing the content of any comment, even where the identity of the participant is not revealed. Participants are permitted only to disclose their own attendance at AALD events and comments they themselves have made. There is strict loyalty to the non-disclosure convention, evidenced by the fact that there have been very few leaks since the AALD's establishment.

The broad objectives of the AALD were set out in the Memorandum and Articles of Division at the time of its establishment. This document stipulates the role of the AALD is to:

---

88 The vast majority of AALD participants I interviewed were personally invited by Scanlan.

89 The Chatham House Rule is an international convention that any forum may choose to invoke as a means to ensure free and frank discussion. It permits participants to use or reveal any comments made at the forum as long as the identity of all participants, bar your own, is not disclosed. For the definition of the Chatham House Rule, see Chatham House, Chatham House Rule, Royal Institute of International Affairs, <http://www.chathamhouse.org/about-us/chathamhouserule>, accessed 1 April 2018.

1. foster better relations between Australia and the United States of America whether they are of a business, economic, political, educational, or cultural nature;

2. establish a platform to maintain and develop peace and prosperity in the future in the Asia/Pacific region;

3. provide a forum to bring together leaders of policy and opinion in Australia and the United States of America;

4. focus on matters of global and regional security, international trade and economics, education, health, issues pertaining to women, management of multi-cultural societies and domestic renewal;

5. oversee the management and encourage the development of programs which endeavour to develop closer links between Australia and the United States of America.[90]

Further indication of the AALD's objectives is provided on the official website of the Dialogue which states that its mission "is to broaden and deepen mutual understanding between Australian and American leaders and to enhance the framework for regional security". The AALD claims to operate according to the "principles of bilateral interest, bipartisanship, voluntarism and leadership in the service of others, frank exchange, intergenerational perspectives, mutual tolerance and personal courtesy".[91]

In the words of Australia's former ambassador to the US and original AALD participant, Don Russell, the Dialogue was established as "a way of cementing the notion that [the US relationship] was a cornerstone of Australia's overall foreign policy".[92] In order to achieve that objective, Scanlan made the decision to focus the AALD exclusively on those in positions of power and influence rather than the general public. The "initial spur to set up the Dialogue", states Hugh White, "was to ensure a deeper body of support [for the alliance] amongst informed and elite opinion" in both Australia and the US.[93]

---

90   Australian American Education Leadership Foundation Limited, Memorandum and Articles of Association, 29 April 1993, p. 22. Note that the constitution was amended in 2006 and the description of these official purposes were deleted and not replaced.

91   Australian American Leadership Dialogue, AALD, <http://www.aald.org/australian-american-leadership-dialogue>, accessed 1 April 2018.

92   Author interview with Don Russell, 21 December 2012.

93   Author interview with Professor Hugh White, 2 September 2011.

As noted above, the AALD emerged in the context of widespread concern about the future of the alliance in the post-Cold War era, and a belief that the next generation of leaders did not have the same degree of emotional attachment and personal commitment to the alliance as those in the past. As President Bush conveyed in a letter to Scanlan prior to the inaugural AALD event in May 1993:

> The ties between the United States and Australia resulting from our shared experiences in the Pacific War were and are real ... You have correctly identified the challenge before us – to engineer a smooth passing of the baton in American/Australian relations from the generation which forged the alliance in the presence of war to the generations which must work together for a permanent, productive, and prosperous peace.[94]

Founding member, David Kemp, recalls that "Scanlan believed ... there was no foundation of personal relationships which could provide links into the future", and so he sought to "develop a whole series of networks between Australians and Americans at the leadership level that would build on and expand the relationships which had come out of the [Second World] War". This perception, Kemp adds, "was widely shared and one he [Scanlan] generated" about the purpose of the Dialogue.[95] This goal is described on the AALD's website as "relationship management between current and likely future leaders from both countries".[96]

Apart from instilling the importance of the alliance into the next generation of elite, discussions at AALD events and personal relationships cultivated there are intended to create tangible benefits for both countries. This is articulated on the AALD's website as "leveraging Australian access in the United States, and American access in Australia, into real influence on matters of respective and designated mutual interest".[97] From an

---

94   Letter from George Bush to Phil Scanlan, Convenor of the Australia-America Leadership Dialogue, dated 31 May 1993. Quoted in Elena Douglas and Diane Stone, The Informal Diplomacy of the Australian American Leadership Dialogue, *Australian Journal of International Affairs*, vol. 69, no. 1, 2015, p. 25.

95   Author interview with David Kemp, 31 August 2011.

96   This version of the website is now defunct. Australian American Leadership Dialogue, Home Page, <http://www.aald.org>, 9 February 2013, original archived at <http://web.archive.org/web/20130209070754/http://www.aald.org/index/index/page/home>, accessed 1 April 2018.

97   Australian American Leadership Dialogue, Home Page.

Australian perspective, Scanlan states the "primary aim" of the AALD is as follows:

> [To] help ensure that Australian policy makers and leaders in the broader community have knowledge of United States decision makers and real time understanding of their views on issues that we, as Australians, determine to be most important for Australia's national interests.[98]

A core purpose of the AALD, according to one board member, is to "keep us both informed – keep both societies informed – on what the other's thinking about so they can more best calibrate their own policy settings".[99] The intent is that information exchange will lead to greater cooperation in pursuing commonly agreed strategies in the world. According to the AALD's website, the "high-calibre of discussion and debate" at Dialogue events "leads to the formation of support for strategic policy in both countries".[100]

The objectives of "relationship management" and "translating access into influence" are accompanied by a third objective of the AALD, which is to provide an open forum for critical discussion and debate. Ostensibly, as a private diplomatic initiative operating in an unofficial capacity, the AALD provides a forum where non-official perspectives on the relationship can be introduced and debated. The views of *The Australian*'s foreign affair's editor, Greg Sheridan, are typical, although not universal, when he claims that discussions at the Dialogue are "frank, fearless, friendly, fierce and intense, with every assertion challengeable and contested".[101] Accordingly, AALD board member Professor Andrew MacIntyre states that participants at the Dialogue "come in with just an incredible range of views ... there's been some of the hardest questioning of different areas where we've got interests that I've witnessed anywhere".[102] When asked if the AALD offered the opportunity for serious discussion and debate about Australia-US relations

---

98 Phillip Scanlan, Australia and the United States, Towards a Deeper Relationship, speech to the Australian Institute of International Affairs (WA Branch), 26 July 2005.

99 Author interview with Professor Andrew MacIntyre, 28 June 2011.

100 Australian American Leadership Dialogue, AALD, <http://www.aald.org/australian-american-leadership-dialogue>, accessed 1 April 2018.

101 Greg Sheridan, Power Talking, *The Australian*, 23 July 2003.

102 Author interview with Professor Andrew MacIntyre, 28 June 2011.

and the nature of US foreign policy, journalist Paul Kelly replied, "that's certainly my view".[103]

However, on rare occasions, the AALD has been publicly criticised for failing to live up to this expectation or apply an adequate degree of scrutiny to the alliance and American foreign policy.[104] Scanlan strenuously denies the allegation that the AALD is a "cheer squad for American foreign policy" or that dissenting viewpoints are pushed out. These criticisms are "just plain dumb", he maintains.[105] Nevertheless, as demonstrated in chapter eight, there is ample evidence to suggest the AALD works assiduously to frame discussion and debate within narrow bounds.

There is no precise method for measuring the impact of the AALD or, for that matter, the success of any private diplomatic initiative.[106] Certainly, AALD participants are almost unanimous in declaring its extraordinary level of achievement in helping to both strengthen personal relationships and reinforce existing sentiments of shared values and interests. Nevertheless, the AALD's impact in relationship management should not be exaggerated, given it operates in the context of already strong, widespread and long-standing feelings of goodwill and friendship between leaders in both countries.

The claim that the AALD has made a substantial impact at the policy level generates far more controversy than its apparent success at relationship management. Former Australian Foreign Minister Alexander Downer argues that while the Dialogue "is a good opportunity for networking ... you can't seriously say it has influenced policy. They sort of sit around

---

103 Author interview with Paul Kelly, 20 January 2012.

104 Scott Burchill, Gillard's Fawning Over Obama a Bad Start on Diplomatic Front, *Sydney Morning Herald*, 30 June 2010, <http://www.smh.com.au/federal-politics/political-opinion/gillards-fawning-over-obama-a-bad-start-on-diplomatic-front-20100629-zj3h.html>, accessed 1 April 2018; David Day, Bowing to Duchess Diplomacy, *Sydney Morning Herald*, 8 June 2012, <http://www.smh.com.au/federal-politics/political-opinion/bowing-to-duchess-diplomacy-20120607-1zysh.html>, accessed 1 April 2018; Flitton, Man of Many Words; Alan Ramsey, The Sermon Bush Wants to Hear, *Sydney Morning Herald*, 12 June 2004, <http://www.smh.com.au/articles/2004/06/11/1086749896060.html>, accessed 1 April 2018; Toohey, The Dialogue Box.

105 Quoted in Flitton.

106 This is largely because most of the benefits of private diplomatic initiatives are intangible and therefore unquantifiable, making any attempt to gauge their success at the policy level "highly problematic". Desmond Ball, Anthony Milner and Brendan Taylor, Track 2 Security Dialogue in the Asia–Pacific: Reflections and Future Directions, *Asian Security*, vol. 2, no. 3, 2006, p. 182.

and shoot the breeze".[107] Another former Australian Foreign Minister, Gareth Evans, holds a similar view. While "strongly in favour" of private diplomatic initiatives and acknowledging the importance of the "substantive discussion" that takes place within the AALD, Evans ultimately views it as a "fairly marginal enterprise in the scheme of things".[108]

On the other hand, strong advocates and long-standing participants of the AALD, such as Peter Hartcher and Paul Kelly, claim it has played a direct role in diplomacy. Two often quoted examples are the AALD's apparent success in helping to convince leaders in Washington to back Australia's 1999 intervention into East Timor and, secondly, its role in facilitating the emergence of the 2005 Australia United States Free Trade Agreement (AUSFTA).[109] In general terms, Kelly argues that if the AALD "had never existed then I think things [between Australia and the US] would have been diminished. I've got no doubt about that".[110]

Those who are more detached from the AALD tend to hold a different opinion. When asked to identify which issues the Dialogue has played a significant role in impacting within either Australian or US policies, the answer from Hugh White is "none". Since its establishment, there has been "no outcome that has occurred which wouldn't have occurred without the Dialogue".[111] In a similar vein, Paul Dibb asks rhetorically, "Is the Dialogue all that influential? Is it really all that powerful? Or is it a figment of the imaginations of Scanlan and indeed, influential journalists like Sheridan and Kelly?" In the final analysis, Dibb argues, the AALD has not substantially altered "the importance, shape and direction of the relationship".[112]

Undoubtedly, the AALD is one small part of a much larger and long-standing established network of close and extensive relationships at the government, military, intelligence and economic levels that ultimately determine the course of the alliance. Nevertheless, it would be wrong to

---

107   Quoted in Toohey, The Dialogue Box.

108   Author interview with Gareth Evans, 10 April 2012.

109   See, for example, Peter Hartcher, Are We Looking Less Like Americans?, *Sydney Morning Herald*, 18 March 2014, <http://www.smh.com.au/comment/are-we-looking-less-like-americans-20140317-34xwx.html>, accessed 1 April 2018. More on the role of the AALD and AUSFTA is provided later in this chapter.

110   Author interview with Paul Kelly, 20 January 2012.

111   Author interview with Professor Hugh White, 2 September 2011.

112   On the two journalists in question, Dibb adds, "One of whom I've got great regard for, that is Kelly, and the other one I don't". Author interview with Emeritus Professor Paul Dibb, 13 September 2011.

dismiss the impact of the AALD. As I relate in subsequent chapters, the AALD's singular success has been in reinforcing and deepening support for the alliance; an achievement which may be limited in scope but is nonetheless highly effective in ensuring the preservation of the status quo.

Embodying the alliance orthodoxy

Although the AALD is singularly dedicated to strengthening the Australia-US relationship, it claims not to advocate any particular agenda or embody a singular, monolithic view of the alliance. Alexander Downer speaks for a number of participants when he says the AALD "is not an organisation with a point of view. It's a whole lot of different points of view".[113] Former board member and participant Sam Lipski concurs that "You can't talk about the Dialogue as if it has a kind of completely united and coherent view. It's not a person. It's not a monolithic organisation. Far from it".[114]

The officially sanctioned view of the AALD is that it merely provides a forum for discussion and debate between both countries on matters of mutual interest. As Greg Sheridan writes, "at Scanlan's insistence and with the enthusiastic endorsement of all its participants, the Dialogue takes no position on any issue beyond the utility of the US-Australia relationship".[115] Much depends, however, on what is inferred by the "utility" of the alliance. In the eyes of former participant Hugh White, the AALD's outlook is based on questionable assumptions:

> [It] embodied from the outset a certain view about what makes the alliance and the relationship strong, what makes it valuable to Australia and what might pose a threat to those strengths and values. It would also be fair to say ... I think the accounts of those things are contestable and quite possibly wrong.[116]

While the AALD claims its goal is to merely strengthen the Australia-US relationship in the interests of both countries, in reality it functions to sustain the orthodox conception of the alliance. As one recent study declared, the AALD "was founded as a means of sustaining an existing historical

---

113   Author interview with Alexander Downer, 14 September 2011.

114   Author interview with Sam Lipski, 25 October 2011.

115   Sheridan, Power Talking.

116   Author interview with Professor Hugh White, 2 September 2011.

narrative of alliance".[117] As detailed in Part I, this narrative subscribes to a view of the alliance as a "special relationship" rooted in shared values and common security interests, first forged in the mutual sacrifices suffered by both nations during World War Two and solidified in every major conflict fought together thereafter. Once again, in the words of Hugh White:

> [The AALD] exposed emerging political leaders to a view of the alliance as something that transcended politics and even policy. It encouraged the view that the alliance was rooted in, and was indeed essential to, Australia's national identity.[118]

As the driving force behind the AALD, Scanlan is steadfast in his belief that "alliances with depth are driven by common and shared values", and it is those "values which today are the glue that binds the US and Australia as strongly as ever".[119] This semi-mystical belief in the importance of values to the Australia-US alliance underpins the central objective of the AALD: to strengthen the personal relationships between leaders of both countries and consequently their commitment to the alliance.

Many current and former participants echo the words of founding member Nick Bolkus, when he states that the purpose of the AALD is to facilitate relationship building where leaders from both countries can "get to know each other and develop strong personal understandings" and "form strong bonds based on common values and interests".[120] For many AALD participants I interviewed, the personal connections it facilitates are what make it such a valuable and effective institution. According to journalist and long-standing AALD participant Peter Hartcher, the Dialogue helps to "strengthen relationships and therefore strengthen the alliance", specifically by "creating familiarity and thickening those [personal] bonds".[121]

Apart from embodying a values-based understanding of the Australia-US relationship, the AALD adheres to the orthodoxy that the alliance is driven by mutual security interests, and specifically that it is indispensable for Australia's defence. Scanlan has repeatedly argued that the alliance

---

117   Douglas and Stone, The Informal Diplomacy of the Australian American Leadership Dialogue, p. 20.

118   Hugh White, Strategic Overreach, *American Review*, 17 August 2014, p. 12.

119   Phillip Scanlan, More Than Just Brothers In Arms, *Australian Financial Review*, 10 October 2001.

120   Author interview with Nick Bolkus, 6 September 2011.

121   Author interview with Peter Hartcher, 29 October 2011.

underwrites the security of Australia and, moreover, that the "defence subsidy" it provides is often unacknowledged and unappreciated[122] – a belief restated on the AALD's website.[123] Australia's national interests, Scanlan wrote in the wake of the 9/11 terrorist attacks, "are fundamentally unchanged: to cement the alliance with the US in order to underwrite the sustained security of Australian citizens".[124]

Scanlan also adheres to the conventional wisdom that US benign hegemony, facilitated in part through the Australia-US alliance, is vital to the security, stability and prosperity of the Asia–Pacific. As he writes:

> [The] Asia–Pacific is a region rich in economic potential and, without a working security network, full of crises waiting to happen. Australia cannot pursue its aspirations in the absence of a comprehensive, multi-layered US strategic engagement across the Asia–Pacific.[125]

These beliefs and perceptions were embedded in the objectives of the AALD on its establishment. Founding member of the Dialogue, Nick Greiner, explains that the "overriding objective, from an Australian point of view, was to ensure the continuing positive engagement of the United States in the Pacific. Australia was, in a sense, a subset of that. That was undoubtedly the overriding purpose".[126] Another founding member of the Dialogue, David Kemp, agrees that one of the objectives was to "keep the American leadership on both sides focussed on the Pacific and East Asia" and to "influence the American strategy" by persuading the US to "stabilise the East Asia region".[127]

The importance of maintaining US engagement in the region remains a consistent theme at the AALD. At the third Dialogue event in 1995, one of the key messages presented to the Americans from the Australian delegation was the following imperative:

---

122   Scanlan, More Than Just Brothers In Arms; Phillip Scanlan, New World Disorder, *Australian Financial Review*, 3 July 2003; Phillip Scanlan, Australia and the United States, Towards a Deeper Relationship; Phillip Scanlan, Australia Must Learn How to Benefit from the US Alliance, *The Age*, 30 January 2007.

123   Australian American Leadership Dialogue, History, <http://www.aald.org/history>, accessed 1 April 2018.

124   Scanlan, More Than Just Brothers In Arms.

125   Scanlan. Also see President's Departure Sets Legacy Deadline, *Australian Financial Review*, 2 January 2007.

126   Author interview with Nick Greiner, 6 July 2011.

127   Author interview with David Kemp, 31 August 2011.

Don't retreat from the region. There is a great and overriding need – strategically, militarily and politically – to continue the US military presence throughout the region. In a post-Cold War world, the maintenance of a forward military presence is a stabilising factor. The visibility of the West, as led by the United States, is critical.[128]

Ten years later, Scanlan reiterated that "confirmation of US engagement in Asia has always been a regular part" of what is described as "the menu at the Leadership Dialogue".[129] Today, the official website of the AALD states that its mission is to "enhance the framework for regional security in a manner that underwrites economic and cultural prosperity for Australian and American citizens".[130]

More recently, the AALD has focused on recreating the policy ortho-doxies of the alliance to fit the new geopolitical realities emerging from China's growing power. From a regional perspective, the AALD is con-sidered to be a "willing camp follower" in America's strategy to hedge against the emergence of an undesirable multilateral regional order.[131] According to White, the AALD's "ethos" is that American primacy can and should be sustained in the face of the Chinese challenge and that Australia's best interests are in supporting them doing so.[132]

When considered as a whole, the agenda of the AALD is not sur-prising given it accords with the long-standing bipartisan commitment among Australian foreign policy-makers and strategic elite to support and strengthen the US alliance and remain committed to a regional security and economic framework underpinned by US hegemony. In terms of ideol-ogy, the AALD clearly embodies the conventional alliance orthodoxy. The salient point is that the AALD's overriding objective is not to challenge this traditional thinking but to protect, strengthen and legitimise it.

---

128   Bruce C. Wolpe, A Message to Clinton, Stick Around, Mate, *Australian Financial Review*, 7 September 1995.

129   Scanlan, Australia and the United States, Towards a Deeper Relationship.

130   Australian American Leadership Dialogue, AALD, <http://www.aald.org/australian-american-leadership-dialogue>, accessed 1 April 2018.

131   Douglas and Stone, The Informal Diplomacy of the Australian American Leadership Dialogue, p. 24.

132   Author interview with Professor Hugh White, 2 September 2011.

Chapter Seven

CORPORATE INFLUENCE

A neoliberal agenda

An important part of the AALD's objective of preserving and deepening the alliance orthodoxy among members of the elite has been a commitment to accelerating the neoliberal economic order strongly promoted by both Australia and the US in the post-Cold War era. As Erik Paul points out, there are mutual interests between Australia's national security elite and corporate leadership regarding America's place as the world's dominant power, in that this "provides the hegemonic stability necessary to maintain a global neoliberal economic order that is favourable to Western economic interests".[1]

Some tension has emerged in recent times between the defence establishment, the intelligence community and those sections of Australia's corporate elite with large business interests in China.[2] Some business leaders have voiced concerns about the fact that Australia's growing strategic relationship with the US appears to be increasingly directed at containing China.[3] Nevertheless, this tension has not fundamentally altered Canberra's commitment to, or the AALD's enthusiasm for, supporting

---

1   Erik Paul, *Neoliberal Australia and US Imperialism in East Asia*, New York: Palgrave Macmillan, 2012, p. 10.

2   When developing the 2009 Defence White Paper, Australia's defence hawks rejected the view of the intelligence community which held that China's military expansion posed little threat to Australia's long-term security. Cameron Stewart, Spy Chiefs Cross Swords Over China as Kevin Rudd Backs Defence Hawks, *The Australian*, 11 April 2009, <http://www.theaustralian.com.au/news/spy-chiefs-cross-swords-over-china/story-e6frg6n6-1225697020657>, accessed 1 April 2018.

3   Vince Scappatura, The US "Pivot" to Asia, the China Spectre and the Australian-American Alliance, *The Asia–Pacific Journal*, vol. 12, issue 36, no. 3, 9 September 2014, <http://apjjf.org/2014/12/36/Vince-Scappatura/4178/article.html>, accessed 1 April 2018.

American regional hegemony. As Nick Bisley points out, Australia is "doubling down on American primacy":

> Although scholarly and public debates have traversed a wide range of policy options, Canberra has made a very clear decision about its strategic future: it will cleave very closely to its alliance with the United States and to the vision of regional order which depends on continued American primacy.[4]

When the AALD first emerged in the early 1990s one of the key messages stressed to the Americans was to immediately "strengthen APEC" and take steps to ensure the "acceleration of the free trade regime".[5] In more recent times, as David Kemp plainly declares, "the Dialogue is free trade. There's no doubt about that. It would be more [pro-] free trade than the Australian political system as a whole or the American political system as a whole".[6] The most conspicuous example of the AALD's neoliberal agenda is the advocacy role it played in bringing about the 2005 Australia United States Free Trade Agreement (AUSFTA). The underlying neoliberal agenda of AUSFTA that sought to increase the rights of corporations and reduce the rights of the Australian government to regulate corporate activity have been well documented.[7]

Advocates of the AALD frequently point to its role in facilitating the emergence of the AUSFTA as evidence of its real impact at the policy level, although this claim has been contested.[8] Speaking in retrospect, Scanlan maintains the AALD "made a significant contribution" in facilitating

---

4   Nick Bisley, Australia and the Region that 1945 Created: The Long History of Contemporary Strategy, *The Journal of Korean Defence Analysis*, vol. 27, no. 2, June 2015, p. 257.

5   Bruce C. Wolpe, A Message to Clinton, Stick Around, Mate, *Australian Financial Review*, 7 September 1995.

6   Author interview with David Kemp, 31 August 2011.

7   Ann Capling, *All the Way with the USA: Australia, the US and Free Trade*, Sydney: UNSW Press, 2005; Linda Weiss, Elizabeth Thurbon and John Matthews, *How to Kill a Country: Australia's Devastating Trade Deal with the United States*, Crows Nest, Australia: Allen & Unwin, 2004; Patricia Ranald, "The Australia-US Free Trade Agreement: Reinforcing Re-peripherisation" in Paul Bowes, Ray Broomhill, Teresa Gutierrez-Haces and Stephen McBride (eds), *International Trade and Neoliberal Globalism: Towards Re-peripherisation in Australia, Canada and Mexico?*, London: Routledge, 2008.

8   Alexander Downer, Australia's foreign minister when AUSFTA was being negotiated, states categorically that the AALD didn't have "any influence over it one way or another". Author interview with Alexander Downer, 14 September 2011. On the other hand, a number of other AALD participants I interviewed refute Downer's claims, dismissing it as an attempt to take all of the credit for the trade agreement.

AUSFTA.[9] Many participants of the AALD from both countries concur with Scanlan's claim.[10] In his in-depth account of the behind-the-scenes lobbying that went on during AUSFTA negotiations, the *Australian Financial Review*'s Mark Davis described the AALD as an "important locus for the unfolding FTA debate", where key American officials strongly promoted the trade agreement.[11]

Whatever the actual impact the AALD had on the emergence of the AUSFTA, Scanlan was certainly a fierce supporter of the agreement. He urged the then Prime Minister John Howard to broaden Australia's push for wider economic integration with the US. He candidly stated that the AALD would put the subject on its own agenda and "strongly advocate" for FTA acceptance at official levels.[12] Scanlan praised AUSFTA as an "act of strategic engagement by Australia that is long overdue", dismissing concerns that it might damage Australia's sugar and dairy industries, labelling them "uncompetitive" and in need of "transformation". Opposition to the agreement by the Labor Party was, in Scanlan's words, merely "political point scoring".[13] Significantly, the reservations expressed by the Labor Party at the time, supported by intense lobbying and debate undertaken by civil society organisations, resulted in a number of important amendments to the final agreement that protected crucial elements of Australia's social welfare system. Arguably, these were ultimately inadequate and left

---

9   Quoted in Brian Toohey, The Dialogue Box, *Australian Financial Review*, 24 April 2008.

10   John W. H. Denton says the Dialogue created the "environment" to make AUSFTA possible. Author interview with John W. H. Denton, 15 February 2012. Stephen Loosley believes "Australia's position was strengthened" because of the work of Dialogue participants. Author interview with Stephen Loosley, 11 January 2012. Sam Lipski argues the Dialogue was a "big factor" during AUSFTA, particularly as a testing ground for anticipating the wider debate in both countries. Author interview with Sam Lipski, 25 October 2011. David Kemp contends that the negotiation of AUSFTA was "one of the instances you could say where the Dialogue actually played a direct role in diplomacy". Author interview with David Kemp, 31 August 2011. On the American side, Robert Zoellick reportedly said that AUSFTA was "really an outgrowth of what the Dialogue was doing". Peter Hartcher, Howard Sets the Trap for a Younger Player, *Sydney Morning Herald*, 18 June 2004, <http://www.smh.com.au/articles/2004/06/17/1087245040341.html>, accessed 1 April 2018.

11   Mark Davis, Quick Dealing at the Business End of Trade, *Australian Financial Review*, 7 January 2005.

12   Peter Hartcher, Push for Broader Deal with US, *Australian Financial Review*, 29 January 2002.

13   Phillip Scanlan, A Trade Pact to Prise US Door Open, *Sydney Morning Herald*, 2 March 2004, <http://www.smh.com.au/articles/2004/03/01/1078117362609.html>, accessed 1 April 2018.

the door open for future changes.[14] In any case, Scanlan "applauded" the Howard government "for pursing FTA talks with the United States" and called on the opposition to "support a comprehensive US FTA".[15]

The most significant private advocate of the AUSFTA from the US side of the AALD was the late Anne Wexler. As previously noted, Wexler was a pivotal influencer in the AALD. Former AALD board member Sam Lipski refers to Wexler as the "anchor person", or the "Phil Scanlan at the Washington end".[16] When Wexler died in 2009, a tribute was placed on the home page of the AALD's website.[17] Commemorating her role as a serving member on the board for fifteen years, she was described as "one of our own" and a "key player … in the development of the Leadership Dialogue." Wexler was one of Washington's important power brokers, dubbed part of the "superlobbyist"[18] elite in Washington and "easily the most influential female lobbyist in a world still dominated by men".[19] She was introduced to the AALD early in its development by her husband Joseph Duffey, director of the United States Information Agency (USIA) at the time.

According to the former president and secretary of the American board of the AALD, Alan Dunn, Wexler was "thrilled and captivated" by her first Dialogue event and subsequently agreed to serve as Treasurer on the board. She proceeded to use her "influence" and "convening power as this uber-lobbyist in Washington to bring people in to participate".[20] Robert Walker, a former Republican congressman and later chairman of the American board of the Dialogue, became a partner in Wexler's lobbying firm, still known today as Wexler and Walker Public Policy Associates. Robert Cramer, a former Democrat congressman and Dialogue board member, also joined the lobbying firm in 2009.

---

14   Ranald, "The Australia-US Free Trade Agreement: Reinforcing Re-peripherisation" in Paul Bowes, Ray Broomhill, Teresa Gutierrez-Haces and Stephen McBride (eds), *International Trade and Neoliberal Globalism*, pp. 42-5.

15   Phillip Scanlan, submission to the Secretary, Senate Foreign Affairs, Defence and Trade References Committee, 3 January 2004.

16   Author interview with Sam Lipski, 25 October 2011.

17   Wexler was also made an Honorary Officer of the Order of Australia by the Australian Government for her work on AUSFTA and the AALD. Note that the tribute to Wexler has since been removed from the AALD's website.

18   Matt Bai, Anne Wexler: Superlobbyist, *New York Times*, 27 December 2009, <http://www.nytimes.com/2009/12/27/magazine/27wexler-t.html>, accessed 1 April 2018.

19   Douglas Martin, Anne Wexler, An Influential Political Operative and Lobbyist, Is Dead At 79, *New York Times*, 8 August 2009, <http://www.nytimes.com/2009/08/09/us/politics/09wexler.html>, accessed 1 April 2018.

20   Author interview with Alan Dunn, 23 November 2011.

After Australia announced its ambition to pursue an FTA with the US in late 2000, Wexler was commissioned by elements of big business to fund a lobbying effort on Capitol Hill. The Wexler Group had previously represented the pro-NAFTA business coalition of Fortune 500 companies in the early 1990s and, together with her husband's efforts at the USIA, employed a sophisticated propaganda campaign to sell the trade agreement to the American public and a reluctant Mexico and Canada.[21] Wexler proceeded to launch the American-Australian FTA Coalition in mid-2001 as the prime US lobbying vehicle in pursuit of the AUSFTA. The coalition consisted of over 300 corporations and business associations including AALD supporters such as Boeing, ALCOA, Coca-Cola, ExxonMobil and Visy Industries.[22]

There was some disagreement about the benefits of multilateral versus bilateral trade agreements within the AALD. However, it can be said there was not "plenty of vigorous debate" on the "merits" of AUSFTA, as Scanlan has claimed. Toohey writes that "apparently, no one in the AALD raised the incongruity of including a highly protectionist measure on intellectual property in the FTA". That is, the extension of copyright protection from 50 to 70 years, which "had nothing to do with trade liberalisation and everything to do with providing a windfall gain for corporations owning a back catalogue of movies, music and books".[23] According to Mark Latham, who was leader of the opposition when AUSFTA was enacted, the role of the AALD was:

[To] just stamp this as approved. They didn't want anyone to question it or amend it as we ultimately did. So they are a voice for American foreign investment and free trade which they are entitled to be but it's partly funded by the commercial proceeds of that agenda.[24]

As Latham suggests, the AALD's explicit "free trade" agenda is underscored by its extensive links to the corporate world, including as the major source of its funding. After its founding in 1993, Scanlan established two parent organisations to secure funds, enlist participants and coordinate each AALD event and associated programs. The Australian American

21 Nancy Snow, *Propaganda, Inc. Selling America's Culture to the World (3rd Edition)*, New York: Seven Stories Press, 2010, pp. 115-122.
22 A similar pro-FTA lobby group was set up in Australia – the AUSTA coalition. Mark Davis, Forging a New Trade Route, *Australian Financial Review*, 5 January 2005; Davis, Quick Dealing at the Business End of Trade.
23 Toohey, The Dialogue Box.
24 Author interview with Mark Latham, 22 November 2011.

Education Leadership Foundation was established to manage the Dialogue's interests in Australia, and its counterpart, the American Australian Education Leadership Foundation, was to manage those operations relating to the US.[25] Both organisations are entirely funded from private sources and declared as non-for-profit educational institutions with tax deductible status in their respective host nations.

Although board members have changed with time, a significant proportion of current and former board members of both the Australian and American foundations have consisted of corporate executives and lobbyists.[26] Contributors to the AALD are mostly confidential but I was able to source a partial list from financial reports submitted to ASIC in Australia and the IRS in the United States, illustrated in tables 1, 2 and 3.

Table 1: Total Fiscal Year Contributions*

Fiscal Year	Contributions (American-Australian Foundation)	Contributions (Australian-American Foundation)
1993	Unavailable	181 000
1994	5 000	142 000
1995	10 000	101 000
1996	28 500	101 000
1997	57 713	Unreported
1998	70 000	112 910
1999	58 500	55 610
2000	65 000	Unreported
2001	11 100	Unreported
2002	87 000	Unreported
2003	97 500	Unreported
2004	195 000	Unreported
2005	77 865	Unreported
2006	165 000	Unreported
2007	80 010	Unreported
2008	190 000	Unreported
2009	148 000	Unreported
2010	365 000	Unreported
2011	340 000	Unreported
2012	150 000	Unreported
Total	**USD 2 201 188**	**AUD 693 520**

* Data for American-Australian Foundation sourced from Form 990 submitted to the IRS, FY1998–2012. Data for Australian-American Foundation sourced from Financial Returns submitted to ASIC, FY1993–2009.

25 Hereafter, the Australian American Foundation and vice versa.
26 These include Amanda Johnston-Pell, Anne Wexler, Fleur Harlan, Heather Podesta, Hugh Morgan, Julie Singer Scanlan, Kevin Nealer, Mehrdad Baghai, Martin Adams, Phillip Scanlan, Richard Pratt, Robert Cramer, Robert Walker, Thomas J. Schneider and Warwick Smith.

Table 2: American Australian Education Leadership Foundation Contributors[†]

Contributor	FY2000	FY1999	FY1998	FY1997	Total
ANZ Bank	-	10 000	10 000	-	20 000
Bank of America	-	-	10 000	-	10 000
Charles Schwab	15 000	-	-	-	15 000
CSR American Companies Foundation	20 000	-	-	-	20 000
EDS	-	5000	5000	15 000	25 000
Peter J Carre	-	5000	5000	5000	15 000
Phillip Morris Co Inc	10 000	15 000	15 000	5000	45 000
Restructuring Associates	-	-	10 000	-	10 000
Sembler Fund	10 000	-	10 000	10 000	30 000
Tampa-Orlando Pinellas Jewish Fund (Sembler)	-	10 000	-	-	10 000
Texas Utilities Australia	-	-	-	10 000	10 000
USA Agri Corp	10 000	-	5000	-	15 000

Contributor	FY2011	FY2010	FY2009	FY2008	Total
ALCOA Foundation	45 000	50 000	25 000	50 000	170 000

† All amounts in USD. Data for FY1997–2000 sourced from Form 990 (FY2001) submitted by American-Australian Foundation to IRS. Data for FY2008–2011 sourced from Form 990 (FY2009–2012) submitted by ALCOA Foundation to the IRS.

Table 3: Australian American Education Leadership Foundation Contributors[‡]

Contributor	FY1996	FY1995	FY1994	FY1993	Total
Terrace Tower Pty Ltd	20 000	5 000	10 000	20 000	55 000
Broken Hill Pty Ltd	40 000	40 000	40 000	40 000	160 000
Westfield Holdings Ltd	-	-	-	25 000	25 000
Kellogg (Aust) Pty Ltd	-	-	5 000	5 000	10 000
David Holdings Pty Ltd	5 000	5 000	10 000	10 000	30 000
Bridge Oil Ltd	-	-	-	20 000	20 000
Burns Philip & Co Ltd	-	-	-	5 000	5 000
Mr Phillip Scanlan	-	-	-	6 000	6 000
CRA Ltd	-	20 000	-	20 000	40 000
Australian Meat & Live-stock Corporation	-	-	20 000	20 000	40 000
Philip Morris Ltd	-	-	-	10 000	10 000
Western Mining Corporation Ltd	-	15 000	15 000	-	30 000
Arthur Anderson	-	-	10 000	-	10 000
Boral Ltd	-	-	20 000	-	20 000
Coopers & Lybrand	-	-	6 000	-	6 000
Caterpillar of Australia Ltd	5 000	5 000	5 000	-	15 000
Norwich Life	5 000	-	-	-	5 000
Korn Ferry	5 000	-	-	-	5 000
Nike Australia Pty Ltd	11 000	11 000	-	-	22 000
Ambassador Bill Lane	-	-	1 000	-	1 000
Richard Pratt	10 000	-	-	-	10 000

Contributor	2012	2011	1990s–2000s (12yrs)	Total
Pratt Foundation	100 000	100 000	660 000 (55 000 p/y)	860 000

‡ Note all amounts in AUD. Data for FY1993–96 sourced from financial returns submitted by the Australian-American Foundation to ASIC. Data on Pratt Foundation is an estimate provided to me by Sam Lipski (Chief Executive).[27]

27   Lipski estimates the Pratt Foundation contributed approximately $55,000 p.a. for twelve or thirteen years and, after a small break, returned with a renewed commitment under the leadership of Anthony Pratt in 2011 for $100,000 p.a. for at least two years.

The information obtained is limited due to the lack of voluntary disclosure. Nonetheless, it provides a reasonable indication of both the sources and amounts of private funding. As might be expected, it is large Australian or American businesses with interests or subsidiaries in each respective country that dominate.

Further confirmation about the corporate backing of the AALD can be gleaned from a brochure celebrating the twentieth anniversary of the Dialogue in 2012. "Supporters" are listed as Qantas, Australia Post, NAB, Visy Industries, Chevron, ConocoPhillips, Corrs Chambers Westgarth, AARNet, ALCOA, ANZ, BHP Billiton, Boeing, Brambles, CISCO, Coca Cola South Pacific, Ernst & Young, ExxonMobil, New Litho, PricewaterhouseCoopers, Visa and Woodside Petroleum.[28] Visy Industries, cited as a "key supporter" in the brochure, has been a central sponsor of the AALD since its early foundation years. Alan Dunn states that the late Richard Pratt played a key role:

> [He] played a very, very important function. He hosted us. He gave us venues where we could get together ... he used what he had a lot of, which was resources and money, to sponsor us. It takes money to make the Dialogue run and he was a generous contributor.[29]

Sam Lipski, a close personal friend of Pratt and Chief Executive of the charitable Pratt Foundation, recalls that Pratt wanted to get involved in the AALD early on because of his many connections with the US and he "was then very much involved in getting the Visy Industries business off the ground in the United States".[30]

Unsurprisingly, big business takes full advantage of their sponsorship and presence at the AALD to pursue their interests. The primary motivation is to gain access to government thinking on issues that may affect their interests and also make representations to government officials on behalf of those interests.[31] The representative of one Australian transnational corporate

---

28   Australian American Leadership Dialogue, Honolulu 2012, 21-23 October Honolulu, Hawaii.

29   Author interview with Alan Dunn, 23 November 2011.

30   Author interview with Sam Lipski, 25 October 2011.

31   It is reasonable to infer that most of the businesses that sponsor the AALD also participate in discussions. Lipski states that during his time as a board member anyone who had made a considerable donation would often be invited to participate or observe "out of courtesy". Author interview with Sam Lipski, 25 October 2011. Corporate tables are available at AALD events for purchase. At the 2011 Dialogue in Perth, for example, corporate tables of ten for the "Gala Dinner" were made available for $5000 per table and included a $3500 donation.

donor, who wished to remain anonymous, provided the following reasons for the corporation's long-standing commitment to the AALD. These are: to support Australia's national interests, to benefit the profile and reputation of the company and, in particular, in order to help understand the environment in which the company operates. According to this senior executive, understanding "what risks are out there, what trends, what debates", and "being able to hear from the US administration, White House level people and, in Australia, from ministers", is "pretty useful" for any company that operates internationally.[32]

Alan Dunn concurs, arguing that business leaders who attend the AALD "get to see who's making policies. They get to hear who's making decisions and what they're thinking about and what the key issues are".[33] When he was an executive at BHP Billiton, Tom Harley brought the company back into the AALD after it had been absent for some years in order to re-energise its US relationships:

> [BHP Billiton] had under baked its US relationships. It had relationships with different communities in the US where it had investments and so on but it had very little engagement with the policy makers ... It enabled us to talk to a whole lot of people that we weren't talking to before ... [34]

While a large company like BHP has no trouble getting access to policy-makers, the AALD has the advantage of bringing them altogether in one room, providing the opportunity for multiple meetings in one trip and in one place that would otherwise take weeks to organise and conduct. Moreover, it is not the access per se which is important but the access to policy-makers in context. In this way, Harley states, business can "see the way these people operate". Rather than just "having a single point meeting and coming away", you're able to have "interaction with them that is broader." By watching political leaders interact with others, business leaders are able to make better judgements about them. Again, in Harley's words:

> I want to have context. I want to know what motivates people. I want to know how consistent they are and how they adapt to different circumstances. You can be more predictive of their behaviours.[35]

---

32   Author interview with participant who chose to remain anonymous.
33   Author interview with Alan Dunn, 23 November 2011.
34   Author interview with Tom Harley, 2 November 2011.
35   Author interview with Tom Harley, 2 November 2011.

While the desire of the AALD to cultivate and represent the interests of big business is entirely legitimate, the interests and concerns of workers are not equally represented. The only union invited to attend the AALD is the right-wing AWU, first represented by Bill Shorten and, later, his successor Paul Howes. "Bill was the first ever union official involved. I'm still the only union official there", Howes declared in 2011. Apart from the fact that Shorten and Scanlan know each other well on a personal level, the AWU's presence, says Howes, "probably reflects" the fact that:

> [The AWU] has always had a very pro-US outlook on foreign policy issues. It goes back to the Cold War. We were the leading anti-Communist union in Australia ... So in the Australian labour movement it's always been well known that the AWU is a pro-US alliance union.[36]

Radical beginnings

It is unsurprising that the AALD holds a bias towards the interests of big business given the founder and driving force of the Dialogue, Phillip Scanlan, is an accomplished corporate executive with a history of neoliberal activism. Prior to his position as managing director of Coca Cola Amatil, Scanlan was the Manager of Corporate Relations and Public Affairs at Amatil (W.D. & H.O. Wills) in the early to mid-1980s.[37] Scanlan assumed a significant public role as defender of the tobacco industry's efforts to delegitimise the link between cigarette smoking and cancer and to thwart a ban on the advertising of tobacco products in Australia.

For example, in 1983 Scanlan declared on national television that the tobacco industry believed smoking did not constitute a health risk.[38] Scanlan also declared on national radio that "the industry believes there is no evidence to substantiate that it [nicotine] is addictive".[39] In an opinion piece in *The Australian* in 1984, Scanlan wrote that proposed legislation to ban tobacco advertising denied the basic right of any citizen to be presumed

---

36   Author interview with Paul Howes, 5 August 2011.

37   W.D. & H.O. Wills was the tobacco manufacturing subsidiary of Amatil, Australia's largest soft drink and second largest food manufacturer. In May 1989, a major corporate reorganisation saw Amatil sell its tobacco subsidiary to British American Tobacco (BAT). At the same time, BAT sold its 41% interest in Amatil to the Coca-Cola Company.

38   Robin Powell, Pressures Are Mounting to Curb Cigarette Advertising Down Under, *Advertising Age*, 12 September 1983.

39   Phillip Scanlan, interview with Jane Singleton, *City Extra*, ABC, 18 June 1984.

innocent until proven guilty.[40] A year later, Scanlan wrote in the *Australian Financial Review* that a proposed bill to ban tobacco advertising breached Australians' individual rights and was in direct contravention of the International Covenant on Civil and Political Rights.[41] In his defence of the right to advertise tobacco products, Scanlan liked to invoke free market principles:

> There is a relationship between competition in the marketplace, enhancement of the principal of consumer sovereignty, freedom of the press no less and civil liberties overall ... people who propose anti-competitive measures such as advertising bans tend to encourage market monopoly and the first loser in monopoly situations is always the consumer.[42]

Scanlan has also been associated with what has been coined the "radical neo-liberal movement" from the mid-1970s until the mid-1990s.[43] The movement was characterised by a loose network of right-wing parliamentarians, businessmen, academics, journalists and other influential sympathisers to the neoliberal economic ideology that was then taking hold in the US, but was still at the margins of political debate in Australia. As part of the movement, a number of corporate funded think tanks and groups were established in an attempt to restructure the Australian economy away from a Keynesian or welfare state into a neoliberal one. By the 1990s, the movement had successfully contributed to a shift in Australian political discourse. Neoliberalism was now elite orthodoxy and, with the election of the Howard government in 1996, the movement had become "an established part of the political landscape with the ear of a sympathetic government".[44]

One of the organisational backbones of the movement was the Crossroads Group, established by Liberal Dry MPs John Hyde and Jim Carlton.[45] Phillip Scanlan was one of its 40 members. It met secretly from 1980 to

---

40   Phillip Scanlan, Rights Threatened, *The Australian*, 14 May 1984.

41   Phillip Scanlan, Tobacco and a Bill of Rights, *Australian Financial Review*, 6 May 1985.

42   Scanlan in interview with Singleton, ABC City Extra.

43   The following discussion of this movement is based on the doctoral thesis by Damien C. Cahill, *The Radical Neo-liberal Movement as a Hegemonic Force in Australia, 1976-1996*, PhD Thesis, University of Wollongong, 2004.

44   Cahill, p. 108.

45   The group was named after the 1980 Shell-sponsored publication, *Australia at the Crossroads*, which had become the movement's manifesto. Wolfgang Kasper, Richard Blandy, John Freebairn, Douglas Hocking, and Robert O'Neil, *Australia at the Crossroads: Our Choices to the Year 2000*, Sydney: Harcourt Brace Jovanovich, 1980.

1986 in order to form strategies to intervene in key areas of public policy and related activities such as placing articles sympathetic to the neoliberal cause in major Australian newspapers. The organisation even conspired to create a cover story to conceal the true nature of its actions in the event of unintended public disclosure. Some activists in this movement subsequently moved into positions of influence in many high profile corporations; these included Scanlan, who became managing director of Coca-Cola Amatil's beverages division.

Damien Cahill, who undertook an in-depth study of the movement, has characterised the Crossroads Group as an important development in the history of the radical neoliberal movement:

> It brought together radical neo-liberals from academia, politics and business and facilitated dialogue between individuals from different movement organisations at a crucial time in the movement's develop-ment. It thus helped to cohere the movement. That it met secretly, and that its existence was deliberately hidden from the public, allowed activists to strategise and debate free from scrutiny.[46]

Shortly after the demise of the Crossroads Group, Scanlan was invited to join the board of yet another radical neoliberal institution, the Institute of Public Affairs (IPA) in New South Wales, as deputy president in March 1988. When the IPA (NSW) decided to close and re-open operations as the conservative think tank The Sydney Institute, in April 1989, Scanlan became the inaugural chairman where until 1993 he played an important role in the early years of its establishment. The Sydney Institute's executive chairman, to this day, is Gerard Henderson, also a member of the now defunct Crossroads Group.[47]

Significantly, the AALD prides itself as an independent private institu-tion able to maintain itself at arms-length from government, operating in the absence of direct government management and funding. The "mantra" that the AALD "be at arms-length from government has been fundamen-tal", says former Australian Prime Minister and long-term Dialogue par-ticipant, Kevin Rudd.[48] However, the extensive corporate connections and foundations of the AALD, including its dependence on private sources of

---

46   Cahill, *The Radical Neo-liberal Movement*, p. 117.
47   Author interview with Gerard Henderson, 7 March 2012; Gerard Henderson, Correspondence: Robert Macklin and The Sydney Institute, *The Sydney Institute Quarterly*, issue 31, September 2007, pp. 15-16.
48   Sheridan, Power Talking.

funding, undermine its claim to be independent and neutral. That is not to say that corporate interests have hijacked the agenda of the AALD. The financial and physical presence of big business is more likely a reflection of the fact that the alliance orthodoxy embodied by the AALD and Australia's political establishment closely aligns with large corporate interests and therefore attracts their support. Evidently, big business has used the opportunities provided by the AALD to their full advantage.

Chapter Eight

PRIVATE DIPLOMACY OR PRO-AMERICAN LOBBY GROUP?

Conceptualising the AALD

The AALD cannot be readily conceptualised or categorised. Ostensibly, as an effort in private diplomacy, the AALD sits within the broad definition of track two (T2) diplomacy. Indeed, the Dialogue has been publicly lauded as the most successful example of T2 diplomacy to emerge from Australia.[1] T2 diplomacy refers to unofficial or informal diplomatic activities that bring current officials, in their private capacities, into discussion with non-officials. It can be contrasted with traditional forms of track one (T1) diplomacy, or government-led diplomatic efforts undertaken exclusively by policy-makers who work through official channels. T2 diplomacy is often employed in either conflict resolution settings or as multilateral cooperation building exercises that help to facilitate mutual exchange and understanding.

T2 dialogues are often viewed as synonymous with "epistemic communities", or "a network of professionals with recognised expertise and competence in a particular domain and an authoritative claim to policy-relevant knowledge within that domain or issue-area".[2] The function of epistemic communities is to "discuss specific issues, set agendas, and formulate policy alternatives outside the formal bureaucratic channels" while serving as "brokers for admitting new ideas into decision-making

---

1   John Denton, Second-Track Diplomacy Aids Foreign Policy, *The Australian*, 17 July 2009, <http://www.theaustralian.com.au/news/second-track-diplomacy-aids-foreign-policy/story-e6frg6n6-1225751155708>, accessed 1 April 2018.

2   Peter M. Haas, Introduction: Epistemic Communities and International Policy Coordination, *International Organisation*, vol. 46, no. 1, winter 1992, p. 3.

circles of bureaucrats and elected officials".[3] Under favourable conditions, epistemic communities claim to be capable of not only framing issues or defining interests but even setting the agenda of policy-makers.[4]

Advocates claim that one of the major advantages T2 holds over T1 is its capacity for discussing and proposing ideas that would otherwise be "too sensitive or controversial" at the official level.[5] Given T2 requires less protocol and is "free of the constraints of official or national positions", there exists greater opportunity to explore "unconventional options" and "challenge current strategies and provide new solutions".[6] In theory, the objective of T2 is to use this greater latitude to critically examine policy options in an "academic fashion" and to challenge "traditional thinking" on security matters rather than simply recite government policy.[7]

Accordingly, one of the key ways T2 claims to have an impact at the policy level is by "generat[ing] dissent" which might "not be to the liking of policymakers" but nonetheless "alerts them to alternative ideas and approaches" against which "their own preferences will be benchmarked and assessed".[8] The rationale of the major T2 initiatives in the Asia–Pacific has been to challenge the status quo and traditional state conceptions of security, including the encouragement of "mutuality rather than power balancing or hegemony".[9]

While challenging official positions and providing alternative perspectives is a fundamental objective and claimed benefit of T2, the failure to live up to this expectation has also been one of its perennial problems,

---

3   Haas, Introduction: Epistemic Communities, p. 31.

4   Sheldon W. Simon, Evaluating Track II Approaches to Security Diplomacy in the Asia–Pacific: the CSCAP Experience, *The Pacific Review*, vol. 15, no. 2, 2002, p. 171.

5   Desmond Ball, Anthony Milner and Brendan Taylor, Track 2 Security Dialogue in the Asia–Pacific: Reflections and Future Directions, *Asian Security*, vol. 2, no. 3, 2006, p. 179.

6   Ian Buchanan and Christopher Findlay, Bolting on the Second Track Key to Regional Cooperation in the Asian Century, *East Asia Forum*, 27 June 2012, <http://www.eastasiaforum.org/2012/06/27/bolting-on-the-second-track-key-to-regional-cooperation-in-the-asian-century/>, accessed 1 April 2018.

7   Brian L. Job, "Track 2 Diplomacy: Ideational Contribution to the Evolving Asian Security Order" in Desmond Ball and Kwa Chong Guan (eds), *Assessing Track 2 Diplomacy in the Asia–Pacific Region*, p. 146.

8   Amitav Acharya, Engagement or Entrapment? Scholarship and Policymaking on Asian Regionalism, *International Studies Review*, vol. 13, 2011, p. 13.

9   Simon, Evaluating Track II Approaches, p.171.

noted in the literature as the "autonomy dilemma".[10] The autonomy dilemma largely derives from the fact that T2 participants are drawn from elite circles, closely intertwined with government and generally holding similar backgrounds and perspectives apart from the rest of civil society. Alternative views are often marginalised because T2 selects "groups and individuals discussing security issues that concern governing elites". By drawing on these elite circles with common worldviews, a kind of "group think" can develop – reinforced through "gatekeeping" – whereby favoured participants are continually reinvited back into the "club" while others remain excluded.[11]

The notion that T2 provides a forum for "thinking the unthinkable" is, it has been argued, an equivocal claim at best, as "non-official diplomatic discourse seems almost always to gravitate to official positions".[12] T2 more often than not functions in a "cheerleading" capacity on behalf of state interests by marginalising dissident perspectives and accommodating "discourses that support a state-centred ontology", or conception of reality, "which aim to maintain the regional status quo".[13]

Ostensibly, as a dialogue-based, private diplomatic process that brings officials and non-officials into discussion with one another, the AALD comfortably sits within the broad definition of T2 diplomacy. On the other hand, virtually all prominent T2 dialogues in the Asia–Pacific are dedicated to conflict management and/or multilateral cooperation building, whereas the focus of the AALD is on the management of bilateral relations between two long-standing allies. Any attempt to study the AALD as an exercise in T2 diplomacy must therefore, as Elena Douglas and Diane Stone note, "address T2 in the absence of conflict and stress long-term consensus-building and friendship engagement".[14]

---

10   Herman Joseph S. Kraft, The Autonomy Dilemma of Track Two Diplomacy in Southeast Asia, *Security Dialogue*, vol. 31, no. 3, 2000. Kraft has since updated his view on the autonomy dilemma, acknowledging that after a decade since first identifying the phenomena, it continues to operate in the Asia–Pacific, and is perhaps something T2 "must necessarily live with and accommodate the effects of". See Herman Joseph S. Kraft, "The Autonomy Dilemma of Track 2 Diplomacy in Southeast Asia" in Desmond Ball and Kwa Chong Guan (eds), *Assessing Track 2 Diplomacy in the Asia–Pacific Region*, p. 176.

11   Kraft, The Autonomy Dilemma, p. 348.

12   See Seng Tan, Non-official Diplomacy in Southeast Asia: "Civil Society" or "Civil Service"?, *Contemporary Southeast Asia*, vol. 27, no. 3, 2005, p. 375.

13   Tan, p. 379.

14   Elena Douglas and Diane Stone, The Informal Diplomacy of the Australian American Leadership Dialogue, *Australian Journal of International Affairs*, vol. 69, no. 1, 2015, p. 21.

More significantly, the problem of using T2 as a conceptual framework for understanding and evaluating the AALD is that it ignores one of the core objectives of T2 which, as just reviewed, is to challenge official government thinking by generating dissent. Although not always successful, one of the central reasons for involving non-officials in discussions with officials is to inject new and unorthodox approaches at the decision making level. The objective of the AALD, on the other hand, is to preserve orthodox thinking and eschew dissenting perspectives. Fearing the alliance might weaken with the loss of personal bonds between the next generation of rising leaders in both countries, the AALD was established to preserve the status quo by reinforcing the alliance orthodoxy in the minds of an elite. In this important respect, the AALD departs from other T2 initiatives and functions more like a lobby group.

There is a clear distinction between T2 initiatives and lobby groups. As "epistemic communities", T2 networks will ostensibly revise their beliefs in light of new or changing evidence. Unlike lobby groups, they do not attempt to define the terms of political debate to ensure only their preferred policy appears legitimate, but rather are committed to articulating expert and policy-relevant advice.[15] The AALD, in contrast, aims explicitly to "help review and refine the parameters of the Australian-American bilateral relationship" and generally views with disdain any opinion outside of the orthodoxy.[16] As demonstrated in the next section, critics of the alliance are not invited to attend the AALD and even strong alliance supporters are shunned when perceived as a threat to the status quo.

By drawing exclusively and carefully from elite circles that subscribe to conventional thinking, the AALD serves as a legitimising platform for existing government objectives. At first glance, this outcome appears consistent with other T2 initiatives that are bedevilled by the "autonomy dilemma", or the tendency of elites to fall into line with official perspectives. However, this criticism does not strictly apply to the AALD given that its objective is not "policy change" but "policy continuity"; the aim being to strengthen and renew the already "relatively stable nature of the ideas and values surrounding the alliance".[17]

---

15   Haas, Introduction, p. 18; M. J. Peterson, Cetologists, Environmentalists, and the International Management of Whaling, *International Organisation*, vol. 46, no. 1, 1992, pp. 148-49.

16   Australian American Leadership Dialogue, AALD, <http://www.aald.org/australian-american-leadership-dialogue>, accessed 1 April 2018.

17   Douglas and Stone, The Informal Diplomacy of the Australian American Leadership Dialogue, pp. 19-20.

Evidently, the AALD is not a traditional interest group or "issue public" that targets participants in the policy process with a set of specific policy objectives and on behalf of a particular constituency.[18] Rather, the term should be applied to the AALD more loosely to describe what amounts to a group of influential pro-American Australians, along with influential Americans, who are devoted to preserving and promoting an orthodox conception of the Australia-US alliance and shaping Australian foreign policy in a pro-American direction.

Rather than engage in direct efforts to persuade elected officials, the AALD brings together leaders in both countries who believe in its alliance orthodoxy in an attempt to mutually reinforce their pre-existing beliefs. The AALD does not "lobby" elites so much as socialise them by facilitating the process whereby its conception of the alliance can be voluntarily accepted or strengthened. While many traditional lobby groups are motivated to shift government policy in their favour, others operate in a "policy watchdog" capacity to prevent adverse changes.[19] The AALD falls into the latter category, acting as a "gatekeeper" for orthodox government policymaking on the alliance.[20]

Although not a direct comparison, the AALD resembles parts of the US-based "Israel lobby" which consists of individuals and groups that actively work to preserve America's "special relationship" with Israel but do not always engage in formal lobbying activities.[21] Although not the focus of this chapter, it is noteworthy that the AALD's most successful spin-off is the Australia Israel Leadership Forum, which in 2009 morphed into the Australia Israel UK Leadership Forum. According to its critics, this Forum engages in "the uncritical boosterism of which Scanlan's group gets accused in some circles".[22] Another relevant comparison is the Australia-based

---

18   Allan Gyngell and Michael Wesley, *Making Australian Foreign Policy*, Cambridge: Cambridge University Press, 2007, p. 166.

19   Gyngell and Wesley, p. 166.

20   The socialisation and "gatekeeping" functions of the AALD, briefly touched on here, are explored in detail in chapter nine.

21   John Mearsheimer and Stephen Walt, *The Israel Lobby and US Foreign Policy*, New York: Farrar, Straus and Giroux, 2007, pp. 112-114;

22   Hamish McDonald, True Friends Must Tell The Truth, *Sydney Morning Herald*, 20 March 2010, <http://www.smh.com.au/federal-politics/true-friends-must-tell-the-truth-20100319-qm1p.html>, accessed 1 April 2018. For an example of such criticism, see Antony Loewenstein, Rudd Helps the Middle East Story Remain One Sided, *Crikey*, 4 December 2009, <http://www.crikey.com.au/2009/12/04/rudd-helps-the-middle-east-story-remain-one-sided/>, accessed 1 April 2018.

"Jakarta lobby", a loose group of academics, bureaucrats and journalists who, in the past, worked to protect Australia's relationship with Indonesia.[23]

The function of such lobbies is not to subvert the normal conduct of government policy. The Jakarta lobby did not cause an Australian subservience to Indonesia. Rather, it assisted in maintaining the relationship in a way that aligned with an orthodox conception of Australia's national interest.[24] The same is true of the Israel lobby in relation to American foreign policy,[25] although others maintain, unconvincingly, that the lobby has successfully hijacked American and even Australian foreign policy.[26] The AALD should be understood along these same lines. It is one small element of what has been described as the "Washington lobby", and what is described in this book as the "US Lobby"; a loose network of elite and institutional relationships that functions to further entrench Australia's "special relationship" with America.[27]

Framing the debate

Scanlan has explicitly rejected allegations that the AALD is a "pro-American lobby group"[28] or a "cheer squad for American foreign policy".[29] As noted in chapter six, many supporters and participants of the AALD reject the label on the basis that the Dialogue has no specific agenda or monolithic view and discussion is open to robust criticism and debate on all matters pertaining to the Australia-US relationship. Contrary to these

---

23   Scott Burchill, The Jakarta Lobby: Mea Culpa?, *The Age*, 4 March 1999.

24   Clinton Fernandes, *Reluctant Saviour: Australia, Indonesia and the Independence of East Timor*, Carlton North, Victoria: Scribe Publications, 2004, pp. 22-24.

25   Noam Chomsky, The Israel Lobby? *ZNet*, 28 March 2006, <https://chomsky. info/20060328/>, accessed 1 April 2018; Stephen Zunes, The Israel Lobby: How Powerful Is It Really?, *Mother Jones*, 18 May 2006, <http://www.motherjones.com/ politics/2006/05/israel-lobby-how-powerful-it-really>, accessed 1 April 2018; Stephen Zunes, The Israel Lobby Revisited, *Common Dreams*, 23 December 2007, <http://www. commondreams.org/views/2007/12/23/israel-lobby-revisited>, accessed 1 April 2018.

26   Mearsheimer and Walt, *The Israel Lobby*; Eulalia Han and Halim Rane, *Making Australian Foreign Policy On Israel-Palestine: Media Coverage, Public Opinion And Interest Groups*, Carlton: Melbourne University Press, 2013.

27   Fernandes, *Reluctant Saviour*, p. 24.

28   Phillip Scanlan, Leaders Dialogue Proudly Bipartisan, *Australian Financial Review*, 21 February 2007.

29   Daniel Flitton, Man Of Many Words, *The Age*, 11 August 2007, <http://www. theage.com.au/news/in-depth/man-of-many-words/2007/08/10/1186530610605. html>, accessed 1 April 2018.

claims, however, there is ample evidence to suggest the AALD is structured in a way to carefully frame discussion and debate within narrow bounds.

Given the AALD is targeted to those who possess, or are likely to possess, a considerable degree of influence over the direction of the Australia-US relationship, participation is largely constrained in political terms to the two major parties. Consequently, criticism at the AALD is limited to that within the politically acceptable mainstream where it is typical to express unquestioning loyalty to the alliance. As former Liberal MP Andrew Robb explains, "Often there is not a lot of disagreement on some of the foreign policy issues between Labor and Liberal so there's often an Australian perspective [at the AALD] … but not always".[30]

Founding member Nick Greiner concurs, stating that:

> [To] some extent, it would be true that while [the AALD] was fiercely bi-partisan, where issues were bi-partisan, which in the United States they often are, and indeed in Australia in foreign policy they often are, the contingents would tend to reflect that.[31]

While Greiner believes discussion at the AALD "was certainly wide open", at the same time, dominant perspectives are rarely if ever challenged because "in many ways it just reflects the prevailing views in both countries in the inner circle".[32]

While one of the official foundational "values" of the AALD is a commitment to "bipartisanship", the AALD appears to attract those from the right and centre-right of politics, particularly with respect to defence and foreign affairs.[33] Carmen Lawrence, former premier of Western Australia and part of the left faction of the Labor Party, although never invited to the Dialogue, got the distinct impression during her time in office that "left-wingers were typically not invited". This is partly because "those from the left tended to have more domestic, social portfolios or opposition spokespeople positions", whereas those in foreign affairs and defence were "typically from the right and very strong on the US alliance".[34]

When it comes to the Labor left, Nick Bolkus believes that Scanlan would probably "rather have them inside the tent". However, Bolkus

---

30 Author interview with Andrew Robb, 15 July 2011.
31 Author interview with Nick Greiner, 6 July 2011.
32 Author interview with Nick Greiner, 6 July 2011.
33 Australian American Leadership Dialogue, AALD, <http://www.aald.org/australian-american-leadership-dialogue>, accessed 1 April 2018.
34 Author interview with Carmen Lawrence, 14 November 2011.

adds, "the broader left is another thing".[35] Indeed, a number of AALD delegates expressed the view that participation from those on the broader left would only serve to "spoil" the Dialogue.[36] Certainly, no member of the Australian Greens has ever been invited to attend, even though there may be some interest to participate.[37] According to AALD board member Richard Woolcott, "I can't speak for Scanlan and the board but I think they'd generally take the view that the Greens really were a bit too far outside what you might call the normal Australian attitude".[38]

The overriding objective of the AALD is not to facilitate critical discussion and debate but rather to foster an environment for building and maintaining friendships among the elite in order to preserve and strengthen the alliance. The cordial environment means that, whatever opportunities there may be for serious criticism of the Australia-US relationship and US foreign policy, participants do not take it very often. According to journalist Peter Hartcher, "people are far too polite".[39] Even on those occasions when participants do hold seriously critical opinions, Hugh White argues "the blush of good companionship at the Dialogue means they're reluctant" to express them.[40]

Former Vice-President of the Liberal Party, Tom Harley, feels that "everyone is terribly polite to each other [at the AALD]. It's all a kind of group hug ... There isn't a diversity of views ... It's all about getting on, which means agreement". Given the notable absence of those who are constructively critical of US foreign policy, the discussion "between Australia and the US [is] almost slavish", Harley adds.[41] Former chairman of the American board of the AALD, Alan Dunn, disagrees with the idea that Australians are "slavish" to the US point of view. Nonetheless, he concedes their criticism is "soft". The Australians are, in his words, "sensitive hosts".[42]

---

35 Author interview with Nick Bolkus, 6 September 2011.

36 Author interview with Nick Bolus. David Kemp speculated that Scanlan would be unlikely to invite anyone from the Greens unless he had "formed the view that there was amongst them someone who was more or less rational. He would be concerned they would take up too much time with their unconstructive projections of ideology". Author interview with David Kemp, 31 August 2011.

37 Correspondence with Anna Reynolds, International Advisor for Senator Bob Brown, 25 July 2011.

38 Author interview with Richard Woolcott, 22 March 2011.

39 Author interview with Peter Hartcher, 29 October 2011.

40 Author interview with Professor Hugh White, 2 September 2011.

41 Author interview with Tom Harley, 2 November 2011.

42 Author interview with Alan Dunn, 23 November 2011.

While he would not describe it as a "cheer squad", Glenn Milne, a former columnist for *The Australian*, concedes that "you're not there as a critic". Particularly when it comes to international and geostrategic concerns, the main function of the AALD is innovative information exchange. Milne claims, "I don't think that precludes criticism or questioning but it's not really what you're there for. You're there to get a deeper understanding of policy direction in Washington mostly".[43]

A number of participants share this view that it is misplaced to assume the AALD is a forum for critical debate. As one former Labor MP and AALD participant explains:

> I would have been surprised if there was serious criticism of Australia or America at the Dialogue ... I don't think anyone's said it's an independent and objective look at American or Australian politics. To view it as something where there should be an independent critique of American defence plans in Iraq or whatever misses the point ... It is of likeminded people. Sort of the US faction, if you like ... It's to promote the positive aspects of it not for us to critique their world view.[44]

Peter Hartcher, a long-time AALD participant, states that while there have been "junctures" in which "very real disagreement and very robust exchange" have occurred, "radicals or opponents or critics probably don't get invited to join. I haven't noticed any turning up". Nevertheless, Hartcher hastens to add, it is not valid to criticise the AALD for excluding critics because the objective of the Dialogue "is not to have robust discussion and debate about whether we should have an alliance. It's to have robust discussion and debate about how to make the alliance work better and work in the national interest".[45]

Accordingly, the claim that the AALD facilitates robust and critical debate comes with an important qualification. As former head of the AWU Paul Howes argues, while the AALD is "one of those forums where you're encouraged to challenge the orthodoxy and speak your mind freely without retribution", at the same time "It's not a forum for critiques of the US relationship; for being an anti-American forum. There are plenty of those forums. It's [sic] called the United Nations".[46]

---

43   Author interview with Glenn Milne, 9 November 2011.
44   Author interview with participant who chose to remain anonymous.
45   Author interview with Peter Hartcher, 29 October 2011.
46   Author interview with Paul Howes, 5 August 2011.

In a similar vein, Professor Andrew MacIntyre, who assumed a position on the Australian board of the AALD in December 2009, does not share the characterisation of the Dialogue as a "cheer squad" for the alliance and American foreign policy. "My experience of it is there's been some of the hardest questioning ... that I've witnessed anywhere", at least between "people who really knew what they were talking about and whose opinions were significant". There are limits to the range of opinion, MacIntyre concedes, with most delegates believing that both Australia and the US are "force[s] for good in the world". Yet "within that range, you get vigorous debate".[47]

Certainly, as Hartcher points out, given the AALD is a "private exercise in second track diplomacy" and not a "tax payer funded public institution", there is no "responsibility to invite the full spectrum of views".[48] Nevertheless, the dangers of repudiating a questioning or critical agenda ought to be apparent. As Carmen Lawrence notes, by facilitating such an environment:

> You create an echo chamber and you hear people saying what confirms your existing views and prejudices. You don't get to hear other voices that might question the conclusions you've reached. In the case of the US-Australia alliance ... that's led to some pretty bloody outcomes.[49]

Indeed, some former participants of the AALD feel that because it is something of a "cheer squad" for the alliance, there was not a lot of opposition within it to the invasion of Iraq.[50]

More recently, the AALD has been criticised for failing to raise important but difficult questions regarding the Australia-US alliance in the face of changing power relations in the Asia–Pacific. When asked how

---

47   Author interview with Professor Andrew MacIntyre, 28 June 2011. MacIntyre was first sought by Scanlan to attend the AALD in 1997 - all expenses paid - to share his thoughts as a specialist on Indonesia. Although today, MacIntyre states, he "find[s] the resources" himself to attend. Incidentally, MacIntyre is considered to have been a part of the "Jakarta lobby". He was a fierce defender of the record of achievements of the New Order regime when he was first invited to attend the AALD, depicting President Suharto as a great leader who brought stability to Indonesia. See, for example, Jamie Mackie and Andrew MacIntyre, "Politics" in Hal Hill (ed), *Indonesia's New Order: The Dynamics of Socio-Economic Transformation*, Sydney: Allen & Unwin, 1994.

48   Author interview with Peter Hartcher, 29 October 2011.

49   Author interview with Carmen Lawrence, 14 November 2011.

50   Flitton, Man Of Many Words; Brian Toohey, The Dialogue Box, *Australian Financial Review*, 24 April 2008.

the AALD might respond to his opinion that US primacy may be bad for regional stability, White says "I can answer … very plainly. I don't think it would go down at all well which probably explains why I haven't been invited for quite a long time". The dynamics of the Dialogue over the last decade in particular, White goes on to say, have resulted in an effort to "conceal, perhaps even to evade, rather than to identify and address" the core questions facing the Australia-US relationship. "For that reason", White concludes, "I think the Dialogue ends up being bad for the alliance".[51]

White's status as a prominent thinker who has departed from the status quo regarding the utility of the Australia-US alliance and US primacy in the Asia–Pacific has raised significant controversy in elite circles in Australia and the US.[52] Noted foreign policy commentator and long-time AALD participant, Greg Sheridan, denounced White's thesis as "distorted", "stupid", "weird" and "positively insane".[53] In one instance, Hartcher reports, White's name was scrubbed from the invitation list of a prestigious gathering of American and Australian elite on account of his "sin" of leading the public debate in Australia "in a direction the superpower didn't like".[54]

In the case of the AALD, former AALD board member Sam Lipski states that he does not "ever recall a conversation with anybody that I overheard in which the conversation went along the lines of we can't have [Hugh White]". Although Lipski doesn't discount the possibility entirely: "Phil's not a child. He's a seasoned political operator and maybe … Ask

51   Author interview with Professor Hugh White, 2 September 2011.

52   Paul Dibb, Why I Disagree with Hugh White on China's Rise, *The Australian*, 13 August 2012, <http://www.theaustralian.com.au/opinion/why-i-disagree-with-hugh-white-on-chinas-rise/story-e6frg6zo-1226448713852>, accessed 1 April 2018; Brad Glosserman, The Australian Canary, *The Diplomat*, 23 November 2011, <http://thediplomat.com/2011/11/the-australian-canary/>, accessed 1 April 2018; Paul Kelly, China Divides Labor Across its Generations, *The Australian*, 11 August 2012, <http://www.theaustralian.com.au/opinion/columnists/china-divides-labor-across-its-generations/story-e6frg74x-1226447870597>, accessed 1 April 2018.

53   Greg Sheridan, Distorted Vision of Future US-China Relations, *The Australian*, 11 September 2010, <http://www.theaustralian.com.au/opinion/distorted-vision-of-future-us-china-relations/story-e6frg6zo-1225917582189>, accessed 1 April 2018.

54   Peter Hartcher, Any China Conversation Better Than None At All, *Sydney Morning Herald*, 14 August 2012, <http://www.smh.com.au/federal-politics/political-opinion/any-china-conversation-better-than-none-at-all-20120813-244vd.html>, accessed 1 April 2018.

him. Ask him directly".[55] Another former board member was equally ambiguous: "He [Hugh White] could be right" about being dropped off the list. "Who would know? Because there isn't a way to test it".[56]

Emeritus Professor Paul Dibb is of the view that the AALD sidelines dissenting views. The central problem of the Dialogue, according to Dibb, is that Scanlan does not tolerate even mild criticism:

> In my experience ... if you make even the slightest of criticisms of the United States you're not invited again. That's not just my experience ... my colleague Hugh White ... he would have the same view. As would former secretaries of defence and chiefs of defence force who I know have been to those occasions and would agree you have to watch what you say. Frankly, I think that is unacceptable. It is a serious problem of an effectively one-man band who determines who will be invited and who won't and who doesn't tolerate criticism.[57]

In Dibb's eyes, the claim by some supporters of the AALD that it holds no particular agenda for how the Australia-US relationship ought to evolve is "bullshit". In his experience, "That's not the way it feels to be there. It is all carefully orchestrated. It is all carefully controlled. It is not an open and frank dialogue. The good part of it is proselytising". While Dibb believes the US alliance is the "most important single security relationship we have by a huge margin", and that Australia receives "enormous benefits from the alliance", the problem he has with the Dialogue "is the way in which this exclusive club is run as a non-critical shop".[58]

The AALD has many supporters who deny these criticisms. Former board member Stephen Loosley, for example, maintains that "The Dialogue is concerned with keeping the relationship with the Americans very healthy, contemporary and strong. Beyond that, it doesn't have any particular ideological or philosophical flavour".[59] Others are less unequivocal. When asked if the AALD sidelines dissenting viewpoints, Nick Greiner responded with qualified uncertainty:

---

55   Lipski was a board member of the AALD from 2004-2009. Author interview with Sam Lipski, 25 October 2011. Note that Phillip Scanlan refused multiple requests to be interviewed or to respond to my questions about the AALD via email.

56   Author interview with participant and former AALD board member who chose to remain anonymous.

57   Author interview with Emeritus Professor Paul Dibb, 13 September 2011.

58   Author interview with Emeritus Professor Paul Dibb, 13 September 2011.

59   Author interview with Stephen Loosley, 11 January 2012.

Well I think that's right and I think Phil exerted ... I mean the truth is Phil was the only one running it. I mean he had some help. And yes, I think that's true. Would he have turned down some foreign affairs critic of the Iraq war if they wanted to come? You'd have to ask him. I don't know. Look that's broadly right. It's not an open slather.[60]

Certainly, the AALD attracts a lot of private criticism regarding the selection process and what is widely perceived as Scanlan's overbearing personality and excessive control over the invitation list. Even among strong supporters of the AALD, there are numerous complaints of the Dialogue being too "top-down driven", while Scanlan himself is described by various participants, though none willing to put these statements on the record, as a "monomaniac", "comrade-leader" and a "one-man band". While the success of the AALD is in part attributed to Scanlan's extraordinary personal contacts and capacity to network,[61] the unfortunate consequence, according to a number of participants, is that the AALD is more or less a gathering of Scanlan and his "mates".[62]

Unsurprisingly, there is an element of convergence between Scanlan's friendship circle and the prevalence of orthodox alliance loyalists at the AALD. When one former senior Australian diplomat and AALD participant was asked if he thought the Dialogue was a cheer squad for American foreign policy, he responded by stating "there is a bit of that". He goes on to explain:

If I were to guess, Scanlan would be very much of the type to not get people on who rocked the boat as he would see it. He sees it as a dialogue with people he knows; right thinking people who are in favour of the Australian-American relationship. Anybody who questions aspects of it he wouldn't favour.[63]

Former Foreign Minister Gareth Evans agrees, stating that during his time at the AALD, Scanlan had a suspicion of anyone "other than those who

---

60   Author interview with Nick Greiner, 6 July 2011.
61   According to those on the inside, "Scanlan's networking abilities are legend". Geoff Elliot and Clive Mathieson, Phil Scanlan and the American Connection, *The Australian*, 16 May 2013, <http://www.theaustralian.com.au/business/the-deal-magazine/the-american-connection/story-e6frgabx-1226641967547>, accessed 1 April 2018.
62   As one former board member, who chose to remain anonymous, phrases it, "There's favourites and there are non-favourites".
63   Author interview with participant who chose to remain anonymous.

fell over themselves to demonstrate passion and affection for the US". The "measuring stick applied" was "not just are you a friend of the US but are you a devotee". Consequently, continues Evans, the AALD is very much a "cheer squad" and a "love-in", not "an environment in which it's comfortable for people to be critical, certainly on any fundamental issues".[64]

Ostensibly, the inclusion of journalists at the AALD ensures greater critical debate is injected into discussions, and important revelations about the inner workings of the Australia-US relationship are conveyed to the public. Although it is "not really attempting to influence public opinion", Paul Kelly argues, by inviting media representatives and key opinion makers into discussions, the AALD has nonetheless indirectly impacted the "the media debate, coverage, analysis and commentary about the relationship" by making it "more intensive" and "sophisticated".[65]

Similarly, Fairfax journalist Peter Hartcher argues that the AALD helps to frame public debate surrounding the alliance, notwithstanding the strict non-disclosure convention of the Dialogue. Specifically, the participation of journalists is crucial for salvaging important disclosures that would otherwise remain private:

> From a journalist's point of view there's only one question: Is it better that journalists are invited and have the opportunity to try to disclose some of the content or is it better that we are not? It's my view that it's better if we are invited which gives us at least the opportunity to bring some of that to the public and that's exactly what I've done.[66]

Hartcher recalls an instance during the 2011 Dialogue in Perth when an interesting discussion erupted regarding clashing interests between the US and China in the South China Sea. "Because of the rules of the game", Hartcher says, "I'm in the room on the condition that I don't rush out and put the whole damn thing in the paper. So I accept the rules and all the journalists there do". After the session was over, Hartcher approached the main American representative, Kurt Campbell, and asked him to state on the record what "the main thrust of the US's concerns" were. Hartcher believes that "What I'm trying to do, and I think succeeding, is bringing [sic] those core concerns and arguments and difficulties that go on inside the relationship and inside the alliance ... to the wider Australian public".[67]

---

64   Author interview with Gareth Evans, 10 April 2012.
65   Author interview with Paul Kelly, 20 January 2012.
66   Author interview with Peter Hartcher, 29 October 2011.
67   Author interview with Peter Hartcher, 29 October 2011.

While certainly important, conveying the concerns of decision makers to the public can come at the risk of acting as a mere scribe or transmitter for official policy perspectives.[68] In any case, it could also be argued the public would benefit from greater critical analysis of the role of the AALD in managing Australia's relationship with the US. In my research, of the more than 1500 news items published with reference to the AALD since its establishment in 1993, less than a handful critically addressed its role in shaping the Australia-US alliance.

The key journalists who are invited to participate in the AALD are generally in agreement with, or are unquestioning of, the alliance orthodoxy that the AALD serves to protect and promote. Paul Kelly and Peter Hartcher are cases in point. Hartcher sees the AALD as a "national asset",[69] while Kelly characterises it as "a distinct and positive force for good".[70] Unsurprisingly, Kelly and Hartcher have been chosen by Scanlan to present an analysis of Australian politics each year to delegates at the AALD.

Foreign editor of *The Australian*, and prominent alliance loyalist, Greg Sheridan, is the other key journalist in attendance at the AALD. In his 2006 book, *The Partnership*, which examines the Australia-US alliance during the Bush-Howard years, Sheridan devotes a small section to praising the successes of the AALD, labelling it "the most significant exercise in private diplomacy ever undertaken in Australian history".[71] Sheridan was the only journalist invited to attend the inaugural AALD event in 1993, and has been to most, if not all, events since.[72] Former AALD board member, Sam Lipski, argues that "of all the people at the Australian end", Sheridan has been one of the most intimately involved Dialogue participants and, in some ways, is "the public chronicler of it".[73]

One of the few investigative articles published about the role of the AALD in managing Australia's relationship with the US was written by

---

68   Indeed, this appears to be what most of the "revelations" from inside the AALD actually are. Key American officials such as Richard Armitage have often used the AALD to relay messages through inside journalists, applying public pressure on Australia to conform to US interests on everything from increasing defence spending to supporting American strategic objectives vis-à-vis China.

69   Author interview with Peter Hartcher, 29 October 2011.

70   Author interview with Paul Kelly, 20 January 2012.

71   Greg Sheridan, *The Partnership: The Inside Story of the US-Australian Alliance Under Bush and Howard*, Sydney: UNSW Press, 2006, pp. 311-318, quote p. 317.

72   As Sheridan declares in his book, "I was the only journalist at that first meeting". Sheridan, *The Partnership*, p. 313.

73   Author interview with Sam Lipski, 25 October 2011.

Fairfax journalist Brian Toohey in 2008.[74] Toohey, who has never been invited to the AALD, characterises the Dialogue as "basically another lobby group for boosting the US-Australia relationship".[75] From the perspective of the AALD, the participation of journalists has the advantage of subjecting them "to what are basically views all in favour of the alliance". Accordingly, Toohey holds some concerns about those journalists who are keen to be heavily involved:

> I do find it a little bit odd that journalists want to be a member of an organisation as dedicated to a political goal such as strengthening the alliance. I would have thought if you were writing about foreign policy or defence you should be a little bit more neutral about these things. Of course, if you are writing an opinion piece you can have an opinion but ... [not those journalists involved in] news analysis and so forth.[76]

While Toohey acknowledges that there are benefits for journalists attending the AALD, he also recognises the costs:

> I can see why journalists want to go. It gives them an inside view of what's happening. I can't see that it's informed many of the journalists who are present to be more critical about things. If anything, I think some of the journalists were probably misled about the value of going into Iraq.[77]

In his investigative report for the *Australian Financial Review*, Toohey discovered the 2002 Dialogue event in the White House – attended by a number of high-level US administration officials – had the "advantage of letting Australians know a war was coming". However, because of the closed nature of the meeting, no journalist revealed to the public what had been said. Nor did anyone query Washington's wisdom of invading Iraq and deposing a secular regime. According to AALD participant and then Fairfax director of Corporate Affairs, Bruce Wolpe, "It was not really that sort of occasion - it was about presenting and listening."[78]

In *The Partnership* Sheridan mentions the private White House meeting in 2002, where Dick Cheney, Paul Wolfowitz, Condoleeza Rice, Karl Rove

---

74   Toohey, The Dialogue Box.
75   Author interview with Brian Toohey, 28 November 2011.
76   Author interview with Brian Toohey, 28 November 2011.
77   Author interview with Brian Toohey, 28 November 2011.
78   Toohey, The Dialogue Box.

and a number of other administration figures conducted half-hour sessions with AALD members; one after another. According to Sheridan, the sessions provided "an opportunity to hear American views from the top, and to express Australian views back into the process" in the lead-up to the Iraq war.[79] He does not, however, mention the fact that, as reported by Toohey, no-one from the Australian delegation spoke out against the war.

There are clearly powerful incentives for journalists to attend the AALD. Most participating journalists view it as a "great gig", in the words of former journalist and Labor MP, Maxine McKew, providing the opportunity to negotiate on-the-record interviews with key decision makers.[80] It is also "very flattering to be mingling with the people who are in these powerful positions", says Fairfax journalist Hamish McDonald. "Some people really get off on that".[81] For one instructive example of how the AALD appeals to the inflated sensibilities of some journalists, witness Greg Sheridan boast about his high-level connections and exclusive access to its "secret" discussions:

> I was seated opposite Dick Cheney and at right angles to Paul Wolfowitz, now US Vice-President and Deputy Secretary of Defence ... The Dialogue lunched informally in the hotel's little back garden. There I shared a table with Brent Scowcroft, who had been the elder George Bush's national security adviser, and Bob Zoellick, who would become George W. Bush's trade representative. At the next table was Karl Rove, now Bush's most intimate adviser, and Rich Armitage, now the Deputy Secretary of State. I can't tell you what was said because it was all off the record.[82]

According to independent author and journalist Antony Loewenstein, "it is obvious why" journalists refuse to challenge the AALD's agenda: "Being close to top officials and politicians makes them feel connected and important. Being an insider is many reporters' ideal position. Independence is secondary to receiving sanctioned links and elevated status in a globalised world".[83]

---

79   Sheridan, *The Partnership*, p. 317.

80   Margaret Simons, Agent of Influence, *Sydney Morning Herald*, 8 November 2003.

81   Author interview with Hamish McDonald, 15 November 2011.

82   Greg Sheridan, Power Talking, *The Australian*, 23 July 2003.

83   Antony Loewenstein, Wikileaks Challenges Journalism-Politics Partnership, *The Drum, ABC*, 10 December 2010, <http://www.abc.net.au/news/2010-12-10/wikileaks_challenges_jounalism-politics_partnership/42042>, accessed 1 April 2018.

The reason more broadly, however, derives from the fact that support for the AALD flows from the wider loyalty the US alliance enjoys as an entrenched part of Australia's elite political culture. Consequently, there are pressures on journalists to conform to the mainstream consensus about Australia's relationship with the US, not least of which is the fear of being marginalised. McDonald notes that for those journalists who work for a mainstream newspaper, as he does:

> If you don't conform you can find yourself on the outside, not getting access to anyone for a long time. Questioning those current paradigms can be a very lonely experience. You might find yourself not in touch with people in the institutions of power but with people on the fringes.[84]

Relatedly, there are many inducements for journalists who conform – study tours, fellowships, grants and so forth – which can quickly vanish for those who depart from overt support for the status quo. As McDonald points out, "There is a lot of money for people who produce work that reinforces what powerful people want to hear".[85]

---

84   Author interview with Hamish McDonald, 15 November 2011.
85   Author interview with Hamish McDonald, 15 November 2011.

Chapter Nine

ALLIANCE MANAGEMENT AND THE SOCIALISATION OF ELITES

Socialisation and public diplomacy

As suggested in the previous chapter, it seems clear the AALD environment excludes perspectives outside the alliance orthodoxy and that challenge the "special relationship" narrative. Even so, the AALD remains committed to open and frank exchange on matters of mutual interest to both countries. Perhaps counter-intuitively, research into belief formation supports the contention that the open exchange of views and debate within the highly insular social environment of the foreign policy community is more likely to produce an enduring impact on one's beliefs than the overt, top-down enforcement of conformity.[1] Belief in the alliance orthodoxy, including belief in the United States as "an overwhelming force for good in the world", exists as an unchallenged assumption that is accepted and reinforced – or rather absorbed and internalised – by virtue of the social consensus created at the AALD.

More than just framing discussion and debate, the AALD socialises members of the elite – inculcating orthodox attitudes about the alliance – by providing a number of important material and psychological inducements to remain committed to the status quo. In this respect, a parallel can be drawn between the AALD and public diplomacy. Specifically, the AALD's socialisation function resembles that of US foreign leader and exchange programs which aim to co-opt members of an elite in the hope of strengthening America's relationships with its closest allies. This socialisation function is a subtle but highly effective process that lays the groundwork for the engineering of consent and, in the case of the AALD,

---

1   Natasha Hamilton-Hart, *Hard Interests, Soft Illusions*: Southeast Asia and American Power, New York: Cornell University Press, 2012, 38.

for preserving and strengthening the alliance orthodoxy in the minds of the Australian elite.

Part of the stated mission of the AALD is to "broaden and deepen mutual understanding between Australian and American leaders".[2] Otherwise known as socialisation, this objective is understood as an important benefit and positive outcome of track two diplomacy (T2), which contributes to the development of shared understandings between participants.[3] Indeed, of all the claimed benefits of T2, "virtually all participants and analysts ... cite its most important role as a socialisation mechanism".[4] In the context of conflict resolution and conflict management, socialisation is a valuable tool for helping to reduce tensions and increase cooperation, including by transmitting alternative norms into the policymaking process.[5]

The socialisation function of T2, however, is very different to that of the AALD which operates to preserve and strengthen personal relationships between two long-standing allies and is grounded in an historical orthodox narrative of alliance. With this goal in mind, socialisation is not so much about developing shared understandings but rather inculcating orthodox attitudes about the Australia-US relationship. As one study on the impact of the AALD points out:

> The AALD represents a distinctive kind of leadership over the long term to *instil a common faith* in the alliance among new generations of policy leaders. The task is consensus-building, norm construction, the filtering and reassemblage of ideas, and the *socialisation of elites*.[6]

---

2   Australian American Leadership Dialogue, AALD, <http://www.aald.org/australian-american-leadership-dialogue>, accessed 1 April 2018.

3   Desmond Ball, Anthony Milner and Brendan Taylor, Track 2 Security Dialogue in the Asia–Pacific: Reflections and Future Directions, *Asian Security*, vol. 2, no. 3, 2006, pp. 180-181.

4   Brian L. Job, "Track 2 Diplomacy: Ideational Contribution to the Evolving Asian Security Order" in Desmond Ball and Kwa Chong Guan (eds), *Assessing Track 2 Diplomacy in the Asia–Pacific Region: A CSCAP Reader*, Strategic and Defence Studies Centre, Australian National University, Canberra and S. Rajaratnam School of International Studies, Nanyang Technological University, Singapore, 2010, p. 143.

5   Ball, Milner and Taylor, Track 2 Security Dialogue in the Asia–Pacific, p. 180-181; Dalia Dassa Kaye, *Rethinking Track Two Diplomacy: The Middle East and South Asia*, Netherlands Institute of International Relations, Clingendael Diplomacy Papers, no. 3, June 2005, pp. 15-42.

6   Elena Douglas and Diane Stone, The Informal Diplomacy of the Australian American Leadership Dialogue, *Australian Journal of International Affairs*, vol. 69, no. 1, 2015, pp. 22-23. Emphasis added.

There is some acknowledgment in the literature on T2 and epistemic communities of the potential for participants to become "entrapped" or "co-opted" by governments because of a fear of losing access and influence.[7] However, when it comes to alliance management, the more important and relevant insights into the process of socialisation, as a conscious mechanism of co-option, can be found in the international relations field of public diplomacy and, specifically, the long-standing and very successful American practice of foreign leader and exchange programs.[8]

T2 and public diplomacy share a number of characteristics. Although typically studied as two distinct fields, the connections between them are acknowledged in the literature, and practitioners often speak of both with similar goals in mind.[9] According to Cull, the fields of T2 and public diplomacy constitute overlapping circles, the exact boundaries between them being unclear.[10] The absence of a clear distinction between the two fields stems partly from the fact that there is no singular definition of public diplomacy, with much scholarly debate about its exact meaning and function. In its simplest and arguably most common interpretation, public diplomacy is defined as "an international actor's attempt to conduct its foreign policy by engaging with foreign publics".[11]

Typically, public diplomacy consists of one-directional information campaigns distributed to mass audiences via news, film, TV and radio

---

7   Amitav Acharya, Engagement or Entrapment? Scholarship and Policymaking on Asian Regionalism, *International Studies Review*, vol. 13, 2011; Sheldon W. Simon, Evaluating Track II Approaches to Security Diplomacy in the Asia–Pacific: the CSCAP Experience, *The Pacific Review*, vol. 15, no. 2, 2002, p. 168.

8   Joseph Nye's concept of "soft power" or "getting others to want the outcomes that you want" is also relevant for articulating the function of socialisation in alliance management. Nye identifies exchanges, among other public diplomacy instruments, as an example of the power of the state to "entice and attract" foreign governments and, especially, foreign publics. Joseph S. Nye, Public Diplomacy and Soft Power, *Annals of the American Academy of Political and Social Science*, vol. 616, March 2008, p. 95. Also see Joseph S. Nye, *Soft Power: The Means to Success in World Politics*, New York: Public Affairs, 2004.

9   See, for example, Gareth Evans, Australia and Asia: The Role of Public Diplomacy, address to the Australia-Asia Association, Melbourne, 15 March 1990, <http://www.gevans.org/speeches/old/1990/150390_fm_australiaandasia.pdf>, accessed 1 April 2018.

10   Nicholas J. Cull, "Introduction" in Joseph J. Popiolkowski and Nicholas J. Cull (eds), *Public Diplomacy, Cultural Interventions & the Peace Process in Northern Ireland: Track Two to Peace?*, USC Center on Public Diplomacy at the Annenberg School, University of Southern California, Los Angeles: Figueroa Press, 2009, p. 2.

11   Nicholas J. Cull, *The Cold War and the United States Information Agency: American Propaganda and Public Diplomacy, 1945-1989*, Cambridge: Cambridge University Press, 2008, p. xv.

broadcasts. It also commonly includes bidirectional activities such as education and cultural exchanges and foreign leader visitor programs that ostensibly operate on the basis of a reciprocal exchange of ideas and information or "mutual understanding".[12] It is these kinds of bidirectional activities, sometimes referred to as "dialogue-based public diplomacy", that are most often categorised as a subset of T2. Indeed, when the original term "track two diplomacy" was coined by William D. Davidson and Joseph V. Montville, "scientific and cultural exchanges" were included as examples.[13]

While the focus of T2 is typically conflict resolution and conflict management, the primary objective of foreign leader and exchange programs is almost exclusively on alliance management and the preservation and strengthening of existing relationships. America's premier International Visitor Leader Program (IVLP) has been extraordinarily successful in solidifying support for American foreign policy objectives among US allies.[14] In his landmark study of the IVLP, Giles Scott-Smith demonstrates that the program had its greatest impact in binding European states to the American transatlantic alliance during the Cold War.[15]

The primary target audiences of foreign leader and exchange programs are foreign elite groups and what is referred to as the "successor generation" of up-and-coming leaders. The IVLP alone attracts more than 5000 international visitors annually and has engaged more than 200 000 people since its establishment in 1940, including over 500 current or former Chiefs of State or Heads of Government. Notable Australian participants include Tony Abbott, Julia Gillard, Quentin Bryce, Paul Keating, William Hayden, Malcolm Fraser and Gough Whitlam.[16]

---

12   Nancy Snow, *Propaganda, Inc. Selling America's Culture to the World*, 3rd edition, New York: Seven Stories Press, 2010, p.88.

13   William D. Davidson and Joseph V. Montville, Foreign Policy According to Freud, *Foreign Policy*, no. 45, winter, 1981-82, p. 155.

14   Prior to 2004, the IVLP was known as the International Visitor Program (IVP).

15   Giles Scott-Smith, *Networks of Empire: The US State Department's Foreign Leader Program in the Netherlands, France, and Britain 1950-70*, Brussels: P.I.E. Peter Lang, 2008.

16   US Department of State, International Visitor Leadership Program (IVLP), US Bureau of Educational and Cultural Affairs, <http://eca.state.gov/ivlp>, accessed 1 April 2018. Although Tony Abbott's name is not mentioned on the IVLP website, elsewhere Abbott has revealed "It was the US Information Agency that organised my first trip to America as a member of parliament", apparently in 1995. See Tony Abbott, the Australia-US Alliance and Leadership in the Asia–Pacific, address to the Heritage Foundation, Washington D.C., 18 July 2012, <http://www.heritage. org/research/lecture/2012/11/the-australiaus-alliance-and-leadership-in-the-asiapacific>, accessed 1 April 2018.

Significantly, the same fear arising from the passing of the World War Two generation of leaders in Australia and America that drove Scanlan to create the AALD also drove US foreign leader and exchange programs to focus more on the successor generation of leaders in Western Europe. As a former US Public Affairs Counsellor explains in relation to US-German relations:

> In the late 1970s and early 1980s, both Americans and Germans concerned with US-German relations began to recognise a problem posed by the gradual passing from positions of power and influence of a generation of Germans and Americans, many of whom had formed a network of human relationships linking the two nations since World War II ... The generation taking their places had no similar formative experiences ... This gap of knowledge and understanding was perceived as posing a danger to the future cohesion of the German-American relationship.[17]

Although exchange programs are predicated on mutual understanding, their approach to socialising elites is more akin to co-option. While socialisation can consist of a mutual transference or two-way exchange of ideas, values and norms, as Ikenberry and Kupchan point out, when relating to a hegemonic power socialisation can also result in a "process through which national leaders internalise the norms and value orientations espoused by the hegemon" and which are consistent with its notion of international order. One of the mechanisms by which this occurs is "normative persuasion". That is, where norms are transferred and subsequently internalised through various forms of direct contact with elites in a target state. Ikenberry and Kupchan identify diplomatic channels, cultural exchanges and foreign study as instruments of normative persuasion.[18]

Scott-Smith details the specifics of the socialisation process employed by the IVLP to bond US allies to American hegemony, describing how the program entices participants to voluntarily accept a pre-laid pathway via the provision of a number of psychological and material inducements. These include bestowing a sense of self-importance; facilitating personal affinities giving the impression everyone is on the same side; providing access to the

---

17   Giles Scott-Smith, Searching for the Successor Generation: Public Diplomacy, the US Embassy's International Visitor Program and the Labour Party in the 1980s, *British Journal of Politics and International Relations*, vol. 8, 2006, pp. 223-224.

18   John Ikenberry and Charles A. Kupchan, Socialisation and Hegemonic Power, *International Organisation*, vol. 44, no. 3, summer 1990, pp. 289-90.

corridors of power and assisting in the development of high-level contacts which create opportunities for career enhancement.[19]

As a result, participants are left with a taste of the benefits they can reap by assuming an attitude consistent with the interests of the hegemonic power and in accordance with their own personal interests and beliefs. As a voluntary and participatory form of persuasion, Scott-Smith describes the IVLP as engaged less in the "engineering of consent than the creation of circumstances for its realisation, and it is often highly effective".[20]

Soft power and psychological warfare

There is a long-standing debate about whether or not public diplomacy equates to propaganda, with attempts to distinguish the so-called "white" or truthful propaganda activities of official public diplomacy from the more deceitful "grey" and "black" varieties.[21] In practice, however, public diplomacy has frequently been used as a euphemism for propaganda. The USIA, the premier public relations agency of the US until its demise in 1999, worked closely with the CIA on numerous covert warfare operations throughout the Cold War;[22] thereafter morphing from an anti-Communist outfit into an instrument of corporate propaganda.[23]

Although not propaganda per se, the main techniques that lie behind US foreign leader and exchange programs today derive from research into propaganda and psychological warfare studies in the post-World War One and early post-World War Two eras. In particular, it was the idea of targeting elite groups and opinion makers that originated in the work of Walter Lippmann, Edward Bernays and Harold D. Lasswell, subsequently revolutionised by social psychologist Paul F. Lazarsfeld, that laid the basis of all future US information campaigns, including education and cultural exchanges. Further research and subsequent practice into the political

---

19   Scott-Smith, Searching for the Successor Generation.

20   Scott-Smith, p. 233.

21   David W. Guth, Black, White, and Shades of Gray: The Sixty-Year Debate Over Propaganda versus Public Diplomacy, *Journal of Promotion Management*, vol. 13, 2008.

22   Cull, The Cold War and the United States Information Agency. A sample of the USIA's more nefarious covert propaganda activities include participation in the US counterinsurgency campaign in the Philippines in the 1950s, the overthrow of Mohammad Mosadegh in Iran and Jacobo Arbenz Guzman in Guatemala in 1953, the US invasion of the Dominican Republic in 1965 and the US invasion of Grenada in 1983.

23   Snow, *Propaganda, Inc.*

effectiveness of exchanges revealed that they were most effective, not in converting critics but in solidifying the opinions of those who already held positive predispositions towards the US.

Lippmann's keystone texts, *Public Opinion* (1922) and *The Phantom Public* (1925), were both largely based on his wartime propaganda experiences with the Committee on Public Information (CPI), the organisation responsible for all aspects of American propaganda at home and abroad during World War One.[24] Lippmann's key contribution was his theory that public opinion could be controlled through the manipulation of symbols implanted into the public mind by those recognised in society to be authoritative figures.[25] Lippmann's work was complemented by Edward Bernays, the so-called "Father of Public Relations", who argued in his seminal work on propaganda in 1928 that "If you can influence the leaders, either with or without their conscious cooperation, you automatically influence the group which they sway".[26]

Like Lippmann, Lasswell viewed propaganda as the "control of opinion by significant symbols".[27] The focus of his dissertation was on the practice of propaganda during World War One. Lasswell aimed to uncover the techniques of American, British, French and German wartime propaganda, not only in demoralising and mobilising hate against the enemy, but also preserving the friendship of allies and neutrals. It was his revelations on the latter that provided the crucial insight into the importance of personal interaction in shaping the minds of elites.

In concluding his assessment on the use of inter-allied propaganda, Lasswell discerned that "among all the means to be exploited, the use of personal influencing is peculiarly important".[28] This was particularly true when it came to London's propaganda efforts aimed at drawing the US into World War One. Rather than preaching entrance into the war directly, the British established myriad associations with influential and eminent Americans. As Lasswell describes it:

---

24   Walter Lippmann, *Public Opinion*, New York: The Free Press, 1922; Walter Lippmann, *The Phantom Public*, New York: Harcourt, Brace, 1925.

25   According to Lippmann, authoritative individuals who possessed the power to give meaning and importance to such symbols; chosen "by birth, inheritance, conquest or election, they and their organised following administer human affairs". Lippmann, *Public Opinion*, p. 144.

26   Edward Bernays, *Propaganda*, Brooklyn: IG Publishing, 2005 [1928], p. 73.

27   Harold D. Lasswell, *Propaganda Technique in the World War*, London: Kegan Paul, Trench, Trubner & Co. LTD, 1927, p. 9.

28   Lasswell, p. 160.

Behind the scenes, and behind the news and pictures and speeches, there flows a mighty stream of personal influencing. The war was more debated in private than public. The doubters were won by friendship or flattery, logic or shame, to fuse their enthusiasm in the rising wave of Allied sentiment.[29]

Lasswell characterises these institutionalised personal connections as "the social lobby", where the "personal conversation, and the casual brush … forged the strongest chain between America and Britain". The power of the social lobby came from "The sheer radiation of aristocratic distinction [which] was enough to warm the cockles of many a staunch Republican heart, and to evoke enthusiasm for the country which could produce such dignity, elegance and affability".[30] Lasswell was describing what the British referred to as "duchessing" as a subtle but effective means of propaganda.[31]

Although Lippmann, Bernays and Lasswell made important contributions, it was the founder and director of the Bureau of Applied Social Research at Colombia University, Paul F. Lazarsfeld, who revolutionised the importance of personal influence in mass communication.[32] While the conventional wisdom held that media messages influenced the public directly, Lazarsfeld hypothesised a "two-step flow of communication" whereby "opinion leaders" mediated the information that came from the mass media.[33] His findings were first published in 1944 in the book *The People's Choice*, and updated after further research in his landmark study with Elihu Katz in 1955, *Personal Influence*.[34]

---

29   Lasswell, p. 157.

30   Laswell, p. 157.

31   George Orwell later famously described duchessing in relation to British MPs "who get patted on the back by dukes and are lost forever more". Quoted in Simon Leys, The Intimate Orwell, *The New York Review of Books*, 26 May 2011, <http://www.nybooks.com/articles/archives/2011/may/26/intimate-orwell/>, accessed 1 April 2018.

32   On the revolutionary nature of Lazarsfeld's work in communications studies, see the collection of articles in Politics, Social Networks, and the History of Mass Communications Research: Rereading Personal Influence, special edition of the *Annals of the American Academy of Political and Social Science*, vol. 608, November 2006.

33   The dominant theory of mass communication at the time was the Hypodermic Needle Model or "magic bullet" theory which suggested that media messages were "injected" or "shot" straight into a passive audience.

34   Paul Lazarsfeld, Bernard Berelson and Hazel Gaudet, *The People's Choice: How the Voter Makes Up His Mind in a Presidential Campaign*, New York: Columbia University Press, 1944; Elihu Katz and Paul F. Lazarsfeld, *Personal Influence: The Part Played by People in the Flow of Mass Communications*, New York: The Free Press, 1955.

The development of the personal influence or two-step model had a profound impact on the practice of public diplomacy. The concept suggested that the key to any information campaign required the successful targeting of local opinion leaders who could serve as the principle channels of influence to the public and provide a multiplier effect into their specific social and professional networks. These and other similar state-of-the-art techniques were all introduced into official American public diplomacy efforts, including foreign leader and exchange programs.[35]

One of the most important discoveries to emerge from behaviourist socio-scientific research on the political effectiveness of foreign leader and exchange programs in securing American foreign policy objectives during the 1950s was their utility in alliance management. Specifically, it was revealed that "instead of converting critics or opponents to a different way of thinking, the most value came from *reinforcing* existing perceptions". The greatest success was realised in exchanges where "conviction, motivation, and capacity to act in accordance with the viewpoint fostered by the program were intensified by the exchange experience".[36]

Although US exchanges have at times been employed to convert hostile participants,[37] the early research, and subsequent practice, made it clear that in international relations "exchanges are primarily a potent weapon for sustaining the status quo rather than changing it", and are most successful "if a certain level of curiosity about cultural affinity with the host country already exists".[38] While participants may not become "converts", nonetheless, a "reorientation in outlook takes place that is all the more subtle, cohesive, and defensible because it is partly driven by individual interests".[39]

Although conventionally portrayed as a product of civilian research, the evolution of the "personal influence" concept from its germination in 1944 to its maturation in the 1950s – and the general development of the area of mass communications studies – grew largely out of US government

---

35   Christopher Simpson, Science of Coercion: Communication Research and Psychological Warfare 1945-1960, Oxford: Oxford University Press, 1996, pp. 72-73; Giles Scott-Smith, Mapping the Undefinable: Some Thoughts on the Relevance of Exchange Programs within International Relations Theory, *Annals of the American Academy of Political and Social Science*, vol. 616, March 2008, p. 177.

36   Scott-Smith, p. 179. Emphasis in original.

37   Snow writes that during her time working with the IVLP in the mid-1990s most participants had a predisposition to support the US, although some were specifically chosen for their strong anti-American feelings. Snow, *Propaganda, Inc*, p. 96.

38   Scott-Smith, Mapping the Undefinable, p. 180.

39   Scott-Smith, p. 182.

and military funded research into propaganda.[40] Innovations such as the "opinion leader" phenomena, although labelled communications research, could just as easily be categorised as psychological warfare studies. As one leading scholar of communications studies points out, "Either description is accurate; the distinction between the two is that the former term tends to downplay the social context that gave birth to the work in the first place".[41]

Reinforcing the status quo

Critics, commenting from the outside, have speculated that Americans use the AALD to socialise or "duchess" Australian leaders into believing American interests and values are always the same as Australian ones.[42] While this certainly occurs, it is also important to note that the AALD is first and foremost an Australian-driven exercise. The result is the rather peculiar situation whereby a group of pro-American Australians facilitate the socialisation of other Australians into acquiescing or reinforcing American political interests.

According to founding AALD participant and former Liberal MP David Kemp, it should not be surprising that the Dialogue functions to deepen support for the alliance among less enthusiastic or even hostile participants. Kemp believes there is a conscious and targeted effort on the part of the AALD to co-opt the anti-American elements in Australian politics. Scanlan, he argues:

> [Captured] in the Dialogue, the very strong pro-Americans and immersed in their company the people who've got a less intuitive liking for the United States. He's provided a forum through which the [pro-]Americans can duchess the anti-Americans and show them they're not so bad after all. It's been highly successful.[43]

---

40   Simpson, *Science of* Coercion, pp. 52-53, 72-74.

41   Simpson, p. 71.

42   Scott Burchill, Gillard's Fawning Over Obama a Bad Start on Diplomatic Front, *Sydney Morning Herald*, 30 June 2010, <http://www.smh.com.au/federal-politics/political-opinion/gillards-fawning-over-obama-a-bad-start-on-diplomatic-front-20100629-zj3h.html>, accessed 1 April 2018; David Day, Bowing to Duchess Diplomacy, *Sydney Morning Herald*, 8 June 2012, <http://www.smh.com.au/federal-politics/political-opinion/bowing-to-duchess-diplomacy-20120607-1zysh.html>, accessed 1 April 2018; Alan Ramsey, The Sermon Bush Wants to Hear, *Sydney Morning Herald*, 12 June 2004, <http://www.smh.com.au/articles/2004/06/11/1086749896060.html>, accessed 1 April 2018.

43   Author interview with David Kemp, 31 August 2011.

Moreover, Kemp argues, there exists a kind of hidden objective of the AALD to target the left-faction of the Labor Party:

> In a way, if the Dialogue was more focused on the Labor Party that's probably one of its main jobs. I suspect Phil wouldn't articulate that. He might. But to concede the work of the Dialogue is more directed to the Labor Party than it is to the Liberals is quite a big concession. And I don't think there would ever be an official concession to that effect.[44]

While he doesn't characterise it as the result of conscious intent, former Liberal MP Andrew Robb also identifies the "somewhat anti-American" component of the Labor Party as one where the AALD has played an important role in helping to remind participants of the value of the Australia-US relationship. Commenting specifically on former Prime Minister Julia Gillard's public emergence as an ardent supporter of the US alliance, Robb argues that, while he "wouldn't just put it down to the Dialogue ... it was certainly a significant contributor".[45]

Despite these observations, it is highly unlikely that the AALD functions to convert "anti-American" critics. As already noted, serious critics of the AALD are not invited to participate. In the words of journalist and long-time AALD participant Peter Hartcher, "I can't think of critics that have been brought in and converted ... I don't think critics are invited ... I just don't know that it works like that. Maybe they'd like it to but I just don't think it's had that effect".[46]

The same can be said of mild critics of Australia's relationship with the US, specifically those in the left-faction of the Labor Party, primarily because they also do not attend the AALD. Their absence is not proof of a specific exclusion policy, but rather more likely due to the fact that those in the Labor Party who inhabit defence and foreign affairs positions are generally from the pro-American right faction. As journalist and AALD participant Glenn Milne points out, "the aim of the Dialogue is to pick future leaders which means, by the nature of ALP internal politics, [that] broadly disqualifies most of the left".[47]

---

44   Kemp qualifies his remarks by stating, "In any case, that is just a point of view I am expressing, not something I have ever gleaned from Dialogue organisers or from Phil". Author interview with David Kemp, 31 August 2011.

45   Author interview with Andrew Robb, 15 July 2011.

46   Author interview with Peter Hartcher, 29 October 2011.

47   Author interview with Glenn Milne, 9 November 2011.

To some extent, the AALD does "preach to the converted", in the words of one former Labor MP and Dialogue participant: "The people who go are the ones who are very interested in the relationship anyway. There is an element of it being self-serving to that extent".[48] Nevertheless, it would be wrong to dismiss the impact of the AALD entirely on account of this fact, as some critics appear to do. Hugh White, for example, although critical of the role the AALD plays in managing Australia's relationship with the US, suggests:

> It's just a group of people who are getting together to have a chat. It's perfectly reasonable they should choose people they want to talk to. All of us are a bit inclined to prefer to talk to people whom we agree with. In a sense it misses the point and kind of buys the Dialogue's own puffery to think there's some requirement that it be representative.[49]

White's states: "If I thought that it had a significant impact on the management of the relationship I'd take a different view, but I don't, so I don't worry about it".[50]

Certainly, there is no evidence to suggest the AALD has a transformative impact on the nature or direction of the Australia-US relationship. The most one could say is that some participants are prodded into taking further steps in a trajectory they were already on. While it may be "subtle", a former Labor MP explains, the AALD "does nudge you a little bit in that [pro-American] direction if you're not already there".[51] When asked if he believed the AALD was useful in encouraging those who may be less enthusiastic about the US alliance to "come over", Richard Woolcott, while careful not to exaggerate its influence, replied, "Yes I think so. Particularly people who haven't been deeply involved in foreign policy".[52]

Many participants attest to the fact that their views have been consolidated by the AALD. The remarks by Liberal MP Kelly O'Dwyer are typical in this regard, when she states that "through the discussions that we had there, my views have become even more solid on just how important that relationship is. Although it did start from a very high base".[53] This

---

48   Author interview with participant who chose to remain anonymous.
49   Author interview with Professor Hugh White, 2 September 2011.
50   Author interview with Professor Hugh White, 2 September 2011.
51   Author interview with participant who chose to remain anonymous.
52   Author interview with Richard Woolcott, 22 March 2011.
53   Author interview with Kelly O'Dwyer, 21 October 2011.

experience is not universal. Former Foreign Minister Alexander Downer concedes that the AALD might hold the potential for shaping participants' perceptions or opening their minds to the US. "It didn't have that effect on me", he adds, "but I knew a lot about America before I ever went to the Dialogue".[54]

It seems apparent the AALD does have a real impact, primarily by reinforcing existing perceptions among current elites and reproducing alliance orthodoxies in the minds of the "successor generation". As further outlined below, the AALD achieves this by providing many of the same material and psychological inducements that have proven so successful in American foreign leader and exchange programs to socialise participants and bind them to the US system of hegemony.

The power of socialisation

One of the primary mechanisms for socialisation identified in foreign leader and exchange programs is the sense of self-importance bestowed upon participants simply for being invited into an elite and prestigious program. While the AALD certainly has its critics, it too is generally held in high-esteem in elite circles. Australians who participate in the AALD, says Kemp, "don't just say, oh well it was good. They say it was fantastic; magnificent; irreplaceable".[55] Consequently, in Paul Howes' words, "it's the type of thing you don't say no to".[56]

According to board member Andrew MacIntyre, "demand exceeds supply".[57] Stephen Loosley, founding member of the AALD and board member from 1999-2010, confirms that:

> [The] Dialogue always has far more applications for delegate status than we're able to accommodate from very senior people. When you've got a queue of people knocking at the door to be involved, that's the best test of how relevant and significant the organisation is perceived to be or actually happens to be.[58]

The potential to be overcome by the sheer stature of the event has been duly noted. Although not a participant herself, former premier of Western

---

54   Author interview with Alexander Downer, 14 September 2011.
55   Author interview with David Kemp, 31 August 2011.
56   Author interview with Paul Howes, 5 August 2011.
57   Author interview with Professor Andrew MacIntyre, 28 June 2011.
58   Author interview with Stephen Loosley, 11 January 2012.

Australia Carmen Lawrence states that during her time as a politician "I certainly remember that a lot of comments made suggested to me that [Dialogue participants] felt this was a really a big treat".[59] More tellingly, a former senior Australian diplomat and AALD participant observes:

> [By] being invited Australians feel a bit privileged. Being let into the inner sanctum and hearing for a couple of days a group of highly articulate and intelligent Americans captures them. And they do become very pro-American. But I don't think it's a conspiracy it's just the way it happens.[60]

The impact of the AALD alone in duchessing Australian elites should not be exaggerated. American leaders are renowned for taking every opportunity to promote the notion of America's "special relationship" with Australia and do so in a number of different forums. Nevertheless, the effect of the AALD is far from incidental, particularly for those who are not used to witnessing American power first hand. As Sam Lipski notes:

> You come [to the AALD in Washington] and it's big. It's the State Department. It's the centre of world power. The Americans do things in impressive ways. There's no question that the Washington end of the Dialogue for Australian participants, the Rudds and the Julias of this world being examples ... it's heavy stuff.[61]

One former ALP parliamentarian, who was a relatively junior person at the time of his first and only AALD event, recalls that:

> [As a] political figure you like to be at the centre of the action so to speak. Even if that's a bit of an unconscious sort of thing. Because of the long period the Dialogue's been around, that it's established, that it's well reputed amongst high officials, I think attendance at that and being part of that does add to your positive view of the alliance ... Everyone who goes basks in the glory of it. I don't mean it literally like that. Everyone who goes there I noticed felt like I'm at the Australia-US Dialogue. It had a degree of cachet in attending ... I think that adds a lot to what people feel about the alliance and so on.[62]

---

59   Author interview with Carmen Lawrence, 14 November 2011.
60   Author interview with participant who chose to remain anonymous.
61   Author interview with Sam Lipski, 25 October 2011.
62   Author interview with participant who chose to remain anonymous.

In the ALP generally, according to Mark Latham, receiving an invitation to attend the AALD is considered to be a necessary ticket for rising through party ranks:

> Sometimes there is a feeling in politics that you want to belong. People coming through the ranks might think oh I've made it now that I've been invited to this club. When I first became a Shadow Minister in 1996, shortly thereafter, people like Gareth Evans, Kim Beazley, Arch Bevis and [a] few others were being whisked off to Washington for a big conference and there were high expectations about it beforehand. Then you wonder, gee, what do I have to do to be invited to that level of seniority in the system? ... For those who do get lulled into it there's that feeling of I've made it now. So it's the peak body for this.[63]

Although Hugh White is unperturbed by what he views as the otherwise incidental impact of the AALD in managing Australia's relationship with the US, he does concede that, "for a young parliamentarian ... an invitation to the Leadership Dialogue is a pretty hefty thing ... this can be quite formative in developing the views of people who are coming into leadership positions". Given that the AALD embodies a values-based conception of the alliance and refuses to confront core questions regarding its future utility, White acknowledges that "it does make it harder for future leaders thus influenced to understand the alliance effectively ... And to that extent its influence has been unfortunate".[64]

The creation of personal affinities, and the accompanying sentiment that everyone is on the same side, is another important aspect of socialisation identified in US foreign leader and exchange programs. Similarly, one of the core functions of the AALD is to create a friendly atmosphere where relationship building can take place. The objective is to solidify the alliance by reinforcing notions of shared values and interests. While Australia is certainly viewed as politically and strategically important to America, many political participants of the AALD share the sentiments of this former Labor MP and Dialogue participant:

> Over my twenty years in parliament, state and federal, I've met a lot of US officials and citizens. I've always detected a strong element of goodwill and friendship towards Australia which exceeds our

---

63   Author interview with Mark Latham, 22 November 2011.
64   Author interview with Professor Hugh White, 2 September 2011.

importance to them in many ways, if one was strictly objective about it ... [The Americans] keep coming back [to the AALD] because they quite like us and there are personal relationships.[65]

Although the AALD is not responsible for creating this attitude, it certainly plays a part in reinforcing it. AALD participants today are almost unanimous in declaring that one of the major achievements of the AALD over the years has been, in Andrew Robb's words, to "constantly reinforce the things we've got in common and the history of our relationship and the value of maintaining it going forward".[66]

Reminiscent of Lasswell's concept of the "social lobby", there exists a number of US "movers and shakers" at the AALD whose job it is to reinforce this view, persistently emphasising the apparent fact of America's "special relationship" with Australia. Over the lifetime of the AALD, the key Americans responsible for cultivating the relationship in this way have been Kurt Campbell, Stanley Roth, Robert Zoellick and, above all, Richard Armitage. The business of such people, Alan Ramsey writes in the *Sydney Morning Herald*, is "in changing political perceptions of Washington's national interest".[67] Describing the atmosphere at the AALD, Ramsey provides his own interpretation of the way the "social lobby" functions:

> What do they do? Well, along with the American 'participants', they have dinners, get squired around the place, meet all the top people, and generally get schmoozed if not duchessed as they hold private talk-fests, among themselves and with members of the US Administration.[68]

Armitage, who received an Order of Australia in 2010 for furthering the relationship between Australian and American defence forces and intelligence services, has been particularly effective in projecting the illusion that the Australia-US relationship is grounded in shared values forged in joint sacrifice. As one astute journalist observed during the 2003 AALD event, Armitage "knows how to make his pitch believable. He is direct, and there is enough candour and humour in it to make him very persuasive".[69]

---

65   Author interview with participant who chose to remain anonymous.

66   Author interview with Andrew Robb, 15 July 2011.

67   Ramsey, The Sermon Bush Wants to Hear.

68   Ramsey.

69   Tim Dodd, Arise Australia, Global Leader ... *Australian Financial Review*, 15 August 2003.

Armitage liked to advertise the fact that his attendance at the AALD comes at his own expense, "not because the State Department wouldn't send me, of course they would, to an important ally like Australia, but because I believe in this".[70] Many Australian participants, such as journalist Greg Sheridan, have taken him at his word: "The fact Armitage, as Deputy Secretary of State, one of the busiest men in the world, makes the effort to travel to Australia to attend a private talkfest is evidence" of America's commitment to Australia.[71]

It is this kind of sentiment fostered by the AALD that Hugh White finds particularly troubling. "It is very easy to slip into the illusion – which of course the Americans are always willing to project to Australians, partly for their own reasons — that this is a relationship that transcends interests and goes to values".[72] In the case of Armitage, White explains that:

> [He] fairly famously has often spoken of the relationship very much in terms of the shared blood sacrifice and all that sort of stuff. That what really matters is that Australians and Americans have bled together in every war since World War I … I'm not one of those who dismisses that sort of stuff. I just don't think that's the basis on which we can either judge the present value of the relationship or ensure its future strength.[73]

The AALD was established, in Scanlan's words, with the intention that it would become "an institution of influence over the next generation".[74] It has since become renowned for its uncanny ability to successfully target future leaders in both countries.[75] Andrew Robb recalls that, in the early years, the AALD did choose "people who were likely to be future leaders … And many of the people that they did invite within seven or eight years were leaders. Either in opposition or in government".[76]

---

70   Peter Hartcher, Forum Plays A Vital Role in Healthy US-Australia Links, *Australian Financial Review*, 10 August 2001.

71   Greg Sheridan, Power Talking, *The Australian*, 23 July 2003.

72   Daniel Flitton, Man of Many Words, *The Age*, 11 August 2007, <http://www.theage.com.au/news/in-depth/man-of-many-words/2007/08/10/1186530610605.html>, accessed 1 April 2018.

73   Author interview with Professor Hugh White, 2 September 2011.

74   Paul Kelly, *The March of Patriots: The Struggle for Modern Australia*, Melbourne: Melbourne University Publishing, 2010, p. 163.

75   Hartcher, Forum Plays A Vital Role; Greg Sheridan, Obama Opts for a Friend of Australia in Key Policy Role, *The Australian*, 19 January 2009.

76   Author interview with Andrew Robb, 15 July 2011.

The drive to engage the younger generation remains crucial to the strategy of the AALD today. Paul Howes, who was no doubt targeted as a potential future leader himself, believes that engaging the younger generation "probably plays more of a role than [engaging] current leaders. I think Phil is really driven on that because he does put a lot of effort on the next generation". Reflecting on his own participation at the AALD since 2007, Howes recalled in 2011: "When you look through the Dialogue, when you look at the young participants, you see five future Prime Ministers sitting there, ten future foreign affairs people".[77]

The desire to reach even further into the next generation of emerging leaders drove the establishment of the Young Leadership Dialogue (YLD) in 2007.[78] According to the AALD's website, the purpose of the YLD is "to secure the long term future of the AALD mission of mutual understanding between Australian and American leaders through a consistently flowing pipeline of young leaders".[79] John W.H. Denton, Partner and Chief Executive Officer of Corrs Chambers Westgrath and Dialogue participant, sees both the AALD and the YLD as an exercise in what he refers to as "succession planning". That is, "seeking to deepen the generational succession for the relationship". In that regard, the YLD has been an "important policy innovation in the organisation itself".[80]

One often quoted example of a well-targeted leader is former Prime Minister Kevin Rudd. He is "such a striking example that the others seem to pale by comparison", declares Sam Lipski.[81] Paul Kelly agrees that Rudd "is a really conspicuous example" of how the AALD has had an influence over the next generation of leaders.[82] Rudd was one of the initial attendees invited to participate in the first AALD event in 1993 "long before anyone had heard of him", Nick Greiner recalls.[83] As a young Queensland bureaucrat, Rudd was unfamiliar with the US and, according to Kelly, "became educated in American ways and built his US networks

---

77   Author interview with Paul Howes, 5 August 2011.

78   Noteworthy political participants of the YLD have included Liberal MPs Jamie Briggs and Kelly O'Dwyer, Labor MPs Chris Bowen and Amanda Rishworth and former head of the AWU, Paul Howes.

79   Australian American Leadership Dialogue, Young Leadership Dialogue, <http://www.aald.org/young-leadership-dialogue>, accessed 1 April 2016.

80   Author interview with John W. H. Denton, 15 February 2012.

81   Author interview with Sam Lipski, 25 October 2011.

82   Author interview with Paul Kelly, 20 January 2012.

83   Author interview with Nick Greiner, 6 July 2011.

virtually entirely from the Dialogue".[84] As Rudd has himself acknowledged, "The truth is, I'd never even visited the US before the first Dialogue, so concentrated an Asianist had I become".[85]

Rudd is a good example of what is perhaps the greatest single contributing factor to the process of socialisation; the access provided to high-level officials and all that entails for career advancement. Rudd used the extensive networking opportunities afforded by the AALD to advance his political career. As Sam Lipski notes:

> Everyone knows that Rudd, from the moment he smelt power in Washington, assiduously cultivated every link and network created by the Dialogue. He didn't just cultivate, he poured water and seed and growth and he just couldn't get enough of it. It became quite important in his growing ambition to become Prime Minister. Look at his relationship with [Hillary] Clinton ... All those doors were opened for him by the Dialogue.[86]

Rudd later evolved into one of Labor's strongest supporters of the alliance and a committed participant at almost every AALD event since its establishment. At the fifteenth annual Dialogue in 2007, Rudd gave an emphatic speech about the importance of the US alliance, where his enthusiasm for American exceptionalism and US hegemonic power were on full display:

> America is an overwhelming force for good in the world. It is time we sang that from the worlds' rooftops ... let there be no retreat of America from the world. Let there be no retreat of America from the Asia–Pacific region. Let there be no retreat of America from our region.[87]

Two years later, in 2009, addressing the AALD for the first time as Prime Minister, Rudd continued in the same vein, declaring that "US global and regional leadership" is something "which we, in this country, Australia, are proud to support, and we intend to be your partners for the future". Rudd concluded: "I salute this Dialogue. I salute each and every one of you

---

84   Kelly, *The March of Patriots*, p. 163.
85   Sheridan, Power Talking.
86   Author interview with Sam Lipski, 25 October 2011.
87   Kevin Rudd, Kevin Rudd's Address, *The Australian*, 24 August 2007, <http://www.theaustralian.com.au/national-affairs/climate/kevin-rudds-address/story-e6frg6xf-1111114253042>, accessed 1 April 2018.

who have been participants in it". For Rudd, and indeed his wife Therese, the Dialogue was more than just "an important informal network" to help strengthen the relationship; it was a place where American participants "have become part of our wider family".[88] Rudd appointed his long-time friend Phillip Scanlan to the position of Consul-General in New York in 2008.

While the impact of the AALD in shaping Rudd's thinking is impossible to measure precisely, it evidently had an impact. As someone who held a positive pre-disposition towards the US, but did not have any personal links and had not visited America, the AALD opened many doors. Consequently, Rudd was able to forge close connections with, and make himself known to, the US political elite. The primary factor behind the development of Rudd's strong relationship with the US was his ambition. The role of the AALD was to help facilitate the realisation of that ambition. The AALD socialisation mechanism was the path laid before him, with no obligations but plenty of benefits, as an inducement to remain committed to the status quo.

Rudd's experience with the AALD has parallels with that of former UK Prime Ministers Tony Blair and Gordon Brown and their experiences with the IVLP. Blair and Brown were ambitious young Labour MPs in the 1980s with very little connection to the US. Brown, like Rudd, had never been to the US, nor did he have any significant personal links with Americans prior to his experience with the IVLP. Blair was also introduced to the Washington elite through the IVLP when he was still relatively unknown in US circles. The experience had a profound impact on the belief systems of both men and, consequently, helped to realign their party's international stance in accordance with American interests and priorities.[89]

Gatekeeping

The socialisation function of the AALD is one part of its "gatekeeping" role to prevent adverse changes to government policymaking on the alliance. In addition, entry to and performance at the AALD is often a means by which Australian political leaders obtain an unofficial stamp of approval as a person able to handle the US alliance. This function appears to be limited to the Labor Party where accusations of "immaturity" or "weakness" on defence matters, and the inability to "responsibly manage" the US alliance,

88   Kevin Rudd, speech to the Australian American Leadership Dialogue, Melbourne, 15 August 2009.
89   Scott-Smith, Searching for the Successor Generation.

are generally directed.[90] The experience of former opposition leader Mark Latham and former Prime Minister, Julia Gillard, are two prominent examples.

Latham was quickly identified as a danger to the alliance orthodoxy, even before he became opposition leader. In July 2002 Latham described John Howard as an "arse licker" with respect to George W. Bush, who he later referred to as the most dangerous and incompetent US president in recent history, with the Australians who followed him "a conga line of suck-holes".[91] However, it was his first major foreign policy speech as opposition leader that sounded the loudest alarm bells, as he implied the Australia-US relationship was an unequal partnership.[92]

John Howard, then Prime Minister, characterised Latham as "indifferent" towards the alliance and a threat to its existence.[93] Similarly, then Foreign Minister Alexander Downer argued that Latham "should not be debating the US alliance in the midst of the war on terrorism" and that his behaviour gave the impression he was "anti-American".[94] Experts in Australian strategic studies identified Latham's position on the alliance as a threat to the long-term bipartisan commitment to the security relationship that Bob Hawke and Kim Beazley had extended during the 1980s.[95]

Latham had in fact declared his party's support for the core aspects of the alliance, declaring that "Labor believes in the value of the alliance not only to Australia and to the United States, but to the international community as a whole", singling out the "importance of the intelligence relationship, based on the joint management and control of facilities in

---

90   Andrew O'Neill, "Regional, Alliance and Global Priorities of the Rudd-Gillard Government" in James Cotton and John Ravenhill (eds), *Middle Power Dreaming: Australia and the World Affairs 2006-2010*, South Melbourne: Oxford University Press, 2011, p. 280.

91   Robert Manne, Little America: How John Howard Has Changed Australia, *The Monthly*, March 2006, p. 30.

92   Mark Latham, Labor and the World, address to the Lowy Institute for International Policy, Sydney, 7 April 2004. Reproduced at Australianpolitics.com, <http://australianpolitics.com/2004/04/07/labor-and-the-world-latham-foreign-policy-speech.html>, accessed 1 April 2018.

93   PM Accuses Latham of "Indifference" to US Alliance, *ABC News*, 11 June 2004, <http://www.abc.net.au/news/2004-06-11/pm-accuses-latham-of-indifference-to-us-alliance/1991070>, accessed 1 April 2018.

94   Latham "Undermining" US alliance, *ABC News*, 13 April 2004, <http://www.abc.net.au/news/2004-04-13/latham-undermining-us-alliance/169506>, accessed 1 April 2018.

95   Rod Lyon and William T. Tow, The Future of the US-Australian Security Relationship, *Asian Security*, vol. 1, no. 1, 2005, pp. 37-8.

Australia".[96] Nevertheless, his position on both the Iraq War and the Australia United States Free Trade Agreement (AUSFTA) were of serious concern to orthodox alliance loyalists. Paul Kelly and Peter Hartcher wrote in their respective newspapers that should Latham be elected prime minister his position on Iraq would likely harm the relationship.[97] When it came to the AUSFTA, Paul Kelly argued that, as the most "vital decision on the US relationship for years", support for the agreement, despite all its "defects", was a "test of Labor's ability to have a successful relationship with the US", and of Latham's "maturity" and capacity to rise above the "anti-Americanism" that he said "infects the ALP".[98]

It is revealing that support for both of these policies was considered a benchmark of Latham's ability to manage the alliance given that Australia's participation in the invasion of Iraq arguably violated the ANZUS Treaty, was contrary to international law and opposed by the vast majority of Australians.[99] During Latham's term as opposition leader, and as the occupation dragged on, support for the war continued to decline.[100] On the AUSFTA too, public support steadily declined from 65 per cent, when negotiations started, to 35 per cent when the deal was concluded in 2004.[101] Lacking popular support, the Australian government was instead driven to conclude the AUSFTA on the back of the lobbying efforts of

---

96   Latham, Labor and the World.

97   Paul Kelly, US, Labor Tense But Talking, *The Australian*, 16 June 2004; Peter Hartcher, Frosty Relations Threaten to Sour Alliance, *Sydney Morning Herald*, 11 June 2004, <http://www.smh.com.au/articles/2004/06/10/1086749840015.html>, accessed 1 April 2018.

98   Paul Kelly, If Push Comes to Shove, *The Australian*, 10 July 2004.

99   Public opposition to Australian participation of an invasion of Iraq, in the absence of UN approval, was consistently high during the 7-8 months prior to the war, but more evenly split in the case UN approval was received. After the invasion began, a majority of Australians shifted to supporting the war, although a substantial minority still opposed it. Brendan O'Connor and Srdjan Vucetic, Another Mars-Venus Divide? Why Australia Said "Yes" and Canada Said "Non" to Involvement in the 2003 Iraq War, *Australian Journal of International Affairs*, vol. 64, no. 5, November 2010, pp. 535-536.

100   46% of Australians were opposed to having soldiers in Iraq in March 2004, 51% in March 2005 and 59% in April 2006. Public Support for Iraq War Hits Low, *Sydney Morning Herald*, 21 April 2006, <http://www.smh.com.au/news/National/Public-support-for-Iraq-war-hits-low/2006/04/21/1145344267763.html>, accessed 1 April 2018.

101   Patricia Ranald, The Australia-US Free Trade Agreement: A Contest of Interests, *Journal of Australian Political Economy*, no. 57, June 2006, p. 40.

certain Australian and American corporate groups who perceived benefits from the FTA.[102]

In response to the "flak" Latham received for his departure from the status quo regarding the alliance, Scanlan warned that the Australia-US relationship needed "hard work and constant nurturing" and that "every Australian political leader needs to develop his or her own understanding of the depth and the breadth of the alliance with the US". Scanlan proceeded to "warmly welcome" Latham to the upcoming AALD event in 2004 which, he proclaimed, was about "achieving mutual understanding between leaders, not merely consensus".[103]

While Latham initially accepted the invitation to attend the AALD, he later retracted his decision for fear of being embarrassed politically on account of his views on the alliance.[104] As Robert Manne wrote at the time, "among this elite group Latham was by now almost the only important dissident on the question of the American alliance".[105] In conversation with me, Latham added that the presence of pro-alliance journalists at the AALD was another reason for his decision to withdraw. As he asked, rhetorically:

> Who wants to rub up against dozens of Sheridan, Kelly and Hartcher articles bagging you for your foreign policy views if you're trying to make your way through the system? Who wants to take on the press establishment in Australia? ... Where would you end up in the system if you took them on?[106]

Alexander Downer responded to Latham's withdrawal from the AALD by arguing that it illustrated his decision to "cut and run from the US relationship". Latham, he said, should have gone and "demonstrated his credentials to manage the relationship in a mature fashion".[107] Similarly, on the American side, Armitage "expressed regret" that Latham had cancelled his planned trip to the AALD in Washington, professing that it would

102 Ranald, p. 42.

103 Katharine Murphy, Latham Cops Flak Over US Stand, *Australian Financial Review*, 13 April 2004.

104 Mark Latham, *The Latham Diaries*, Melbourne: Melbourne University Publishing, 2005, p. 281.

105 Manne, Little America, p. 31.

106 Author interview with Mark Latham, 22 November 2011.

107 Alexander Downer, Latham Cuts and Runs From US Relationship, press release from the Minister for Foreign Affairs, 12 May 2004, <http://foreignminister.gov.au/releases/2004/040512.html>, accessed 1 April 2018.

have been an occasion for him to "get exposure to the length, the breadth, the depth of this relationship". Armitage had "made plain that he thought Mr Latham neither understood nor appreciated the alliance".[108] According to Richard Woolcott:

> The Americans [at the AALD] probably wanted to influence [Latham] in a more pro-American direction, and I suppose some other Australian members of the Dialogue wanted to see him more committed to the alliance. But that never happened so in a sense, that's hypothetical.[109]

When Kevin Rudd assumed the position of leader of the Labor Party in December 2006, participation at the AALD was once again viewed as a litmus test for indicating the necessary maturity to manage the relationship. Rudd was "strongly urged to attend" the upcoming AALD in January 2007 by other members of his party as a symbol reaffirming Labor's rejection of Latham's attitude towards the alliance.[110] Similarly, Bob Carr's long-standing attendance at the AALD was widely cited in the media as evidence of his capacity to responsibly manage the alliance after he was appointed foreign minister in the Gillard government in 2012.[111]

While Latham illustrates how the AALD operates to censure those who depart from the status quo, Julia Gillard demonstrates what is required to gain approval. Gillard's performance at the 2008 Dialogue event, where she gave her first foreign policy address as deputy Prime Minister, was carefully watched and assessed in elite circles. Gillard looked to reassure her audience of 300 Australian and American elites that the alliance transcended the power of any single leader or party; a subtle reference to

---

108   Peter Hartcher, Think About Life Without the US: Armitage, *Sydney Morning Herald*, 11 June 2004, <http://www.smh.com.au/articles/2004/06/10/1086749842549.html>, accessed 1 April 2018.

109   Author interview with Richard Woolcott, 22 March 2011.

110   Cynthia Banham, US Meeting May Provide A Potent Symbol for Rudd, *Sydney Morning Herald*, 11 December 2006, <http://www.smh.com.au/news/national/us-meeting-may-provide-a-potent-symbol-for-rudd/2006/12/10/1165685553923.html>, accessed 1 April 2018.

111   Greg Sheridan, Bob Carr Right Choice for Foreign Job, *The Australian*, 3 March 2012; Laurie Oakes, Julia Gillard Finds a Spine, Turns Defeat Into A Breathtaking Win, *Herald Sun*, 3 March 2012, <http://www.heraldsun.com.au/news/opinion/julia-gillard-finds-a-spine-turns-defeat-into-a-breathtaking-win/story-fn56baaq-1226287818689>, accessed 1 April 2018; Simon Benson, How Suicidal ALP Spawned a Saviour, *The Daily Telegraph*, 2 March 2012; Stefanie Balogh, US Had No Concerns About Bob Carr's Appointment As Foreign Minister, *The Australian*, 1 April 2012.

both Latham's ambivalence towards the alliance and the dangers posed by George W. Bush's immense unpopularity. Gillard reassured her audience that the alliance was "bigger than any person, bigger than any party, bigger than any government, bigger than any period in our history together". The AALD, Gillard added, is "full of committed advocates, of true believers", in the Australia-US relationship.[112]

Gillard's address to the AALD was recognised, in Andrew Robb's assessment, as "one of the most, not strident, but positive statements of the value of the alliance that anyone has given on either side of politics".[113] According to Mel Sembler, former US ambassador to Australia, Gillard "wowed the Americans" with her content and presentation and "everybody loved it".[114] Peter Hartcher, reporting on the event for the *Sydney Morning Herald*, wrote that propositions such as Australia and the US working together "to help build a world where civilisation will persist", as Gillard phrased it, was "music to American ears". Hartcher concluded his assessment of Gillard's performance at the AALD by stating:

> Julia Gillard has come a long way since the Victorian Socialist Left. She has made a sophisticated and successful international debut, and moved herself credibly into a new category of leadership … In doing so, she has reaffirmed Australia's place as America's uniquely reliable ally.[115]

The specific role played by the AALD in assisting Gillard's elevation to leadership material in the eyes of the establishment is perhaps best articulated by Kelly, who, immediately after the 2008 AALD event, wrote:

> Coming from the Labor Left and once a loyal supporter of the anti-American Mark Latham, Gillard has been inducted into the political culture and rituals of the alliance. This is a prime function of the dialogue. She has become a true believer.[116]

Kelly later elaborated on what he meant, pointing out that Gillard's address to the AALD "was in the Benjamin Franklin room at the State Department … It's a very special event, in a very special forum, in a very special room.

---

112 Peter Hartcher, Curtin Call and Excellent Debut, *Sydney Morning Herald*, 27 June 2008, <http://www.smh.com.au/news/peter-hartcher/curtin-call-an-excellent-debut/2008/06/26/1214472672972.html>, accessed 1 April 2018.

113 Author interview with Andrew Robb, 15 July 2011.

114 Hartcher, Curtin Call and Excellent Debut.

115 Hartcher.

116 Paul Kelly, The Rudd Alliance, *The Australian*, 28 June 2008.

That's what I meant when I talked about Gillard being inducted into the rituals of the relationship".[117]

In other words, according to Kelly, Gillard had both been assisted and affirmatively judged by the AALD on her transition as an orthodox alliance loyalist. Any question over her commitment to the status quo arising from her affiliation with the left could be laid to rest now that she had been unreservedly accepted by the AALD. Journalist Hamish McDonald believes that Kelly's remarks are "astonishingly frank as an admission or almost a boast" that showed how the AALD welcomed Gillard into "the inner priesthood of the highest strategic circles".[118]

Upon assuming the prime ministership, Gillard's performance at the AALD was once again recalled and heralded as evidence of her maturity and capacity to manage the alliance relationship. Sheridan wrote that Gillard had moved her "national security identity bang in[to] the middle of the mainstream". The evidence provided was her attendance for several years at the AALD and her speech at the 2008 Dialogue event where she was "clear and declarative about her attachment to the US alliance".[119] The *Australian Financial Review* wrote Gillard was careful to indicate that her government would be a "safe transition", promising to honour Australia's alliance with the US, and that she had "impressed [by] taking part in such forums as the Australian American Leadership Dialogue and the Australia-Israel forum".[120] The *Sydney Morning Herald*'s editorial on Gillard's foreign policy agenda claimed it promised little change "as the former campus radical has made the transition to the safe mainstream consensus without a ripple". The editorial concluded by stating:

> [Gillard] has been a participant in the second-track diplomacy effort known as the Australian-American Leadership Dialogue, and in the newer Australia-Israel forum set up last year. In these two sensitive areas, where politicians are carefully watched for deviation by powerful lobbies, she has flagged her adherence to the norm.[121]

---

117   Author interview with Paul Kelly, 20 January 2012.

118   Author interview with Hamish McDonald, 15 November 2011.

119   Greg Sheridan, Leader to Stay True on Foreign Affairs, *The Australian*, 25 June 2010.

120   John Kerin and Greg Earl, Gillard Sticks to Her Guns on Foreign Affairs, *Australian Financial Review*, 26 June 2010, <http://www.afr.com/news/politics/gillard-sticks-to-her-guns-on-foreign-affairs-20100625-iva7m>, accessed 1 April 2018.

121   Julia Gillard Gives Labor a New Start, Sydney *Morning Herald*, 25 June 2010, <http://www.smh.com.au/federal-politics/editorial/julia-gillard-gives-labor-a-new-start-20100624-z3jh.html>, accessed 1 April 2018.

Australian elite circles and the American establishment carefully watch future Australian leaders at the AALD for adherence to the status quo. The AALD is "almost an American veto on who is acceptable to be a political leader in this country and who's not", argues Mark Latham. "You can be absolutely assured", Latham continues, that if Gillard hadn't proven herself at the Dialogue "she wouldn't have been a candidate for the leadership ... that got rid of Rudd".[122]

Certainly, a number of leaked diplomatic cables revealed by WikiLeaks suggest that the US embassy viewed acceptance at the AALD as an important indicator of Gillard's commitment to the status quo. A cable sent on 13 June 2008, under the sub-heading, "Gillard the Pro-American", describes how previous concerns about Gillard's apparent "ambivalent" feelings towards the alliance were assuaged since she became the Deputy Leader of the Labor Party and indicated "an understanding of its importance". Apart from going "out of her way to assist the [US] embassy", the other evidence provided was her attendance and performance at the AALD where, it was noted, she "is now a regular attendee ... and will be the principal government representative to the AALD meeting in Washington at the end of June".[123]

A comment added to the end of the cable by a US diplomatic staff member reveals reservations about the authenticity of Gillard's alliance loyalty: "it's unclear whether this change in attitude reflects a mellowing of her views or an understanding of what she needs to do to become leader of the ALP. It is likely a combination of the two". However, a year later, after a lengthy character assessment of Gillard recorded in a cable sent on 10 June 2009, these reservations became irrelevant as the embassy felt confident her "pragmatism" would ensure compliance to the alliance orthodoxy. In a cable sub-headed, "A Left-Winger Now a Pragmatist", Gillard's performance at the 2008 AALD event was once again highlighted as evidence of this fact.[124]

While performance at the AALD was certainly viewed as an important indicator of Gillard's alliance loyalty, the degree to which it also influenced her transition into a "true believer" of the alliance is a more difficult question

---

122 Author interview with Mark Latham, 22 November 2011.

123 US Embassy Canberra, "Gillard the Pro-American", cable #58001, 13 June 2008, reproduced at *The Age*, <http://images.theage.com.au/file/2010/12/15/2096934/Cables.htm?rand=1292396653979>, accessed 1 April 2018.

124 US Embassy Canberra, "A Left-Winger Now a Pragmatist", cable #1074, 10 June 2009, reproduced at *The Age*, <http://images.theage.com.au/file/2010/12/15/2096934/Cables.htm?rand=1292396653979>, accessed 1 April 2018.

to answer. Citing the influence of the AALD and US political exchange programs, Mark Latham credited Washington for Gillard's transformation into an orthodox alliance loyalist:

> You have to hand it to those guys in Washington, they have a way of making lefties like Gillard change their minds on foreign policy. Within the space of two years, they converted her from a highly cynical critic of all matters American into yet another political sycophant. The poor woman has been brainwashed.[125]

While Gillard might have formally placed herself in the left faction of the Labor Party, there's no indication that she actually subscribed to that ideological position, particularly on foreign policy issues. Gillard famously declared in 2010 that she did "not have a passion for foreign affairs", and it was not foreign policy that caused her "to get active in the labour movement".[126] Even Kelly concedes that he would not use the word "transformative" to characterise the AALD's impact on Gillard, although, in his mind, there was not "any doubt at all that the Dialogue influenced Gillard's attitude towards the alliance and facilitated her own involvement with the alliance and with the United States".[127] It appears as though, at most, being a part of the culture and rituals of the AALD helped Gillard to "learn the foreign policy game" that requires strict adherence to the alliance orthodoxy.[128]

Whatever impact the AALD might have had on Gillard's attitude towards the alliance, it was certainly utilised by her as a tool to demonstrate publicly her acceptance of its orthodoxy. As Hartcher argues, "it wasn't the Dialogue that persuaded Gillard to embrace the alliance or move to the right. That was the journey that Gillard was on. The Dialogue gave her the opportunity to parade her credentials and to, if you like, seal the deal".[129] The AALD helped Gillard to demonstrate that she was not a "left-winger or a Lathamite or a Victorian", as Paul Howes observes, but instead that she

---

125 Mark Latham, At America's Beck and Call, *Australian Financial Review*, 20 August 2009.

126 Mark Kenny, Gillard Lacks "Passion for Foreign Affairs" that Rudd had, *The Australian*, 6 October 2010, <http://www.theaustralian.com.au/national-affairs/politics-news/gillard-lacks-passion-for-foreign-affairs-that-rudd-had-story-fn59nqld-1225934581534>, accessed 1 April 2018.

127 Author interview with Paul Kelly, 20 January 2012.

128 In the words of one former senior Australian diplomat who chose to remain anonymous.

129 Author interview with Peter Hartcher, 29 October 2011.

held "a very mature calibre of opinion on the understanding and nature" of the Australia-US relationship.[130]

The AALD is perfectly suited to help current and future leaders refute those critics who might cast doubt upon their alliance loyalty. Writing in *The Australian* after Gillard had been elevated to prime minister, Sheridan wrote that the right faction of the Labor Party had, until shortly before, placed a veto on her as leader. However, as he notes:

> From at least the time she became deputy leader, Gillard shrewdly and effectively set about removing that veto on herself. She did this in part by attending the Australian American Leadership Dialogue and another similar dialogue with Israel. On a couple of occasions at the Australian American dialogue she was the senior Australian politician present, and she was fulsome in her endorsement of the US alliance.[131]

John W.H. Denton explains what participation in the Dialogue projects to establishment forces:

> Continuous participation in the Dialogue is a clear manifestation of your support for the prime role of America in Australian foreign policy concerns. It puts you mainstream in foreign policy thinking ... [The mainstream thinking] with the US is the primacy of the ANZUS relationship to Australia's defence and geo-strategic concerns ... Gillard has been able to position herself in the mainstream by affiliating herself with the Dialogue ... It's like, well that's fact. You can't say I'm anti-American. I participate in the Australian American Leadership Dialogue ... So you're able to position yourself, therefore, clearly and unmistakably in the middle of mainstream Australian foreign policy thinking. It also sets mainstream thinking about foreign policy.[132]

The case of Mark Latham suggests that the AALD is not always successful as a socialisation mechanism. One of its central objectives, after all, is to strengthen the importance of the alliance in the minds of the next generation. Latham, however, represented "a younger strand of ALP

---

130   Author interview with Paul Howes, 5 August 2011.

131   Greg Sheridan, Continuity in Foreign Affairs but Questions Remain, *The Australian*, 1 July 2010.

132   Author interview with John W. H. Denton, 15 February 2012.

opinion that, surprisingly, is not steeped in the alliance".[133] Although Latham was "unsteepable", in the words of Sam Lipski, the AALD played an important role by censuring his insistence on departing from the status quo.[134] For a "pragmatist" like Gillard, on the other hand, the prime function of the AALD was to provide an endorsement of her transition into the mainstream consensus and her induction into the alliance orthodoxy.

Significantly, neither Latham nor Gillard ever posed a serious threat to the alliance. While Latham held a critical position on the alliance that was atypical in modern Australian politics, the reality was that he continued to support its core elements. Latham was also surrounded by pro-alliance loyalists who would not have permitted him to depart very far from the status quo if he were to become prime minister. Indeed, just three months after his first foreign policy address questioning Australia's dependence on the US, Latham began to soften his position, particularly with regard to Australia's involvement in Iraq. Although Latham delivered the new position, Kim Beazley revealed that "the policy is based on discussions with me and Kevin Rudd".[135]

After Latham retired from politics and revealed in his memoirs that he believed the Australia-US relationship was "just another form of neo-colonialism", and questioned the "the long-term need" for the alliance, the Labor Party quickly distanced themselves.[136] Then opposition defence spokesman, Robert McClelland, claimed that Latham would have been "rolled" if these attitudes were known at the time.[137] When Rudd became opposition leader, he chose McClelland for his replacement as shadow foreign minister because he was considered "a safe pair of hands on the alliance".[138] McClelland was also a participant of the AALD.

In my interview with journalist Glenn Milne he argued that although the AALD has not faced a formidable challenge thus far in terms of dissident political elites in Australia, it "will have to start muscling up" and

---

133 Kelly, If Push Comes To Shove.

134 Author interview with Sam Lipski, 25 October 2011.

135 Latham's softened policy, along with his decision to elevate the solidly pro-American Beazley to shadow defence spokesman, was hailed as evidence the alliance was back in safe hands. Peter Hartcher, Big Kim a Sturdy Bridge to the US, *Sydney Morning Herald*, 16 July 2004.

136 Latham, *The Latham Diaries*, p. 393.

137 Phillip Hudson, Latham A Threat To Security, *The Age*, 18 September 2005, <http://www.theage.com.au/news/national/latham-a-threat-to-securi ty/2005/09/17/1126750170163.html>, accessed 1 April 2018.

138 Banham, US Meeting May Provide A Potent Symbol for Rudd.

really "prove its worth" if, in the future, there were to arise any "high level questioning of the value of the relationship and the place of the United States in the Pacific".[139] Since Milne made those comments in 2011, there has indeed been increased debate in Australia about the value of the alliance, particularly with Trump in the White House and, in the longer term, in the face of China's growing power. According to its supporters, the AALD is successfully fulfilling its function by reassuring Australians of America's commitment to the alliance during these difficult times.[140] Nevertheless, while there continues to be broad and deep support for the alliance among members of the Australian elite, the AALD may yet come to face its biggest challenge in the years ahead.

139   Author interview with Glenn Milne, 9 November 2011.
140   Greg Sheridan, All Credit to Turnbull for Trying to Seal Deal with a Troubled Trump, *The Australian*, 5 August 2017, <https://www.theaustralian.com.au/news/inquirer/all-credit-to-turnbull-for-trying-to-seal-deal-with-a-troubled-trump/news-story/087207c447ef65c24a754f080f147246>, accessed 1 April 2018.

CONCLUSION

Power and influence

Australia's alliance with the United States is, first and foremost, understood in terms of its defence value. It has variously been described as an insurance policy or deterrent against attack, essential for maintaining regional stability and, since the 1970s, as crucial to Australia's self-reliant defence posture. Much more than just providing for the defence of Australia, however, the national security elite has long emphasised the benefits of the alliance in bolstering Australia's regional status as a "leading middle power", an "Asia–Pacific power" and "a player of significance" on the global stage. By ensuring Australia maintains an "edge" over Southeast Asia in military and intelligence capabilities, and elevating Canberra's status in regional and global governance regimes, the alliance is seen to augment Australia's capacity to favourably shape its strategic and economic environment.

Allying to the greatest power in world history has undoubtedly provided some defence benefits to Australia, as well as incurring risks. During the Cold War, Australia's desire to restore and expand Western influence in Asia played out within the very real and dangerous great power competition between the US and the Soviet Union. However, the conventional view that Australia's security was bound to the outcome of a global conflict between Western democracies and communist totalitarianism was deeply flawed. The objective of checking Soviet and Chinese aggression was the lesser of two central US foreign policy goals during this period. The much larger game was the extension of American capitalism and the efforts to crush those nationalist independence movements that threatened Washington's influence in the Third World.[1]

The major security threats to Australia in the post-World War Two era have, somewhat paradoxically, resulted from Australia's alliance with

---

1   While the conventional view of the Cold War, including some sharply critical variants, contends that it was primarily a confrontation between two superpowers, the central dynamic was, for the Soviet Union, a war against its satellites, and for the US, a war against the third world. See Noam Chomsky, *Deterring Democracy*, London: Vintage Books, 1992, especially pp. 9-68.

the US.[2] The threat of direct nuclear attack during the Cold War and, to a lesser extent even today, has been a consequence of hosting sensitive American intelligence and communications bases, especially Pine Gap. The threat of a terrorist attack in Australia after 11 September 2001 was greatly exacerbated as a result of Australia's participation in America's "war on terror". Today, there remains the possibility of Australia being drawn into a wider US-Sino conflagration as Canberra ties itself to Washington's vision for retaining its hegemony in Asia.

While providing some defence benefits, given the enduring absence of actual or potential threats to Australia, the alliance today serves primarily to bolster Australia's power-projection capabilities and regional influence rather than to ensure Australian security. While increasing Australia's defence capabilities and enhancing Australia's regional power are potentially complementary objectives, they are also distinct. When considering the alliance in the context of Australia's relatively benign security environment, the primary consideration for national security policymakers is not defence and security but credibility and influence.[3]

Ostensibly, Australia's desire to play a regional leadership role, under the auspices of its superpower ally, is motivated by a long-standing commitment to maintaining and furthering peace, stability and prosperity, as well as promoting freedom, human rights and the rule of law. However, Australia has consistently acted in concert with the United States to undermine these professed interests and values when they have come into conflict with the preservation of American hegemonic power.

The key debates about Australia's alliance with the United States have typically revolved around the issue of independence versus dependence. Supporters argue that the alliance reflects a fundamental expression of Australia's independent decision making and national security interests. Moreover, supporters contend, the alliance is informed by a rational

---

2   As Beeson writes, "For a country with no obvious enemies, the main threats to Australian security since World War II have, paradoxically enough, actually resulted from its US alliance". Mark Beeson, American Hegemony: The View from Australia, *SAIS Review*, vol. 23, no. 2, 2003, p. 117.

3   Significantly, this point has also been argued with respect to Singapore, the only other country in the immediate region apart from Australia whose armed forces are externally oriented. Given that any immediate threat to Singapore's sovereignty is "far-fetched", its formidable defence capability and its cultivation of defence relationships with great powers is best understood as a means to augment its non-military instruments of power – particularly diplomatic and economic – thereby increasing its regional and international influence. Yi-Jin Lee, *Singapore's Defence Policy: Essential or Excessive*, Master's Thesis, US Army Command and General Staff College, Fort Leavenworth, Kansas, June 2010.

calculation of the costs and benefits to Australia, the balance of which overwhelmingly falls to the latter.[4] Critics, on the other hand, argue that the alliance is characterised by a fundamental imbalance in the relationship, with decision makers in Canberra sacrificing Australia's national interests on account of an insecurity complex and other cultural predispositions that lend themselves to dependency on "great and powerful friends".[5]

I would contend that, in contrast to the views put above, Australia's alliance with the United States is primarily the result of independent decision making on the part of members of an elite in Canberra, whose fundamental interests are the expansion of state power and influence and the preservation of a pro-Western capitalist order. Australia's enthusiasm for America's foreign policy objectives and military adventurism reflects a shared global outlook between elites in both countries, along with a willingness on the part of Canberra to pay the premium required to reap the benefits that derive from a privileged connection to the dominant global power.

Managing elite opinion

The alliance orthodoxy, which helps to sustain elite support for Australia's "special relationship" with the United States, is important precisely because there is nothing inevitable about the centrality of the alliance to Australian defence and foreign policies. Despite the breadth and depth of this orthodoxy, public opinion can swing quickly with events, and members of the strategic elite are always cognisant of the possibility of an "ultra-left wing Labor government" emerging that might decide to follow the "New Zealand model" of the mid-1980s and effectively withdraw Australia from the ANZUS Treaty.[6]

As has been noted, it was partly in response to these concerns that a number of private initiatives were established in the 1990s and 2000s with the objective of strengthening the Australia-US relationship and insulating

---

4   Commonwealth of Australia, *Australia's Defence Relations with the United States*, Canberra: Joint Standing Committee on Foreign Affairs, Defence and Trade, 2006, pp. 8, 87; Gary Brown and Laura Rayner, *Upside, Downside: ANZUS After Fifty Years*, Foreign Affairs, Defence and Trade Group, Department of the Parliamentary Library, Current Issues Brief, no. 3, 2001-02; H. G. Gelber, *The Australian American Alliance: Costs and Benefits*, Baltimore: Penguin Books, 1968.

5   For a summary of the independence versus dependence argument see, Andrew Carr, "ANZUS and Australia's Role in the World Affairs" in Peter J. Dean, Stephan Fruling and Brendan Taylor (eds), *Australia's American Alliance: Towards a New Era?*, Kindle Edition, Melbourne: Melbourne University Publishing Digital, 2016.

6   Paul Dibb, "Australia-United States" in Brendan Taylor (ed), *Australia as an Asia Pacific Regional Power: Friendship in Flux*, London: Routledge, 2007, p. 45.

it from change in the post-Cold War world. Primary among these was the AALD, established explicitly to preserve the centrality of the Australia-US relationship into the future at a time when personal relationships between powerful elite individuals in both countries were perceived to be at risk.

For supporters of the alliance the emergence of the AALD was timely. In the aftermath of the Cold War, a number of critical international relations scholars recognised that the time was ripe for challenging the orthodoxy in Australia's security thinking and the "institutionalised habits of mind" that posed an obstacle to reform.[7] The AALD's objective was precisely the opposite: to entrench the alliance orthodoxy in the minds of elite individuals and prevent any change to the status quo. The AALD was the embodiment of Australia's formal approach to regionalism in the 1990s, operating on the "assumption that economic and military security ... is best pursued through a dialogue of elite officials and academics".[8]

The AALD's agenda has been somewhat obscured by its self-identification as an effort in T2 informal diplomacy, ostensibly dedicated to the benign objectives of relationship building and mutual understanding. However, it is clear what the outcome is likely to be from a gathering of carefully selected participants drawn from elite circles discussing mutual concerns behind closed doors in an institution dedicated to preserving the status quo. Upon its establishment, critics of the alliance presciently warned that the AALD could turn into "another instance of Australia trying to ingratiate itself with the United States, instead of trying to form a genuinely independent foreign policy".[9]

Much later, critics commenting from the outside speculated that the private and exclusive nature of the discussions at the AALD, and the sense of prestige associated with privileged access to powerful American policy-makers, bred an unhealthy and uncritical relationship on Australia's part. According to this critique, the AALD operated as a mechanism for "duchessing" Australian leaders into behaving as if American interests were the same as Australian interests, much in the same way the British had achieved this behaviour from Australians in the past.

---

7   The Authors and Editors, "Introduction - Breaching Institutionalised Habits of Mind" in Graeme Cheeseman and Robert Bruce (eds), *Discourses of Danger & Dread Frontiers: Australian Defence and Security Thinking After the Cold War*, Sydney: Allen & Unwin, 1996, pp. 1-9.

8   David Sullivan, "Sipping a Thin Gruel: Academic and Policy Closure in Australia's Defence and Security Discourse" in Cheeseman and Bruce (eds), p. 62.

9   Dennis Phillips, then lecturer in American history and politics at Macquarie University, quoted in Kate Cole-Adams, Born Again Allies, *Time*, 7 June 1993.

In the absence of any serious critical investigation into the AALD, I have set out in this book to investigate these claims and to critically evaluate the AALD's role in managing Australia's relationship with the US. The existing literature on T2 diplomacy provided important insights into the institutional structures inherent in the AALD, and other T2 dialogues, that lead it to eschew critical debate and adopt official or orthodox policy positions. Nevertheless, the T2 literature ultimately proved limited in providing an adequate explanatory framework for a bilateral private initiative dedicated to alliance management.

Consequently, I turned instead to the literature on lobby groups. Lobby groups are distinguishable from T2 by their pre-existing agenda to define the terms of political debate in ways that suit their own preferred policy outcomes. In the case of the AALD, the agenda is to preserve the alliance orthodoxy and the notion of Australia's "special relationship" with the US, dictating an ever-closer alignment of foreign policies. In effect, the AALD functions in a "policy watchdog" capacity to prevent changes to the status quo. However, unlike traditional interest groups, the AALD preserves and promotes the alliance orthodoxy not by lobbying decision makers directly but rather by facilitating the socialisation of elites. The notion of the socialisation role of the AALD is supported by the evidence presented in this book, drawn from numerous interviews with present and former participants.

While a number of critical voices affirm this view, others dismiss the notion that the AALD socialises elites or otherwise has a significant impact on elite orientations towards the alliance. However, the socialisation techniques utilised by the AALD, consciously or not, constitute a sophisticated form of co-option developed over decades of research into psychological warfare studies and public diplomacy practice. The AALD, although a uniquely private initiative, exhibits many of the same material and psychological inducements identified in scholarship as being successfully employed to preserve America's alliance relationships.

It is not my contention that, as some critics of the AALD suggest, the US has effectively hijacked Australian foreign policy, by convincing political elites to defend American strategic and economic interests that Australia does not share.[10] Critics of the alliance are not converted at the AALD into "true believers". The reality is far more subtle. The AALD functions to solidify a set of orthodox beliefs that are deeply embedded in domestic

---

10   See, for example, David Day, Bowing to Duchess Diplomacy, *Sydney Morning Herald*, 8 June 2012, <http://www.smh.com.au/federal-politics/political-opinion/bowing-to-duchess-diplomacy-20120607-1zysh.html>, accessed 1 April 2018.

institutions, ideologies and historical legacies, and long shared by elites in both countries. Although limited in scope, the AALD does have a real impact in shaping the preferences of the Australian elite who already hold a predisposition towards the alliance orthodoxy.

The AALD is only one small element of what I have described in this book as the much larger US Lobby. Together with prominent voices in the media, academia, defence, think-tanks and non-government organisations that promote the alliance orthodoxy, this loose network of elites and institutional relationships functions to further entrench Australia's "special relationship" with America. It undoubtedly constitutes the dominant voice in Australian national security discourse and it plays a significant role in sustaining the security consensus that ideologically constrains political elites from departing too far from the status quo.

Future prospects

Turning to the future, one of the indicators of success of the AALD, according to supporters, is its capacity to continue to attract influential and well-targeted up-and-coming members of the elite in both countries. Today, the AALD remains by far the top non-Australian government sponsor for parliamentarians travelling to the United States.[11] Nevertheless, given the success of the AALD is largely attributed to the personal dedication and energy of its founder, Phillip Scanlan, some participants have raised questions about its long-term survival in his absence. The AALD, Kemp believes, "has depended very heavily on Scanlan and I think in my own mind there's always been a question of whether the Dialogue would survive [Scanlan's departure]".[12]

On the other hand, because Scanlan's centralised management style evinces criticism among some participants, his eventual departure is also viewed as a potentially positive development. In particular, there is the perception among some members of the Liberal Party that Scanlan holds a bias towards the Labor Party.[13] In one instance, an influential Liberal

---

11   Jessica Clarence, Who Funds Federal Parliamentarians' Overseas Travel? *Australian Strategic Policy Institute*, 26 June 2018, <https://www.aspi.org.au/report/who-funds-federal-parliamentarians-overseas-travel>, accessed 20 September 2018.

12   Author interview with David Kemp, 31 August 2011.

13   According to Kemp, many in the Liberal Party believe Scanlan is "closer to people like [Kim] Beazley and the other Labor pro-Americans", even though Scanlan himself probably "identifies as a Liberal." Author interview with David Kemp, 31 August 2011.

Party figure threatened to discourage members of the Party from attending the AALD unless a strict protocol of bipartisanship was implemented.[14]

More recently, Scanlan's perceived partisanship has fuelled speculation about the AALD's demise,[15] a charge strongly refuted by Scanlan who insists the Dialogue's trajectory "remains onward and upward".[16] Interestingly, in early 2016 there was an apparent split with the American board of the AALD, the official reason being "the Americans want to build a broader and more independent institution so senior political and business figures can strengthen the US-Australia alliance outside of Scanlan's orbit".[17] The newly established American Australian Council consists of numerous high-profile members of the strategic and corporate elite, and its founding chairman is Tony Podesta, one of America's most powerful lobbyists.[18]

Management issues aside, the prospects for genuine reform of the AALD in ways that address the major concerns raised in this book are slim. Genuine dialogue requires not just a commitment to mutual understanding but "spirited debate" and the willingness on the part of Washington (and Canberra) to "consider the real possibility that its thinking, policies, and actions might be wrong".[19] Even so, the hope that fundamental change might occur by "speaking truth to power" is doubtful and wrongheaded. As critics of American public diplomacy argue, "to imagine that significant pillars of American foreign policy ... will be modified through engagement is, in practice, a fantasy".[20]

Significantly, in the case of T2, scholars have suggested potential remedies to the "autonomy dilemma" so that perspectives outside of the politically acceptable mainstream might be seriously entertained. Specifically,

---

14   Although Scanlan eventually relented, according to this senior Liberal figure, he did so while "spitting chips and raving and foaming at the mouth". Author interview with participant who chose to remain anonymous.

15   Will Glasgow and Joe Aston, The Demise of Phil Scanlan and the Australian American Leadership Dialogue, *Australian Financial Review*, 4 February 2015.

16   Phillip Scanlan, Leader Dialogue Still Strong, *Australian Financial Review*, 5 February 2015.

17   Will Glasgow, Will Turnbull Save Scanlan's Australian American Leadership Dialogue with a DD?, *Australian Financial Review*, 9 March 2016.

18   The American Australian Council still has listed as its parent foundation the American Australian Education and Leadership Foundation. American Australian Council, Foundation Structure, <http://americanaustraliancouncil.org/about/>, accessed 1 April 2018.

19   Edward Comor and Hamilton Bean, America's "Engagement" Delusion: Critiquing a Public Diplomacy Consensus, *International Communication Gazette*, vol. 74, no, 3, 2012, p. 214.

20   Comor and Bean, p. 213.

greater collaboration with T3 initiatives, or grassroots civil society organ-isations, has been offered as a means to break the monopoly of elite views and interests at the official level.[21] Unlike T1 and T2, discussions at the T3 level are "often based on a critical perspective that tends to oppose mainstream government policies. They question the hierarchy of priorities and the assumptions that underlie the framework behind these policies".[22] However, attempts to utilise T2 as a bridge between T1 and T3 have ended in failure, partly because elites have proven unwilling to undertake a genu-ine dialogue with civil society.[23] In the case of the AALD, the fact that it exists solely to sustain the alliance orthodoxy means there is little hope of reform along the lines some scholars have suggested.

Finally, there is the larger question of whether the AALD is a benign or malign force in the management of Australia's relationship with the US. The answer to that question largely depends on one's belief in the value of the alliance and its role in the world. For alliance loyalists who hold the "special relationship" sacrosanct, the AALD plays a crucial role in supporting the infrastructure of personal relationships that helps to keep it strong. On the other hand, for those who adopt a critical approach along the lines I have taken in this book – and are deeply concerned about the many pernicious impacts of the alliance as it has historically functioned – the AALD has not served the interests of Australians well.

---

21   Amitav Acharya, Democratisation and the Prospects for Participatory Regionalism in Southeast Asia, *Third World Quarterly*, vol. 24, no. 2, 2003, p. 386; Brian L. Job, "Track 2 Diplomacy: Ideational Contribution to the Evolving Asian Security Order" in Desmond Ball and Kwa Chong Guan (eds), *Assessing Track 2 Diplomacy in the Asia–Pacific Region: A CSCAP Reader*, Strategic and Defence Studies Centre, Australian National University, Canberra and S. Rajaratnam School of International Studies, Nanyang Technological University, Singapore, 2010, p. 150; Herman Joseph S. Kraft, The Autonomy Dilemma of Track Two Diplomacy in Southeast Asia, *Security Dialogue*, vol. 31, no. 3, 2000, p. 353.

22   Herman Joseph S. Kraft, Track Three Diplomacy and Human Rights in Southeast Asia: the Asia Pacific Coalition for East Timor, *Global Networks*, vol. 2, no. 1, 2002, p. 52.

23   Alan Collins, A People-Oriented ASEAN: A Door Ajar or Closed for Civil Society Organisations?, *Contemporary Southeast Asia*, vol. 30, no. 2, 2008; Katherine Marie G. Hernandez, Bridging Officials and the Peoples of ASEAN: The Role of the ASEAN People's Assembly, a paper prepared for the Anniversary Conference of the Centre for Southeast Asian Studies, University of Michigan, Ann Arbor, 22 October 2010.

CPSIA information can be obtained
at www.ICGtesting.com
Printed in the USA
LVHW010225160819
627851LV00003B/4/P